D0393808

The House of
Twenty Thousand Books

The House of
Twenty Thousand Books

Sasha Abramsky

NEW YORK REVIEW BOOKS

New York

THIS IS A NEW YORK REVIEW BOOK
PUBLISHED BY THE NEW YORK REVIEW OF BOOKS
435 Hudson Street, New York NY 10014
www.nyrb.com

First published in the United States in September 2015
by New York Review Books

First published in 2014 in Great Britain by Halban Publishers Ltd
22 Golden Square London W1F 9JW

Library of Congress Cataloging-in-Publication Data

Abramsky, Sasha.
The house of twenty thousand books / Sasha Abramsky.
pages cm
Includes index.
ISBN 978-1-59017-888-1 (hardback)
1. Abramsky, Chimen, 1916–2010. 2. Abramsky, Miriam. 3. Abramsky, Chimen,
1916–2010—Library. 4. Booksellers and bookselling—England—London—
Biography. 5. Antiquarian booksellers—England—London—Biography. 6. Book
collectors—England—London—Biography. 7. Jewish historians—England—
London—Biography. 8. London (England)—Intellectual life—20th century. I. Title.
Z330.6.L6A27 2015
381'.450020922421—dc23
[B]
2015006798

ISBN 978-1-59017-888-1
Available as an electronic book; ISBN 978-1-59017-889-8

Printed in the United States of America on acid-free paper
1 3 5 7 9 10 8 6 4 2

This book is dedicated to Chimen and Miriam Abramsky.
You were, quite simply, extraordinary.
I miss you and mourn for you every day.

*What a piece of work is a man! How noble in reason, how infinite
in faculty! In form and moving how express and admirable!
In action how like an angel! In apprehension how like a god!
The beauty of the world! The paragon of animals!
And yet to me, what is this quintessence of dust?*
—William Shakespeare, *Hamlet*, Act II, Scene 2

Contents

PROLOGUE I:
SAYING GOODBYE

He looks upon himself as a part of the books, or the books a part of him, I don't know which.
—William Morris, News from Nowhere (1890)

THERE IS NO *sound on earth like that of a quiet man, a dignified man, exploding in primal grief. Nothing compares to it—not fingernails scraping on a blackboard, not the whir of a dental drill through enamel. Nothing. It is the howl of absolute horror, a keening black hole of noise that sucks in everything else. It pulls you into the abyss—extraordinary, out of character, it brooks no dissent. This, the sound announces, is about forever.*

I heard this noise as I cradled the phone to my left ear in March 2010. I was at home, in Sacramento, California, perched desolate on a sofa in the TV room, my wife and children in another room. Six thousand miles away, my father was sitting next to his father's body at his North London home at 5 Hillway, in Highgate. A few minutes earlier my grandfather Chimen Abramsky had finally died. Of what? Old age? He was ninety-three years old. Complications from Parkinson's disease? He had been deteriorating for years, a frail, deaf old man, a widower increasingly locked, stony-faced, into a broken, frozen body. Or the aftermath of a horrifying series of late-life illnesses and infections, each of which in and of itself ought to have killed him? In the end, the cause didn't really matter. What mattered was that the last of my grandparents had died, a man who had been my teacher, mentor, and guru, as well as my "Nye"—the name I coined for him when I was a toddler, because he always wore a tie and I couldn't pronounce that word. My wonderful, at times playful granddad—the old man who would dance around his dining room with a great stack of colorful plastic cups, each one fitting neatly into the next, balanced atop his head to entertain me when I was a young child—was gone. The man who had surrounded himself with tens of thousands of wondrously rare books, bought over the better part of a century, had disappeared, everything that made him him replaced with the waxen, impersonal stillness of death.

As I started to weep, the sobs shaking my body, part of me floated up above the scene and, looking down, wondered why I was so shocked. After all, I had had plenty of time to practice my grief: Chimen's decline had been slow, his final months painful and humiliating, every phone call to my parents or siblings begun with an update on his tenuous hold on life. He had become, during those last few months and years, a coda to his own story.

———

In the seventeenth century, René Descartes had famously concluded "I think, therefore I am." For much of Chimen's life, as he methodically constructed his House of Books, the reverse had held: He was, and therefore he thought—had he not thought, read, analyzed the world around him, and the history from whence that world grew, he would have been a lost soul. He was, after all, never very good at twiddling his thumbs. But now, in his nineties, with his body wrecked by Parkinson's, with his hearing gone, unable to leave his house to go on the walks he used to love, he became a prisoner; his mind was locked in his failing body, and that body was cloistered in his House of Books. Bit by bit, the world closed in on him; eventually, he could no longer make it up the stairs. His world was reduced to the small, book-filled rooms of his home's ground floor. The house that had once served as one of left-wing London's great salons, which still contained one of England's most important private libraries, now became utterly claustrophobic. The home that had sparkled with intellectual life when I visited it as a child became a little frightening, decrepit, a place I took my own children to out of obligation rather than joy. Animated conversation was replaced by the long silences of deaf old age; the bustle of a crowded kitchen and a gaggle of diners and overnight guests gave way to the stillness of Parkinson's.

Then, the Cartesian equation righted itself: Seeking to maintain a hold on life, on sanity, Chimen became even more obsessed with the world of books he had created for himself. Like a man who pinches himself to make sure he still has feeling, Chimen read to reassure himself that he was still alive. He thought, therefore he was. For years, as he declined, his ability to think sustained him; he clung to his extraordinary intellectual facilities, to his near-photographic powers of recall: When a social worker, attempting to ascertain his mental acuity, asked if he knew who the prime minister was, Chimen responded witheringly that he could list every prime minister from the past two hundred years. But at the very end, even his memory abandoned him. Physically broken, he finally became confused.

I had been grieving over Chimen's dissolution for months, years even, the partial grief for the living that emerges at unexpected times and in unwanted places. But, as I listened now to my father keening in the book-filled living room of my grandfather's house near Hampstead Heath, the room my grandfather had eventually slept in after he could no longer climb the stairs to his bedroom, something snapped. The ghastly permanence, the irrevocability of the iron door that separated death from life, sliced me up, left me in pieces.

———

A day later, I was in London, helping the family to prepare for my grandfather's funeral. We roamed Chimen's house, starting the grim process of sorting out a lifetime's accumulation of papers, completing financial documents, and, in doing all the other standard activity that accompanies death, filling up the hours in the days leading to the funeral. Solace came from Chimen's library, an extraordinary collection of fifteen to twenty thousand volumes. Even leaving aside the quality, the rarity of these books, many of them hundreds of years old, their sheer physical presence was overwhelming: If each book weighed, on average, a pound—a fair estimate, given that many were slim little volumes just a few ounces in weight, while others were huge tomes easily weighing ten pounds—then at a conservative guess the house contained upward of ten tons of books, the weight of at least five large cars. There were, in addition, several tons of manuscripts, letters, and newspapers stacked around the house. I would stop in front of one bookshelf or another, take out an old book, smell it, touch it, examine its publication date, reacquaint myself with it as with an old friend; I would talk about it with my younger brother, Kolya, who of all of the five grandchildren knew the most about Chimen's collection.

During those sad hours, I looked for particular books that we had been introduced to in happier years, or particular authors whose importance Chimen had hammered into our heads, young apprentices in his world of ideas. And I remembered conversations from decades earlier, the conversations that in so many ways had formed the basis for my intellectual identity. I remembered the gatherings that throughout my childhood my grandparents had presided over.

My grandmother Miriam (Mimi to us kids; Miri to Chimen) was extremely intelligent. Unlike Chimen, however, temperamentally she was neither an academic nor an obsessive scholar. Instead, she put her energies into her career and, above all, into nurturing a vast, extended network of family and friends. During my early childhood, in the 1970s, she was the head of the psychiatric social work department at the Royal Free Hospital. She would come home from work— long days spent counseling disturbed, sometimes suicidal individuals —to cook fabulous, heavy, Old World meals with which to feed the endless array of guests who made their way to the house. One could not refuse her food; she simply would not accept an unwillingness to eat. She created an ambience in their home that would outlive her, would survive in somewhat muted form into the new millennium. When, during the last years of Chimen's life, I brought my children to visit their ailing great-grandfather in his increasingly dilapidated house, he was still welcoming academics and old comrades—those few whom he had not outlived—for brief cups of coffee, bread and herring, and snippets of conversation.

Now, with Chimen dead, I could not stop pacing about the house, trying to imagine a world without my grandfather. Every time I descended the staircase, I was confronted by the grotesquerie of Picasso's *Guernica*, a copy of which had hung above these stairs for my whole life. One of my earliest memories was waving Mimi and Chimen off for a Spanish holiday in the late 1970s; they had waited forty years to visit Spain, refusing to go until General Franco, on whose behalf the Nazi bombers had attacked Guernica in 1937, was dead.

One evening, my oldest friend, Ben, came to visit to cheer me up. He reminded me of the many times I had invited him to play at Chimen and Mimi's. "How lucky you were," he said. "Most kids regard their grandparents as burdens, as old-timers to be endured, maybe even respected and loved in an abstract sort of way, but certainly not to be emulated or considered a part of one's daily life. You," he told me, "your grandfather was your hero."

It was true. Chimen was, in so many ways, larger than life. The atheist third son of a famous rabbi, Yehezkel Abramsky—who in 1956 won the first Israel Prize for rabbinic literature; the grandson of another famous rabbi, Moshe Nahum Jerusalimsky; and the great-grandson of yet a third renowned rabbi, Yaakov David Willowski (known affectionately as "the Ridbaz," a nickname built around the acronym of his title and initials), Chimen was like a character out of an Isaac Bashevis Singer story, or an antiquarian out of a Dickens novel, or an eccentric eighteenth-century salon host, or, more accurately, a chimera of them all. It was impossible to pigeonhole him: Too many stories flowed through his person simultaneously. While his father was head of London's Beth Din, the chief religious court for Jews in Britain, Chimen was a leading member of the Communist Party of Great Britain, and he also ran, with my grandmother, a Jewish bookstore and publishing house named Shapiro, Valentine & Co., around the corner from Yehezkel's office. Later on, he became an outspoken critic of the Soviet Union and came to count the liberal philosopher Isaiah Berlin among his closest friends and champions. Lacking a university degree, Chimen nevertheless, in middle age, was acknowledged as one of the world's great experts both in Socialist history and in Jewish history. After decades of buying and selling books for a living, he spent the latter part of his career as an academic, first lecturing on Marxism at St. Antony's College, Oxford, and then as the chair of the Jewish and Hebrew Studies Department at University College London; he also spent time as a visiting professor at both Brandeis and Stanford—and he lectured at many other institutions on both sides of the Atlantic. Rounding out his career,

Chimen became a leading consultant on manuscripts for Sotheby's auction house.

He was, across all of these incarnations, one of England's most extraordinary book collectors and one of the great letter-writers of his age, penning letters in English, Hebrew, Russian, and Yiddish, sometimes as many as ten and even twenty missives in a day, to a vast array of acquaintances.

Chimen was a diminutive figure, five feet one inch tall, with great, sturdy arms and a bullish neck, quite possibly the legacy of his years in charge of Shapiro, Valentine & Co., years during which he regularly schlepped heavy boxes of books around the great metropolis. One of my father's oldest friends, writing about his childhood memories of postwar London, described Chimen, with great affection, as a "little Russian gnome." He would, in his later years, almost always wear a ready-made charcoal-gray suit and tie; if he was feeling particularly casual, on a rare visit to the beach perhaps, he might replace the jacket with a woolen sweater. When he was outdoors, his head, bald on top, adorned with a ring of unruly white hair around the back, always hosted either a cloth cap or a tweed homburg. He had a wonderful Eastern European accent, an accent somehow almost as musty, as imbued with echoes from the past, as the books that he collected; and he spoke a patois of English, Hebrew, Russian, and Yiddish, sometimes reserving particular languages for specific friends or acquaintances, and on other occasions blending the languages in a most singular manner.

Chimen at his bookshop, Shapiro, Valentine & Co., early 1960s.

In notes that he had sketched out in his

mid-eighties, for an autobiography that he ultimately found himself unable to write, he asked himself the question: "Why should a person feel the need to write about his own life?" Part of his answer was that his life covered "a long period in our turbulent century of Revolution, civil war, pogroms, ruthless dictatorship, World War Two with its terrible tragedies, culminating in the genocidal destruction of six million Jews.... Life is to a large degree a lottery, whose fate is decided by forces frequently by chance, outside our will, but to whose decisions we contribute, willy-nilly." He would, he averred, "endeavour to write on days gone, on a past which was colourful, full of contradictions, conflicts, and, in a word, some ordinary and some startlingly original and colourful personalities." It was an echo of the words of one of the thinkers he most admired, the nineteenth-century Russian radical writer and revolutionary Alexander Herzen, who had given a similar rationale for writing his own memoirs nearly a century and a half earlier. In 1855, in exile in London, Herzen had begun publishing a series of essays about his life in *The Pole Star*, a Russian-language journal that he ran. (The essays were later reprinted in book form under the title *My Past and Thoughts*.) "Who is entitled to write his reminiscences?" the exiled writer asked his readers. He answered, "Everyone. Because no one is obliged to read them. In order to write one's reminiscences it is not at all necessary to be a great man, nor a notorious criminal, nor a celebrated artist, nor a statesman—it is quite enough to be simply a human being, to have something to tell, and not merely to desire to tell it but at least have some little ability to do so." In his old age, Chimen concluded that he lacked the ability to tell his own story; yet that story, as he knew, as I knew, as all who were close to Chimen knew, was one that needed to be told.

Several months after Chimen's death, his library was sold. My family kept back only a small number of volumes—those of sentimental value to my father and his sister, and those specifically requested by my brother and myself. A couple of months later, the mailman arrived at my house in California with a large, heavy cardboard box. In it were my books, the ones I had asked for from the House of Books. A set of Past Masters pocket paperbacks, published by Oxford University Press, outlining in brief form the philosophies of great thinkers from Blaise Pascal and Thomas More to Herbert Marcuse and Che Guevara. They had occupied perhaps a foot of shelf space about five shelves up, in the hallway just by the front door, next to a rather austere oil painting of my grandmother's father. And a set of crumbling old Everyman Classics, consisting of political philosophy texts from Plato's *Republic* and Aristotle's *Ethics and Politics* to Ernest Renan's *The Life of Jesus* and the religious writings of Saint Thomas Aquinas; from Machiavelli's *The Prince* to classic texts by Rousseau and Voltaire; More's *Utopia*; Spinoza's *Ethics*; Immanuel Kant's philosophical works; Hobbes's political treatises; Hume's philosophical musings; Adam Smith's economics; Hamilton's *Federalist Papers*; Marx's *Das Kapital*; and Macaulay's *Historical Essays*. These books occupied one of the shelves in the front living room, halfway up the wall backing onto the hallway.

Arriving separately—to be delivered personally by my mother on her next visit—was an 1841 fourth edition of Tocqueville's *Democracy in America*, published in New York, Boston, and Philadelphia, the original tracing-paper map of his American journeys bound into the volume as accompaniment to the thick, rough-hewn, water-damaged printed pages. The spine of the thick black binding was missing, and the inside of the binding that remained was stained brown, the shadow of a now-missing library-borrowing list, perhaps. The exquisitely thin map folded up next to the title page showed the

9

United States when the states ended at Missouri and Arkansas, and much of the southwest on the map was colored yellow, indicating that it belonged to Mexico. Alaska was colored pink and listed simply as "Russian America." There is no California in this world, no Nebraska or Arizona. Texas's population is listed on the map as twenty thousand.

Also delivered by my mother: An early edition of *The Working-Class Movement in America*, co-authored by Marx's daughter Eleanor and her common-law husband, Edward Aveling, which had been owned by Herbert Gladstone, a son of the British Liberal prime minister William Gladstone. And a little red Workers' Library book, *Memories of Lenin*, by Lenin's wife, Nadezhda Krupskaya.

Fifty volumes, maybe one hundred, out of the thousands in that house. Mere fragments. But those fragments told a story, they delineated a set of core beliefs—philosophical schools of thought, explorations of democracy and of revolution—ways of understanding human behavior and society. They were Chimen's guides through life, his search for meaning, for purpose, for structure in human existence. They were like a seed bank out of which his world could be resurrected, or shards from an archaeological dig—the older layers buried underneath newer, fresher levels—allowing vanished histories to come back to life.

"Whatsoever moved Saint Jerome to call the journeys of the Israelites in the wilderness, mansions," wrote the metaphysical poet John Donne in his eerie sermon, "Death's Duel," written shortly before his death in 1631, "the word...signifies but a journey, but a peregrination." For Chimen, too, his mansion of ideas, his House of Books, was more a journey, a never-ending voyage of discovery, than a physical abode. Perhaps that was why he cared so little for its creature comforts, living with hopelessly outdated plumbing, a leaky roof, flaking window frames, and, hidden under fraying rugs, floorboards that were more coarse planks than carefully carpentered, tightly fitted slats. His home was to be experienced like a trip to far-off lands—difficult, challenging, unpredictable—rather than to be reveled in like a luxurious penthouse apartment.

———

Over the decades Chimen had become so addicted to the printed page, to the texture of his books, to the feel of old manuscripts, and to the material contained within his written correspondence, that he ended up surrounding himself with walls of words. They provided protection from the madness of the world outside—or, at the very least, a road map for navigating the chaos.

By the end of his life, every single room in the house, except the bathroom and kitchen, was lined from floor to ceiling with shelves double-stacked with books, with only a few bare spots left in which paintings and photographs hung. If you pulled a few bricks out of the wall of books, you found a second, hidden wall behind it. And when the shelves were filled, first the floors and then the tables succumbed to great, twisting piles of tomes. In a home that remained largely unrenovated during the sixty-six years Chimen inhabited it, becoming more dilapidated with each passing year, ideas were the mortar holding his biblio-bricks together: notions of progress, understanding of civility and culture, explanations of how and why great cultures and civilizations decline, theories of history.

As the House of Books rose, volume by volume, shelf by shelf, room by room, so the connections became more complex. Adam Smith's free market ideas segued into the economic theories of Marx's *Das Kapital*. Macaulay's and Carlyle's theories of history stood alongside Hegel's dialectic, Marx's notions of structure and superstructure with Frantz Fanon's rants about the cleansing role of blood-letting.

The conservative late-eighteenth-century historian and parliamentarian Edmund Burke paved the way for the antirevolutionary French cleric Joseph de Maistre, whose dark views on the human condition in turn led to an intellectual movement that eventually culminated in Fascism and the maniacal theories embodied in Hitler's *Mein Kampf*. Nineteenth-century working men in England protesting against harsh conditions in the factories of the Midlands shared a shelf with fellow nineteenth-century Russian anarchists such as Mikhail Bakunin. Above them would be perched twentieth-century Russian Bolsheviks. Plato could serve as the foundation for the medieval Jewish scholar Maimonides, who found echoes centuries later in Spinoza; and Spinoza's *Ethics* helped hold up secular liberal theorists such as John Locke, Montesquieu, and Tom Paine. Eighteenth-century Jewish mystics shared a wall with nineteenth-century English utopian Socialists. And so on.

———

Hillway held two libraries. The first was Chimen's Socialist collection; the second his Judaica volumes. The Judaica collection, even after five thousand books and two thousand offprints had been removed in the 1980s to join other volumes in a specially endowed section of the library in the imposing nineteenth-century buildings at University College London, was utterly comprehensive, detailing every conceivable aspect of Jewish life over the centuries. Of the seven thousand items purchased by the university, Chimen's colleague Mark Geller, in internal correspondence with the university's provost, wrote that they made up "probably the best Jewish History library in Europe." The Socialist collection was in all likelihood the most complete privately owned collection of eighteenth-, nineteenth-, and early twentieth-century Socialist literature anywhere in the world. Certainly it was the most complete collection of its kind in Britain.

Taken as a whole, these two separate but interconnected libraries were of vast range, the fruit of a collector's obsession nurtured in the late 1940s by Chimen's friendship with the rare-book dealer Heinrich Eisemann. A German Jew, Eisemann had learned the mysteries of his trade at the hands of fin de siècle experts in Frankfurt, Paris, and Rome, and had been the novelist Thomas Mann's book dealer. He had left Germany prior to the Second World War, settling first in the East End of London and later moving to the more affluent St. John's Wood neighborhood. The German refugee knew so much about his trade that, Chimen recalled in a conversation with Eisemann's grandson sixty years later, when he walked into a Sotheby's auction room all the top buyers would stand up out of respect.

Under Eisemann's tutelage, Chimen made connections with dealers in England, including a number of specialists along Farringdon Road and Maggs Bros Ltd, dealers in "rare books, autographs, manuscripts, engravings," who boasted a fashionable Berkeley Square address and counted royalty in England, Spain, and Portugal among their clients. He established relations, too, with dealers in Israel, Denmark, France, Germany, Switzerland, Italy, Holland, and the United States. He would order books by mail and, in a somewhat chaotic manner, kept all of the receipts and invoices. In bureaus in his house, in random folders at his university office, he would stuff all of his correspondence with these dealers: requests for payment; disputes over lost checks; notes informing Chimen of rare books that had just gone on the market. So important were these book-dealing connections that, over the years, he filled in several address books just with their contact information. When Chimen traveled to America in 1948, Eisemann also happened to be there. One evening, he called Chimen to his hotel room in New York to show him something.

There, in the room, was a handwritten manuscript, a complete movement from Beethoven's Ninth Symphony, just purchased by Eisemann on behalf of an American collector. "The greatest symphony ever written," Chimen remembered near the end of his life, his reedy, ancient voice still conveying the awe he felt at that moment. "It was something exceptional."

Well into the 1950s, Chimen regarded himself as Eisemann's apprentice, acting as his literary procurer. In one typical transaction, using £500 put up by Eisemann and an anonymous investor, Chimen bought five letters by Karl Marx, and one from Marx's wife, Jenny, in 1951. The conditions were as follows: If Eisemann could not resell the letters, Chimen would refund him half of the money that he had put up, but if they sold for a profit, Chimen agreed that the profit would "be equally shared between the anonymous person who lent for the purpose of the letters two hundred and fifty pounds, yourself, and myself." At some point, however, Chimen gained both the knowledge and the confidence to strike out on his own. He would, on occasion, still act on Eisemann's behalf—such as when he traveled to Stuttgart in 1957 to evaluate and purchase a rare Hebrew Bible (Eisemann, who had lost many relatives in the Holocaust, refused to set foot in Germany after the Second World War)—but as the years progressed he expected more of a share in the profits. Eventually, Eisemann slid into senescence, recognizing neither Chimen nor the treasures that, together, they had bought and sold; Chimen was left to continue without his mentor. He did so with a passion.

That passion produced something extraordinary: an architecture to the House of Books that was infinitely complex, its crystalline structure largely obscured to the untrained eye. When an estate agent came around to evaluate the property shortly after Chimen's death, he looked at all the books, laughed, and said that my father and aunt should consider selling the whole lot to one of those dealers who take stuff in bulk, sight unseen. *You never know, all that old paper might be worth a few bob,* was the clear implication. *But you had better clean it out quickly so that prospective buyers can get a glimpse of the size of the place.* With some knowledge of the subject, however, and with a bit of deductive effort one could actually work out, through the architecture of the library, how Chimen's interests had evolved. Moving from room to room at 5 Hillway, one could travel through hundreds of years of European political history, and thousands of years of philosophy and Jewish history; one could see which individuals and which events particularly enthralled Chimen, which artists and poets inspired him, which languages he understood, and which cities and their publishing houses especially intrigued him. And as one came to understand *when* each room was populated with books, one could get a sense of how Chimen's interests and priorities had changed over the decades.

Some of Hillway's rooms had, by the time my generation came on the scene, ceased to have any functional purpose; the bibliographic flora had simply run rampant. In the diabolically cluttered little upstairs "office" or "study"—a room that Mimi's mother, Bellafeigel, had inhabited in the 1950s for the last four years of her life—spirals of reference books, Jewish art volumes, and bound collections of newspapers reached up toward the ceiling, surrounded by mountains of miscellaneous papers and handwritten correspondence. At some point, the room had become simply unusable; Chimen's response had been to lock it from the outside and hide it from view. It was "the jungle room," he mischievously told his friend David Mazower (the great-grandson of the Yiddish playwright and novelist Scholem Asch, whom Chimen had known in London decades earlier), when diving into one of the piles to find a bound volume of rare Yiddish newspapers and into another to retrieve an armful of precious Bundist pamphlets, printed in late-tsarist Russia on onionskin. He always carried little black leather pouches full of numerous keys—to safes, to hidden rooms, to filing cabinets. Only he knew which keys opened which locks, so it was a sure bet that no one would trespass into his deathtrap of an office accidentally. That said, when one of my cousins *did* sneak in behind him on one occasion, she saw him disappear into a tunnel through the piles that, she swore later, was carved out to just fit his form. In that room, after his death, my father and aunt found, buried under stacks of papers, old Russian folk art, as well as a small eighteenth-century Armenian Bible, perhaps four or five inches high and almost as thick, posted to Chimen decades earlier, the envelope in which it was contained never opened.

Elsewhere, order still seemed to reign. In the smaller bedroom to the rear of the house—the room that had once belonged to Jenny, my dad's younger sister, and which, as a result, was not vacated until the late 1960s—were the catalogs and other tools of the trade that Chimen needed to consult when working for Sotheby's in the last decades of his career. That was the room I slept in when I was a child spending the weekend with my grandparents. On a wall opposite the bed hung a copy of a Marc Chagall painting depicting a whimsical scene of a circus, the clowns in pointed hats floating through their magical landscape. Next to it was another Chagall, this one portraying a beautiful woman holding what looked like an urn filled with water in her right hand, her left hand raised skyward, toward an orb, just out of reach. She was surrounded by other women, each of them with their own unexplained circles to carry. In the corners of the painting were what appeared to be olive branches. In the top left, a dove fluttered its wings. Years later, leafing through a Liberal Haggadah one Seder night, I came across a reproduction of that same painting. It was titled *Miriam the Prophetess at the Red Sea.*

As the number of books expanded, the order became more tenuous, more precarious. In the airing closets, cupboards, and wardrobes around the house, more random heaps of books were stored. And on the dining-room and living-room floors unstable towers of additional volumes gathered.

———

I do not think anyone ever counted the number of books in the house, although Chimen made partial efforts over the years to catalog his collection, and various book experts, some flown in from New York and others from London, spent weeks studying it after he died. Looking at the shelves, I estimated that there were probably close to twenty thousand volumes in the house at the time of Chimen's death. My father believed it was more like fifteen thousand. Whatever the exact number of books at Hillway, it was staggering. And what made it more staggering was their quality. Chimen did not simply aim for numbers; he collected books and editions that were extraordinarily hard to find and, by extension, were worth their weight in gold. More important, they were the stuff of rebirth, ways to bring vanished pasts to life.

It was, quite simply, a magnificent intellectual enterprise, both a working library that Chimen could access while researching his essays and books, and also a work of love, of respect for the past, preserving the memories and ideas of men and women now long dead, their worlds as vanished as their voices, their smiles, their bodies. Inside Hillway, one could embark on journeys into that past, to see the fighters of 1848 take to the streets in Vienna or Berlin or London; to witness the Paris Communards on the barricades; to visit the Russian revolutionaries in Petrograd in October 1917 or the displaced Yiddish-language journalists and theater impresarios who, a century earlier, had printed London East End newspapers with such whimsical names as *Der Poylisher Yidl* and had entertained homesick immigrants.

Chimen himself was not a particularly good storyteller—he frequently gave away the punch line of humorous anecdotes too early or, with more serious stories, got bogged down in too many details. Yet he knew so much about history and was so precise with his usage of names, his memory of places and dates, of who knew whom and who feuded with whom, that with a bit of imagination one could create one's own vivid, three-dimensional plotlines to accompany his scholarly historical conversation. He provided the raw materials and empowered his guests or students to imagine the rest for themselves.

My grandfather was not parsimonious with his collection, but one had to earn the right to see his bibliographic jewels, one had to have the right introductions. When a stranger wrote to University College London, shortly after Chimen had been made a professor, asking to see one of his William Morris letters, Chimen had his secretary type out a sniffy response: "I regret very much that my library is strictly private and I only allow very few people to have a look at it. Paul Meier, an old friend of mine, used my library for his article on Morris as well as for his great book on Morris in which he refers to it many times. I regret very much that the manuscript is not available to anybody else." Chimen would gauge your interest, see how much knowledge you brought to the table or how much enthusiasm you had for the world of ideas, and then, gradually, he would begin to give you entrée into the library. On one visit he might show you an early edition of one of Lenin's books; then, on the next encounter, he would let you glimpse a handwritten document by Lenin or something penned by the martyred German revolutionary Rosa Luxemburg. Perhaps, eventually, you would even see the original William Morris illustrated manuscripts kept in the very Bible box in which Morris had stored them during the latter part of the nineteenth century. Or you might get to handle a first edition of William Godwin's 1793 treatise, *Enquiry Concerning Political Justice*, the earliest published anarchist policy tract. It was a heavy volume, its thick, yellowing pages sandwiched within a majestic black binding; a volume similar to the one the teenage William Hazlitt, later to be counted among England's leading essayists, would have read in the mid-1790s. "No work in our time gave such a blow to the philosophical mind of the country as the celebrated Enquiry concerning Political Justice," Hazlitt wrote later in his collection of essays on famous men, *The Spirit of the Age*. "Tom Paine was considered for the time as a Tom Fool to him, Paley an old woman, Edmund Burke a flashy sophist. Truth, moral truth, it was supposed, had here taken up its abode; and these were the oracles of thought."

All of this was an exercise in trust—not that Chimen was fearful that one of his guests would flee Hillway with the box of Morris under his or her arm, or with Godwin's tract secreted in a briefcase but rather, that he believed intellectual favors ought to be reciprocal. He was more than happy to show visitors documents that in some cases they could see nowhere else on earth, but he would do so only in exchange for meaningful questions and thoughtful comments, or at the very least an expression of admiration and awe in response to the ideas and documents at hand. In 2006, to commemorate Chimen's ninetieth birthday, the documentary filmmaker Christopher Hird and the British New Left activist and scholar Tariq Ali made a film about Chimen and his books. As Chimen took Ali deeper and deeper into the collection, eventually bringing out such treasures as Marx's membership card from the First International—the organization set up in London in 1864 with the aim of uniting trade unions and left-wing political parties around the world into a structure capable of promoting a coordinated working-class revolution—and editions of *The Communist Manifesto* with Marx's and Engels's personal, handwritten annotations, Ali's eyes got wider and wider. "Oh my gosh, oooooh my gosh Chimen," he kept spluttering, overwhelmed by the historical relics he saw before him, by the proximity to extraordinary historical events Chimen was allowing him to experience. "Oh my gosh!"

"Marx is much more important in his political comments than as an economist of lasting value. This is what keeps me interested in Marx. His interpretation of history is brilliant. He realized before the word 'globalization' came into being that the capitalist system is becoming bigger and bigger, and not attached to individuals. This point he noticed already in *The Communist Manifesto*," Chimen told Ali during the shooting of the documentary, the old spark momentarily reignited in his tired, watery, antique eyes, as he lovingly presented book after book from his collection to his awed interviewer. Even then, all those decades after he had left the Communist Party, Marx remained my grandfather's intellectual icon. "He opened my eyes to understanding history." For those minutes, time fell away, and Chimen was no longer crippled by Parkinson's disease. Instead, he was the still-vibrant man who would take me on walks up the hill to visit Highgate Cemetery where Marx is buried. For those minutes the emergency medical assistance button hanging from his neck was simply a *vanitas*, a delicate reminder of mortality, rather than an urgent part of his daily wardrobe. "His sharpness of style, writing in English, German, French, absolutely brilliant in all three languages. It captured my imagination." Chimen smiled a crooked, chipped-tooth smile as he said this, shuffled over to a shelf, pulled an 1886 anarchist edition of *The Communist Manifesto* from his shelf, and laughed as he showed Ali how the anarchists, the self-proclaimed desperado freedom fighters, had censored passages they disagreed with.

The House of Books that my grandparents lived in, as well as the lives they lived and the people who made up their vast social circle, drew me across the generational lines and into their world. As a result of the gatherings I took part in at Hillway, for all of my life the shadows and ghosts of history have peered over my shoulder.

From my early childhood days, Chimen taught me how to interpret the world around me, how to use ideas carefully to create patterns out of chaos. He made me realize that we are, in large part, defined by our pasts—both our individual pasts and our collective histories. We are the aggregate of generations of experiences lived by our ancestors; but we are also, inevitably, products of our times, influenced by wars and revolutions, by social upheavals, by economic turmoil, by scientific advances and so on and so forth. The nineteenth-century German philosopher Ludwig Feuerbach famously noted that "Man is what man eats." True, but man is also what man's ancestors ate and what man's surrounding community eats. However much we try, we cannot entirely escape the past. What I consumed at the House of Books was not just Mimi's food but also the grand feast of ideas that accompanied every meal.

And so, we come back to Chimen's death. When my books arrived —Plato, Thomas More, Aristotle, Marx, Tocqueville—I put them on the top shelf in my study. There they sat, just within reach if I stood on a chair and stretched my arms up high. Close enough to take down when I needed them. Just far enough away that I did not feel compelled to plow through them all instantly. They were, I reminded myself, still really my grandfather's books, not mine. In addition to those volumes, I reclaimed a huge photo album that I had made for Chimen on his seventieth birthday, a collection of family images going back to the mid-nineteenth century. I was fourteen when I made that album; with hindsight I realize it was the first serious history project that I ever embarked upon, scavenging family contacts around the globe, writing to them, asking them to rummage through old boxes for photos of people now long dead, and then coaxing them to conjure up biographical information on those individuals.

The books and the album, together, represent to me a vision of stewardship. Of understanding how history is both deeply personal and collective. They help me see how it is made up not only of memories but also of documents. They force me to appreciate the role in history both of great doers and thinkers and of anonymous individuals. I look at them, and my past comes alive.

PROLOGUE II:
SAYING HELLO

Everything must be recaptured and relocated in the general framework of history, so that despite the difficulties, the fundamental paradoxes and contradictions, we may respect the unity of history, which is also the unity of life.
— Fernand Braudel, *On History* (1980)

GROWING UP, I was always presented with my grandfather's story in almost mythological terms, a series of inadequate, somewhat simplistic snapshots of a life too large to chronicle properly. I knew, according to the summaries of his life that I gathered in conversation, that Chimen had been born in the autumn of 1916 in Minsk, then a White Russian region and now in the Republic of Belarus, near the small town of Smalyavichy in which his family lived; that his birth had only been registered several months later; and that he had, therefore, at least two different birthdays. I knew, too, that Chimen had grown into his teenage years in Moscow and, when he was fifteen years old, his father—who had served two years in a hard-labor camp in Siberia for religious proselytizing and the ostensibly treasonable activity of talking to an American human rights fact-finding mission—had been sent into exile in England. Chimen, his younger brother, Menachem, and his mother were also allowed to leave. His two older brothers were kept as hostages in the Soviet Union for several years. In London, despite Rabbi Abramsky's recent experiences at the hands of the Soviet secret police, Chimen became involved in left-wing politics, and surreptitiously acquired and read copies of Karl Marx's writings with the glee of discovery and youthful rebellion.

In the mid-1930s, the young man enrolled at the still-new Hebrew University in Jerusalem, in what was then Palestine. He traveled there by train and ship: ships from England to France, trains south to the Mediterranean, then another ship, on which he had a steerage ticket, across the sea to Palestine. His vessel, like so many others bringing Jews to the mandated territory in the mid-1930s, docked at the port town of Haifa. On similar voyages it is recorded that many of the passengers, as they readied themselves to disembark, sang the Zionist anthem that later became Israel's national anthem, "Hatikvah":

> As long as the Jewish spirit is yearning deep in the heart,
> With eyes turned toward the East, looking toward Zion,
> Then our hope—the two-thousand-year-old hope—will not
>   be lost:
> To be a free people in our land,
> The land of Zion and Jerusalem.

Chimen might have sung along, although he never mentioned it when reminiscing about these years; more probably, however, he would have stayed silent. His political beliefs, at this point, did not include supporting the creation of a Jewish state. He arrived in a city in the throes of reinvention. In the old quarters of the town, the narrow, cobblestone streets were lined with buildings hundreds of years old. In the newer parts of Jerusalem, large numbers of modern apartment complexes were being erected at speed to accommodate the influx of new residents.

The university was a strange place, still trying to establish itself. Chaim Weizmann, the leading figure behind modern Zionism, had sunk its foundation stones in the summer of 1918, but the university had not opened for classes until 1925, and when Chimen arrived in 1936 its position in the academic firmament was still uncertain. Many of the faculty members were refugees from Nazi Germany; a fair number of them, as described in S. Y. Agnon's novel *Shira*, spoke almost no Hebrew. When they were short of cash, they sold their German books to dealers for a pittance; some of those books ended up in Chimen's early collection.

Shortly after he arrived, Chimen joined the Haganah (Jewish Defense Force) in response to the Arab revolt which broke out that year. Rioting throughout the summer months resulted in the deaths of numerous Jews, among them six students and several faculty members. The university's library was also attacked. "There was," wrote Agnon (one of whose original manuscripts subsequently made its way into Chimen's collection), "a new round of violence known as the riots, in which Jewish blood flowed unrestrained, and there were so many murders and massacres that no self-preserving Jew would venture out at night." Buses were fitted with iron window bars to deflect the rocks thrown at the vehicles by rioters. Yet, if his letters are any guide to his actions, Chimen spent his time in the Haganah arguing fine philosophical points rather than learning military drills. He became, during this period, friends with three other intense young men—Shmuel Ettinger, Jacob Fleischer, and the Silesian-born Abraham "Abby" Robinson—who would play major roles in his life in the years to come. And he dreamed of success in the world of academia.

But the Second World War interrupted his studies. In the summer of 1939, he had come to London to visit his parents, leaving from

Haifa and transiting through Marseilles on July 11, carrying a certificate of naturalization from the government of Palestine, written in both English and Hebrew, and also a brown Palestinian government passport, number 103907, issued the previous June. Chimen entered the United Kingdom on a four-month tourist visa, fully intending to return to Jerusalem after the summer; instead, he was left stranded and stateless by the outbreak of war. He remained stateless until late in 1947, when he received a short typewritten notice that his application to become a British citizen had been approved. He swore the oath of allegiance to the United Kingdom six days into the new year. As for his undergraduate university studies, he never returned to them. Henceforth, he would be an autodidact.

And so instead of claiming what he surely thought was his rightful place in a respected university, over the next several decades Chimen and Mimi (whom he married in 1940) ran Shapiro, Valentine & Co., a respected, albeit rather claustrophobic, Jewish bookshop in London's East End. Thwarted and frustrated in his academic ambitions, he looked for other avenues for his intellectual curiosity. During these early years with Mimi, Chimen embraced two passions: First, no longer religious and searching for an alternative set of certainties, he threw himself into the world of Marxism. And second, apprenticing himself to Heinrich Eisemann, he began to collect and deal in rare books.

Like so many of his peers, and like my grandmother and both of her sisters, Chimen had been drawn ever-closer to Communism during the early years of the Great Depression, and most particularly with the onset of the Spanish Civil War, years in which progressives in Europe dreamed of a popular front while the great Western democracies stood by and watched the demise of the Spanish Republic. Mimi formally joined the Communist Party in the mid-1930s. Chimen took slightly longer to so do. Growing up, I believed this delay was perhaps out of deference to Rabbi Abramsky. It was, however, merely conjecture; my grandfather never really explained to me either why he had joined the Party (the *p* was always uppercased) after his father's experiences or why it had taken him longer to join than it did many of his peers—although, I found out subsequently, he did tell researchers late in his life that in the 1930s, before he became a British citizen, the Communist Party did not admit foreigners as members. He did, however, acknowledge that he had become an intellectual Marxist as a teenager while he was still living in the Soviet Union. Whatever the reasons for the delays, he formally became a member only after the Nazis invaded Russia in June 1941.

Chimen never told me, either, how he rationalized joining a political organization that had defended the Nazi–Soviet Nonaggression Pact only two years earlier; how he justified to himself his defense, even hero-worship, of Joseph Stalin; or how he could continue to glorify the Soviet Union (albeit with less enthusiasm in the years after "Uncle Joe's" death) until the late 1950s, two years after Stalin's successor, Nikita Khrushchev, had acknowledged the scale of Stalin's horrific crimes. Perhaps he felt that others had already explained it for him. As the English politician Richard Crossman wrote in his introduction to the collection of essays *The God That Failed*, there was a "terrible loneliness" that progressive intellectuals felt during the 1930s. "They had a premonition of catastrophe, they looked for a philosophy with which they could analyze it and overcome it—and many of them found what they needed in Marxism."

Once Chimen joined the Party, he rapidly became a committed activist. During the war years and the decade that followed, he was one of the leading figures in the party's National Jewish Committee, as active—perhaps, I fear, even as fanatical—as any other Party leader. In his contributing essay in *The God That Failed*, Arthur Koestler compared his own original commitment to Marxism to a religious conversion. "From the psychologist's point of view," he noted, "there is little difference between a revolutionary and a traditionalist faith. All true faith is uncompromising, radical, purist.... All Utopias are fed from the sources of mythology; the social engineer's blueprints are merely revised editions of the ancient text." So it was with Chimen. He embraced Marxist orthodoxy with a messianic passion. In January 1947 he wrote a critical review of Koestler's book *Thieves in the Night*, on Jewish terror groups such as the Stern Gang, which had embarked on a violent campaign in Palestine, and prefaced his clever critique of the author's support for the violent organizations with a jargon-filled denunciation of his politics. Koestler, he opined under the ludicrously flimsy nom de plume "A. Chimen," was a "former revisionist, once a fellow-traveller in the Communist Party, [who] has now returned to the revisionist fold."

Yet, as for so many others of Chimen's generation, the adherence to the all-or-nothing political vision ultimately could not last. The word *utopia*, coined by Thomas More, comes from the Greek word *ou-topos*, meaning "nowhere." In the early 1950s, in the face of Stalin's purges of Jewish intellectuals and a rash of anti-Semitic show trials and campaigns throughout the Warsaw Pact countries—most famously the Doctors' Plot in Moscow, in which nine prominent doctors, most of them Jewish, were accused of poisoning, or planning to poison, top Communist Party officials; and the trial of prominent Jewish Communists in Prague who had been accused of the catchall crime of "Trotsky–Titoism"—Chimen gradually came to feel that he was indeed stuck in a nowhere-land. When the Jewish doctors were freed after Stalin's death, and their confessions voided—they had been tortured into admitting to nonexistent crimes—it became all but impossible for Communists in the West to continue to deny that anti-Semitism had flourished in Stalin's Soviet Union. Chimen's unease grew. And yet, somehow, he remained a Party member.

In 1956, when, in quick succession, the post-Stalin leadership in the USSR made public a long list of Stalin's atrocities and then committed their own outrage by sending troops into Hungary to suppress the anti-Soviet revolution, Mimi and her sisters left the Party. Chimen, inexplicably, stuck it out for two more years. For the rest of his life my grandfather was dismayed at his lack of judgment in supporting an abysmal, bloodthirsty system for so long.

Why Chimen remained in the Party during these years is beyond my powers of explanation—and possibly his own. But being a man who did nothing by half measures, once he left, he left with a vengeance, and in the decades following, both he and Mimi grew increasingly critical of left-wing politics. Chimen, long a member of the influential historians' unit within the British Communist Party, feuded with friends like Eric Hobsbawm for their continued embrace of Communism. Over time, Chimen reinvented himself as a serious liberal thinker. Politically, he came to align himself with Cold War liberals such as his close friend from his Hebrew University years, Jacob Fleischer (who had subsequently changed his surname to Talmon), whose worldview Chimen had, at the height of his Stalinism, scorned.

———

From middle age onward, Chimen became, temperamentally, ever more of an intellectual, an interpreter of events rather than a participant in them. In his little pocket diaries, in place of Communist Party meetings, were listed the minutiae of everyday family life: £26 and change spent on buying food, drink, and clothing for Yasha's (his and Mimi's nickname for my father) bar mitzvah; notes to pay insurance bills; dates on which school terms began. Yet unlike so many others in full flight from Communism, Chimen did not ever really withdraw from public life. Instead he pivoted, embracing academia where once he had embraced slogan-filled pamphleteering; declaring his fealty to liberal values and promoting the rights of individuals where once he had placed his hopes in the class struggle.

His knowledge was beyond panoramic. Chimen knew things that not only were rare nuggets of information but were literally unknown to other scholars. And he knew just when to reveal his hidden intellectual treasures and when to play coy and let other people take the spotlight. Well into his nineties Chimen retained a photographic memory, a remarkable range of knowledge, and an engagement with the world of ideas that was reminiscent of participants from the great salons of bygone centuries. His last published work was a letter to the editor of the *London Review of Books* in 2007, when he was ninety years old, providing hitherto unknown details of the ill-fated attempt by the literary critic Walter Benjamin to escape over the Pyrenees to elude his Nazi pursuers in 1940; Benjamin did get over the mountains but was found dead shortly afterward, the victim either of suicide or of murder. Chimen wrote about how he had discovered, through conversations with the niece of the woman who had tried to smuggle Benjamin to freedom, that Benjamin was carrying with him a black briefcase containing a manuscript "more important than his life." Neither the briefcase nor the manuscript was ever found. It must, wrote Chimen sadly, have been "destroyed by whoever found it immediately after Benjamin's suicide." Shortly after Chimen wrote this letter, Carl Djerassi (an emeritus professor of chemistry from Stanford University, who had been instrumental in the development of the contraceptive pill and steroids) visited him. In retirement, Djerassi was writing novels and plays, and he was currently doing research for a theater piece—*Four Jews on Parnassus*—in which four famous Jews, from different walks of life, would get into a conversation. One of his characters was Benjamin, and one of the themes he wanted to explore was the missing briefcase that Chimen had detailed. Chimen and Djerassi spent time together at Hillway. Afterward, the chemist wrote, enthusiastically, that my grandfather had "bewitched" him.

Mention anyone connected with anything to do with Socialism or modern Jewish history (which, it being an ancient culture, meant anything from about the last five or six hundred years) and almost anything to do with the Enlightenment, and Chimen could give you the equivalent of an encyclopedia-entry answer as to who they were and why they mattered. Steven Zipperstein—a protégé of Chimen's, who went on to become a professor of Jewish history and culture at Stanford—would come to Hillway after a long day of studying at the British Library and proceed to mention which Russian-language Jewish newspaper articles he had been reading. Every time, Chimen would recall the article and explain its contents in detail. Fascinated by this feat of memory, Zipperstein decided to test how deep the well went: He began to drop cryptic clues about what manuscripts he had been perusing, waiting to see how long it took Chimen to guess the documents. Invariably, it did not take long. Chimen was like the mythological students celebrated in yeshiva lore, who had become so adept at studying texts that one could stick a pin into a book and they would know, from seeing how far it had sunk in, what page the point was resting on and what text was on that page.

In other words, he was like his father.

———

Rabbi Yehezkel Abramsky, the son of a small-time timber merchant Mordechai Zalman Abramsky and his wife, Friedl, had reputedly been born and survived childhood as the result of a blessing bestowed on his parents—they had earlier lost several infants to childhood diseases—by a renowned rabbinic scholar and miracle worker known as *Der Moster Zadik* ("the Holy Man from Most"). As a result of this intervention, his God-fearing admirers later hypothesized, Yehezkel, optimistically nicknamed Alterke ("the old one") by his parents to cement further his chances of a long life, had memorized every book of the Hebrew Pentateuch by the time he was eight years old. When the family walked to the town of Most from the tiny village, or *dorf*, of Dashkovtski, in what is now Belarus—so small that it could not rustle up the ten men required to form a minyan (quorum) for religious services—to attend synagogue on the High Holy Days, Yehezkel would astound audiences by reciting from memory any Jewish religious text he was asked to perform. They would shout requests from the rooftops; he would oblige. He was a Mozart of Torah. Within a few years of these public performances, he had attended every top yeshiva in the region, doing a sort of grand tour of the Orthodox equivalent of the Ivy League, and in the process establishing for himself a reputation as a Talmudic wunderkind without peer in the Jewish communities of Byelorussia and Lithuania in the dying years of the nineteenth century and the opening ones of the twentieth.

The young Yehezkel was so remarkable in his knowledge of the Babylonian Talmud, and all the great rabbinic codes of history, that Rabbi Chanoch Henekh Eygish suggested to his famous cousin Rabbi Israel Jonathan Jerusalimsky that Yehezkel might make a suitable husband for Jerusalimsky's daughter, Genia "Hendel" Raizl. Jerusalimsky was the rabbi of Ihomen and a scion of a rabbinic dynasty dating back five hundred years (a dynasty so fabled among the religious Jews of the region that they referred to it as "the silk family"); he invited the young scholar to his house, quizzed him on complex questions about the Holy Books, and promptly offered his seventeen-year-old daughter's hand in marriage. Over the next decade, Jerusalimsky would be instrumental in securing his son-in-law a series of increasingly prestigious rabbinic posts, as well as blessings from famous rabbis and Talmudic scholars, throughout the Byelorussian region. Rabbi Jerusalimsky's daughter, now married to a prodigy, would encourage her husband to realize his potential, to become as successful as her own ancestors. "Without her, my father would not have become so famous," Chimen averred in a filmed interview a few years before his death, the sunlight streaming into his dining room, a vase of red tulips perched on his dinner table as he talked. "She made him famous. She pushed him," he said, to use his extraordinary memory and understanding of the Talmud to maximum effect.

Yehezkel's preternatural memory was a trait that he would pass on to his third son, Chimen, who was named after a long-departed great-grandfather who had been born around the time that Napoleon's armies were invading Russia. The mnemonic tricks that yeshiva students such as Yehezkel learned in order to master the Gemara (the part of the Talmud made up of rabbinical commentaries on the Mishnah, which was a compilation of the Oral Law transmitted down the centuries by early Judaism's great sages), including a form of the call-and-response method, in which tutors called out verse numbers and students then recited the verses back at them, and in which instant translations from Hebrew to Yiddish and back to Hebrew were chanted, were shared with Chimen. Later, when he had his own children, Chimen would impress them by shouting out long lists of numbers, which they would write down and he would repeat back a few minutes later with no mistakes. They thought he was simply remembering the numbers that he had conjured up randomly. In fact, he later explained—a magician finally revealing his tricks— he was simply converting the letters that made up the words of particular Bible verses into their equivalent numeric placement in the

Hebrew alphabet. And, when asked to recall the stream of numbers a few minutes later, would rapidly translate into numeric form, once more, the biblical verse he had previously chosen. It might have been numbers that came out of his mouth, but it was the words of the Bible that triggered their release.

In the rare instances when Chimen could not respond to a question off the top of his head, he knew exactly which of his tens of thousands of books contained the answer, what page the information was on, and where along his many double-stacked bookshelves the volume could be located. "I'm just a little man," he would say, "but I know something about..." and, a smile of pride growing as he talked, as he gauged his audience's level of wonder, he would rattle off a stream of information about whatever the issue or event in question might be.

When Chimen talked about Voltaire or Maimonides, about the self-proclaimed seventeenth-century Jewish messiah Sabbatai Zevi, or about Marx, one half expected these historical giants to knock on the door and saunter down the hall and into the dining room to plunge into the discussion. There, in my fantasies, they would be joined by history's chorus singers, second-rank thinkers such as Harold Laski or the German Socialist Karl Kautsky, revolutionaries such as David Riazanov and Clara Zetkin. For Chimen, a man who had been born in prerevolutionary Russia, whose childhood had encompassed civil war and famine, and whose formative adult years had involved a world war and the Holocaust, these theories and philosophies, words and books provided structure to his world; they staved off the chaos, the anarchy, the fearsomeness of daily existence.

It did not happen often, but when he did not know something, my grandfather could bluster. Hence the time he assured my younger brother that butterflies turned into caterpillars; or the day he stopped England's boxing superstar Frank Bruno, who lived nearby, on the street to talk about boxing, a sport I doubt very much Chimen was acquainted with in any way, shape, or form other than via newspaper headlines and photos. From then on, when the two men bumped into each other Bruno would affectionately call out to "the Prof." Or the learned conversation that, as a very old man, Chimen engaged in with my father's cousin Peter about whether or not the English soccer star David Beckham ought to move to Los Angeles to play for the LA Galaxy. While Peter had been obsessed with soccer for his whole life, Chimen had almost certainly never once kicked a ball and, as certainly, had never ventured into a stadium.

From the time I was a very small child, I met people like Isaiah Berlin or the great modern Jewish historian Salo Baron, the New York rabbi Arthur Hertzberg or Chimen's best friend, the Israeli historian Shmuel Ettinger, at the House of Books, and I was absorbed into their conversations. In hindsight, I realize this was a gift as great as any I would ever receive. I was treated like an adult, maybe allowed a few sips of wine for the experience, was expected to have opinions on the great issues of the day, was argued with and consulted with as if my views genuinely had importance. It taught me self-confidence, and it taught me the wonders of curiosity, of knowledge. With some of the most profound thinkers of the age, I would talk about—sometimes shout about—nuclear disarmament; the 1984 miners' strike in England, which utterly captured my attention the year I turned twelve; Israel; the Soviet Union; interpretations of the Second World War; the Holocaust; great museum exhibitions and theatrical productions.

There, too, I would see my grandparents' nephew, the social historian Raphael Samuel. He would often come to visit Mimi and Chimen and, on occasion, to needle them. Raph had been a central figure behind the emergence of the New Left in England in the late 1950s. Like as not he had mapped out its formation with his Oxford chums while sitting at the dining-room table in Hillway amid the wreckage of the Communist dream, as a way to breathe new life into a demoralized radical movement. And he remained a true and unrepentant radical until his death in 1996. While Chimen and Mimi had become increasingly sympathetic to Zionism, Raph continued to believe that Israel was a fundamentally flawed project, and that the Middle Eastern wars from 1967 onward were wars of occupation. The result, at my grandparents' house, was often a form of spectacular intellectual and ideological fireworks, made all the more tense by the interjection of family emotion into the passion play. Raph and Chimen sometimes fought so heavily that they would not speak to each other for months afterward.

Children take the environments they are familiar with for granted. And so it was that for many, many years I simply assumed that all old people lived in book-houses, every wall lined with musty old tomes containing the secrets of history, politics, philosophy, religion, art. I assumed that it was entirely normal to spend one's time arguing the merits of various obscure Socialist doctrines in between the matzo ball soup and the roast duck. I concluded—wrongly I subsequently learned—that most children had Spinoza and Marx, Rosa Luxemburg and Hegel quoted to them as morality tales by their grandfathers. Nearing forty as I write this, I can still recall Chimen's fabulous

Chimen and Sasha in Jack and Lenore's garden. Southampton, 1974.

Eastern European accent, his wagging finger, his earnest expression as he urged moderation on me, commanded me, "Meester Sasha," to read Spinoza—the brilliant autodidact from Amsterdam who had been excommunicated by the Jewish community, who had spent much of his life underappreciated, and who for decades had ground glass lenses to make a living—and to learn the fine arts of intellectual subtlety.

"The attainment of true intellectual values, that is perfect intellectual ideas, is impossible except for a man whose moral character is properly trained and who possesses dignity and balance," wrote the Spanish Jewish philosopher and ethicist Maimonides in 1190, in *The Guide for the Perplexed*. Only such a person would have a chance at true enlightenment, at understanding the great mysteries of life and of the moral code upon which society rested. God, for Maimonides, existed outside of time, unchanging, not a person, a physical presence, so much as a concept; but it was this unchanging essence that allowed the world to exist, that provided a wellspring for all the dynamism within it.

For Chimen, Maimonides was the lodestar, one of the great philosophers out of whose ideas modernity could emerge. Substitute "forces of history" for God, and one could start to understand Chimen's approach to life. He believed that these big forces shaped everyday lives; and he believed that only through strenuous intellectual effort could one come to fathom the immensity of these forces. Where Talmudic scholars were preoccupied with interpreting God's will in the aftermath of Creation, Chimen was obsessed with the interpretation of history's will. He was a historian-cum-metaphysician, fascinated by Hegel's idea of the dialectic of history, of clashing opposites bringing new worlds to life—the holy trinity of the thesis, the antithesis, and the synthesis; and by Marx's delineation of the driving forces of history—great, impersonal, economic forces operating on human societies with something approaching inevitability.

Chimen himself, as he was all too aware, had been born into the crucible of history: his family caught between warring armies on the eastern front during the First World War, the communities out of which they had emerged ravaged by pogroms, their lives further upended by revolution and civil war. Indeed, for the first years of Chimen's life, he knew nothing but the deprivation and terror of the front line.

In July 1920, when Chimen was nearly four years old, Smalyavichy, the town in which his father, Yehezkel, was the rabbi, was besieged. It had changed hands several times during the civil war that had broken out following Lenin's October Revolution and the Russian withdrawal from the First World War. This time, it was a triumphant Red Army that readied itself to push Polish nationalist soldiers, allied with the pro-tsarist White Armies, out of the town and the broader region. As the Polish soldiers retreated, they set fire to large parts of town, especially in the Jewish quarters, indulging in a last frenzied bout of pogrom-like brutality. Yehezkel was not present as the flames rose skyward—he had, according to his biographer Aaron Sorsky, an appointment in the nearby city of Minsk. But his wife, Raizl, was at home, and so were his four young sons: Moshe, Yaakov David, Chimen, and an infant who died shortly afterward. (A fifth son, Menachem, would be born four years later.) The flames caught hold of their house, and Raizl barely had time to grab her children, rush them out into the street, and run for safety before their home was reduced to ash. Inside, Yehezkel's books, as well as his large personal correspondence with the leading rabbis of Byelorussia and Lithuania, went up in smoke.

Yehezkel was born in a tiny village in the forests outside the town of Most in 1886 and had been trained in the Musar schools, a particularly rigid and austere form of religious training, which stressed breaking down the self and a continual battle against "the evil inclination," be it the libido, pride, or possessiveness. In his classic novel about this vanished world, *The Yeshiva*, Chaim Grade has one of his characters make the following statement: "I've also heard it said that a Musarnik occasionally goes out in the street in the summer wearing a fur coat, a scarf, and galoshes. Is this some kind of religious observance?" The rabbinic scholar Tsemakh Atlas responds by saying: "They do this to train themselves to disregard other people's opinions and to ignore ridicule." So, the questioner continues, "What's a Musarnik?" Atlas, who was schooled in many of the same yeshivas as was my great-grandfather, thinks about it for a while and eventually answers, "A Musarnik is a man who lives the way he thinks he should live."

In these yeshivas, the Israeli historian Shaul Stampfer wrote in *Lithuanian Yeshivas of the Nineteenth Century*, "most of these students came from small towns, and this was their first taste of city life. Relatively few of them came from large cities, since by the late nineteenth century talented young men from the affluent families in larger urban centers were usually more attracted to the local secular schools than to a distant yeshiva." Indeed, Russian records from the year that Yehezkel was born do suggest that more Jewish students were enrolled in secular universities than in the yeshivas. The Musar schools—no-nonsense in their discipline, determined to build a cadre of ethically pure religious students who could protect the broader Jewish culture from what they saw as the ravages of secularism—were in many important ways a countermovement against modernity. They were somewhat akin, in the zealotry of their moral beliefs, to the born-again movement in American Protestantism in the late twentieth century and were often run by people who had been tempted by secular texts and newfangled scientific and philosophical notions, but who had returned, with resurgent enthusiasm, to the religion and belief systems of their forefathers.

Groomed for greatness within this self-enclosed religious world in which he had been identified as a rising star, Yehezkel's education had not stopped with Musar. He had also spent time in Lithuania, studying with the fabled scholar Chaim Soloveitchik, who had pioneered a technique known as the Brisker method, which pushed students to understand and analyze Torah commentaries through the precise analysis of key terms in various rabbinic debates. The challenging nature of Brisker teachings, the ability it gave its best students to understand their lives and ideas as part of a continuum of millennia of Jewish experience, must surely have helped men like Yehezkel to put life's ups and downs into perspective.

Soloveitchik's famous Slobodka yeshiva had been closed, by order of the Russian authorities, in 1892. And so, instead of attending group lessons there, Yehezkel studied privately with Soloveitchik and his sons, absorbing knowledge that previous generations of students had received from the *shiurim* (lectures) in the yeshiva's large halls. Yehezkel also took lessons from the Vilnian rabbi Hayyim Ozer Grodzenski. While still a student at Slobodka, he was initiated into the rabbinate by Rabbi Yehiel-Mihel Epstein, who, at nearly one hundred years old, had witnessed pogroms and upheavals from the French Revolutionary period through to the rise of the Russian bomb-throwers of the late nineteenth century. Barely eighteen years old, Yehezkel had already entered the elite tier of Eastern European rabbis. He moved on to Telz in Lithuania, which was the most competitive of the great yeshivas, with complex entrance exams on rabbinic writings, monthly follow-up examinations, and an emphasis on manners and deportment. There, he acquired the yeshiva equivalent of a graduate education, combined, in some small way, with the presentational touches of a finishing school: He learned how to conduct himself in public. Yehezkel spent two and a half years there. During the famines that accompanied the Russo-Japanese War of 1904–05 and the pogroms that followed in its wake, he and his fellow students were reduced to living on bread and water.

Yehezkel was thus no stranger to deprivation and loss. Yet even with such a training and a history, such an ability to put his own story into the context of the larger story of human and, in particular, Jewish history, human tragedy and the quest for an understanding of God, losing the bulk of his library in 1920 must have been a bitter blow. Of course, in rabbinic lore the words from burned holy books and scrolls find their way to heaven—but even so, in his heart of hearts Yehezkel must have deeply mourned their loss. Perhaps it was the story of the fire, repeated in subsequent years around the family dinner table, which triggered in Chimen (who was a toddler at the time) his lifelong obsession with collecting books. Two things, however, mitigated the loss: Yehezkel's family had survived the fire, and his manuscript, painstakingly handwritten in elegant Hebrew lettering—the early volumes of a sprawling set of commentaries on a body of teachings called the Tosefta, which he would write over six decades, titled *Chazon Yehezkel*—had been with him in Minsk and had thus avoided the conflagration.

Chimen spent a lifetime insulating himself from the flames, surrounding himself with so many books and so much knowledge, that something could be guaranteed to survive out of the ashes, out of the chaos of history. "When it came to books," his friend Dovid Katz, a Yiddish scholar whom Chimen had first met when Katz enrolled to study with him in 1976, believed, "there could be no left or right, no good or bad, for Chimen: they were part of a magical sphere of life that he had command of like no other. How he loved to show the works of a rabbi and a radical philosopher on the same shelf, showing how the bookshelf is the true territory of human harmony."

In the late 1970s, a family friend of my mother's came from Los

Angeles to visit us in London and was taken to see Chimen and Mimi's house. An artist, he immortalized that evening with a black-and-white ink drawing titled (for some reason in French) *Maison Livres des Shimin Abramski* [*sic*], or *Chimen Abramsky's House of Books*. It showed a house, the walls and—a flurry of artistic exaggeration—even the ceilings of which consisted entirely of books, a house whose occupants sat around cluttered tables in old chairs drinking endless cups of tea while engaged in animated conversation.

To me, that house, so ordinary from the outside—with its white plastered walls and tiled roof, its TV antenna perched next to the chimney, it looked like one of countless thousands of North London semidetached houses built in the early decades of the twentieth century—was my school, my university, my library, my sanctuary when the going got tough at home. It was the place I retreated to when I fought with my parents or found my younger siblings too annoying.

Chimen Abramsky's House of Books, sketch by Theodor Thomas, 1975.

From a very young age, I'd take a train from the station near our house in West London to Gospel Oak, walk along the side of Hampstead Heath, make a left on Highgate Road, a right on Swain's Lane, and then another left on Hillway. I'd walk down the dull red-brick front garden path, between my grandmother's rosebushes, and climb the three steps to the door. I'd ring the doorbell, and there Chimen would be. "Ah, Meester Sasha," he'd announce, pretending to be surprised. "Miri, it's Meester Sasha. Come on in." And he'd kiss me quickly on both cheeks, his breath slightly stale, then pull me into the House of Books and close the door behind me.

MASTER BEDROOM:
THE CITADEL

We do recognize our brave friend, Robin Goodfellow, the old mole that can work in the earth so fast, that worthy pioneer—the Revolution.

—Karl Marx, speech at anniversary of
The People's Paper (1856)

MY EARLIEST MEMORY of Hillway is not one of entry, of coming up the garden path and through the red front door, but rather of the citadel: Chimen and Miriam's bedroom.

I was three years old, old enough to call my grandfather "Nye" and my grandmother "Mimi," and old enough to be taken to a party at University College London, where Chimen was chair of the Hebrew and Jewish Studies Department. If memory serves, it was, ironically enough, a Christmas party. I have a vague recollection of a small room with what seemed to be a hobbit's door, through which one entered to get a present from a bearded Santa Claus; it had to have been made for hobbits, since even Chimen, at barely five feet tall, had to stoop to enter. And I have another half memory—maybe from the same day, maybe from another—of Chimen taking me to see a paleontologist friend who plied me with trilobites and spiraling ammonites, and then sent me merrily on my way. I was the oldest grandchild, and my grandfather loved showing me off to all his colleagues. As soon as I learned to walk, he started taking me to the university, parading me through its marbled hallways on our way to eat at the faculty cafeteria, and past the glass case in which resided the embalmed body of the philosopher Jeremy Bentham.

After that party, Nye brought me back to Hillway, where Mimi cooked us dinner. At some point that evening, thick fog rolled in—a pale imitation of the foul and deadly Dickensian pea-soupers that blanketed London into the 1950s, but nevertheless dense enough to bring traffic to a standstill. Chimen tried to get me home to my parents' house, twelve miles away in West London, and failed. An appalling driver at the best of times, the fog simply overwhelmed him. He turned around and, at a snail's pace, brought me back to Hillway.

I screamed bloody murder that night. Lying between Mimi and Chimen, in their musty old bedroom, surrounded by so many books they were impossible to count, I sobbed for hours. Long before dawn broke, Chimen had had enough. As soon as the fog lifted, he bundled me into my coat, put on his own bulky sheepskin jacket, dumped me into the backseat of his rickety old white Ford Cortina, and headed toward the Westway overpass and then on to Chiswick. By five o'clock, my bleary-eyed parents had reclaimed me.

Books cast strange shadows in a bedroom. Crammed next to one another, the varied heights and colors and textures of the spines reflect and absorb light in different ways.

Chimen and Mimi's bedroom had one little window, grimy with soot. If you pushed it hard, it opened outward onto a view of the back garden and, behind that, the tall spire of a North London church. The holes of a painted white latch placed over white pegs in the frame determined how much fresh air would be let in, but it was seldom open. To the right of the window were piles of books and papers and a series of metal filing cabinets. To the left was a tiny wardrobe, where Chimen's clothes hung, as well as a small chest of drawers for my grandparents' underwear and shirts. Next to that, on the wall facing the bed, was a huge old wooden rolltop desk, every inch covered with ancient books, handwritten correspondence, and a vast array of crumbling, antiquated documents. Above the desk were wooden bookshelves bracketed into the wall and sagging with the weight of photograph albums, books dating back to the eighteenth century, and old newspapers. Up on those shelves, and in waterproof plastic bags atop more shelves in the upstairs hallway, was a collection of William Morris books and manuscripts, including the original woodcut for Morris's book *News from Nowhere*, and a complete set of *Commonweal* newspapers that Morris had both published and, in this case, owned. It was, in sum, Chimen asserted proudly and perhaps a touch bombastically, more important than the Morris collection owned by the British Library. On the other side of the desk was the bedroom door. Down the far wall were more bookshelves, these books inside sturdy cabinets with glass doors. Behind the doors, which I don't remember being locked, were hundreds of the rarest Socialist books and manuscripts in the world: books with Marx's handwritten notes; volumes annotated by Lenin; treatises by Trotsky and by Rosa Luxemburg (including the typed manuscript of her doctoral thesis); original documents from the revolutionary Chartist movement of the 1830s and '40s, whose members had marched, and ultimately fought, for the right to vote, for economic dignity, for the ability to organize into trade unions, and for a Parliament that represented the people instead of corrupt, moneyed interests. "For three-and-twenty years," the original Chartists wrote in

Handwritten letter by Rosa Luxemburg from Chimen's collection.

their petition to Parliament in July 1838, nearly a quarter of a century after the Napoleonic Wars had ended, "we have enjoyed a profound peace. Yet with all these elements of national prosperity, and with every disposition and capacity to take advantage of them, we find ourselves overwhelmed with public and private misery."

In homage to working-class martyrs from earlier revolutionary epochs, Chimen had, at some point in time, bought at auction a sword made to commemorate the cutting down of protestors at St. Peter's Field in Manchester in 1819, a generation before the Chartists. The Peterloo massacre, as it was known, had resulted when the cavalry rode into a huge crowd that had gathered to demand parliamentary reform and tried to forcibly disperse them; eighteen people were killed and hundreds more were injured. It was a long, slightly curved saber with a set of floral motifs painted onto the metal near its hilt. Its handle was striped. The point, even after nearly a century and a half, was still murderously sharp. Chimen had kept the totemic weapon just long enough to realize that should his young children— Jack was a teenager, Jenny still in primary school—stumble upon it while exploring the nooks and crannies of Hillway, they might accidentally shed blood once again with its blade; and so he sold it.

The shelves of Chimen and Mimi's bedroom were double-stacked, hidden jewels invisible to the naked eye. Like genies waiting to be released from their bottles, the revolutionary ghosts of hundreds of years of human struggle lay in Chimen's tomes, waiting, waiting for someone to open the volumes; waiting, waiting for the chance to leap into the light once more. Every so often, a reader would indeed release these genies, and then hidden worlds would be revealed. Open those books and the Rights of Man would come alive; the cruelties inflicted on nineteenth-century workers would be laid bare; the aspirations of generations of revolutionaries would be explained. Contradictory and contentious programs for the improvement of humanity jostled one another on Chimen's shelves, just as their authors had sparred at political meetings, in cafés and taverns throughout Europe. Volumes calling for universal suffrage could be found alongside detailed justifications for the dictatorship of the proletariat; celebrations of liberal individualism were shelved next to texts that referred to those same individuals, in the mass, by slogans—the glorious proletariat, the filthy bourgeoisie.

By the late 1950s, Chimen's greatest intellectual joy lay in his ability to find and to purchase rare books. Part of that joy flowed from what he knew he would read in those books; he had the passions of a true historian, was a connoisseur of little details. When he read a book, he read it not simply for the main text but for the footnotes, the name of the publisher, and the location of the printer. All were clues; all helped him to understand the milieu in which the book was crafted. The differences between editions gave him a glimpse of the author's evolving thoughts on a topic. The bibliographies enabled him to chart an intellectual odyssey.

But another part of the joy resided simply in the hunt. He would scour the annual *Book Auction Records*, exploring what had been sold at which auctions and to whom over the past year. He would examine the prices carefully—and thus be able to calculate how much he would likely have to pay for books and manuscripts that he wanted to add to his collection. On Mondays and Tuesdays, he would attend

Sotheby's sales. On Wednesdays, Christie's held their auctions. He would turn up on Chancery Lane when Hodgson was selling books that he was interested in purchasing. In those postwar years, explained the rare-books dealer Christopher Edwards, who knew Chimen decades later, "There were so many books coming onto the market. It was a more liquid market. There was a greater supply." And because of that, prices were suppressed. In the 1950s, Chimen could indulge his passion for book-buying in a way that he never could have done had he started out collecting a generation later. And like London's other knowledgeable dealers, he could take advantage of the auction houses' ignorance to buy books cheaply and then resell them to private purchasers for a handsome profit. "It was," noted Edwards, "a bit like the diamond business. It was a group to which a relatively small number of people had access. There was a well-established, not very well-known market to which only the dealers were admitted."

Chimen approached books with the tenderness of an artisan, cognizant of every little detail, every flaw, every unique blemish. "You can recognise the edition by the little woodcut on page 31 and also on the title page," he wrote to his friend and fellow rare-books collector, the economist Piero Sraffa, on November 23, 1959, of a particularly rare 1888 edition of *The Communist Manifesto*. "In some copies there is also a misprint; after Fleet a comma follows and then the word St. There are many reprints but they have slightly different woodcuts. I could easily recognise it if I could see it." To a layperson, the misprint would have been unnoticeable; to Chimen it was as important as a misprinted stamp might be to a philatelist. He boasted in his letters that he had acquired "the rarest pamphlet of Marx in English." He mourned being outbid, by £20, for a Marx letter he had sought to buy at auction. He competed with Sraffa for the privilege of purchasing Marx esoterica. "I ordered heavily from Douglas, in Edinborough [*sic*], but missed all the items," he wrote in a hurried note to his friend in early April 1966. "Probably you succeeded in getting them."

Much later in his life, Chimen turned his eye to cataloging his own library. It was a task he stubbornly refused to finish, despite having cataloged many of the world's most important Judaica libraries for Sotheby's, despite having even compiled a catalog of catalogs that he would occasionally show to fellow bibliographers. "It takes the magic out of it. It becomes a thing to sell, not a real collection. Once you catalogue the book, it becomes a dead object almost," was how Edwards interpreted this reluctance. Chimen loved being courted by would-be buyers; adored being taken out to restaurants and clubs, such as the Garrick in central London, where dealers could flatter him by talking about the importance of his collection. But when push came to shove, he did not want to admit that, apart from a few missing pieces (he bemoaned the fact that he did not have any original issues of Marx's newspaper the *Neue Rheinische Zeitung*, published in Cologne during the revolutionary year of 1848 and into 1849), his collection—his life's project—was complete. Even when his insurance agent, Will Burns, repeatedly wrote him letters requesting that he provide a catalog of his library, Chimen managed to find one excuse after another. He was too busy; he was traveling; he was ill; he would do it next month. "I had hoped to do it during the summer vacation," he informed Burns in late October 1981, "but unfortunately, as Miriam had an accident in Israel, I was unable to do so. I hope to complete it towards the end of January." He did not, and Burns wrote him several more letters on the matter before eventually giving up. The collection remained insured only as general contents; had disaster struck and the House of Books burned to the ground, Chimen would have found, to his horror, that his inability to provide a catalog was a costly oversight.

What Chimen did do, though, was pen a series of memoranda

about how he had acquired some of his rarest prizes. He wrote, for example, about how, in the early 1950s, he had managed to buy William Morris's complete collection of the Socialist League's journal, *The Commonweal*, along with the wooden box, with a rexine cover dyed blue and lined with a white feltlike material, that Morris himself had constructed to house a 1539 Bible, and in which, ultimately, he kept his copies of the revolutionary newspaper. The pages of the publication—its words printed in double columns originally on a monthly basis, then later weekly, from 1886 until 1895, and filled with the revolutionary musings of Morris, Marx's daughter Eleanor, and other radical luminaries of the late-Victorian years—had passed from Morris to his close friend, the typographer Emery Walker; from Walker to his daughter; and from her to a poet named Norman Hidden. Chimen eventually bought it from Hidden for £50. And there they stayed, in their Bible box, high on a wooden shelf in the upstairs hallway at 5 Hillway, for more than half a century.

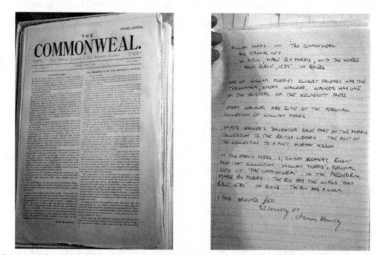

Left: Page from William Morris's complete collection of *The Commonweal*, owned by Chimen. Right: A memo Chimen wrote late in life explaining how he acquired his Morris materials.

Those pages were some of Chimen's most treasured possessions, their crinkly texture and age-browned color conjuring images of the cultured, tea-drinking revolutionaries who had made up Morris's coterie. I imagine that, in many ways, Chimen saw himself in their stories. The front-page manifesto in *The Commonweal*'s first issue, sold to readers for one penny in February 1886 and signed by the twenty-three founders of the Socialist League, put the mission simply: "We come before you as a body advocating the principles of Revolutionary International Socialism; that is, we seek a change in the basis of Society—a change which would destroy the distinctions of classes and nationalities." On May Day the following year, the date on which it was announced that the paper would be published weekly, Morris and his friend Ernest Belfort Bax wrote an editorial: "We are but a few, as all those who stand by principles must be until inevitable necessity forces the world to practise those principles. We are few, and have our own work to do, which no one but ourselves can do, and every atom of intelligence and energy that there is amongst us will be needed for that work."

In his lectures—at Oxford in the early 1960s; at Sussex University, where he delivered an epic series of talks in 1967 to commemorate the fiftieth anniversary of the Bolshevik Revolution in Russia; and at the numerous other universities and clubs which, from the time he reached middle age, began asking him to speak—Chimen took audiences on panoramic journeys through the landscape of nineteenth- and early twentieth-century European upheaval. He ranged from the early and mid-nineteenth-century writings of Nikolai Gogol and Alexander Herzen, and of the anarchist/terrorist Mikhail Bakunin—denizens of what Isaiah Berlin termed the "remarkable decade" —through to the later nineteenth-century revolutionaries such as the early Marxist Georgi Plekhanov, and into the twentieth century with the life and times of Lenin.

Marx's titanic battles during the 1860s and '70s with Bakunin (whom he had accused, in print, of being a tsarist agent provocateur as early as 1848—the year Europe teetered on the brink of wholesale revolution) for the soul of the First International acquired form in Chimen's lectures. One could imagine the two patriarchs of revolution frothing at the mouth with rage, spittle flecking their copious beards, hands clutching their large brows, as each made his gambit for the loyalties of Europe's awakened working classes. The extraordinary drama of Russia's changing position in revolutionary thought also came alive: It moved from being the lodestar of reaction, the great bear that had crushed Central Europe's revolutions in 1848, and a country that Europe's revolutionaries ardently believed had to be brought low before a more general revolution was possible, to becoming the beacon for an international revolutionary movement. "To quote Pushkin," Chimen told the Sussex students at the tail end of 1967's summer of love—trying to flatten his Russian accent and making it sound, in the process, almost Dutch—"Russia was lying in wait for a spark to light the flame." His words were precise, clipped; in listening to the recordings, all these decades later, I can visualize him desperately forcing himself to slow down, to enunciate each syllable, each word correctly.

In Chimen's library the great dramas of generations of revolutionary struggle were tucked away. Enter into this secluded suburban household and a diorama of revolutionary images—from Russian peasant communes and revolutionary committees, to the more sedate imagery of Victorian English radicals—was there for the viewing. Take, for example, the small purple book, surprisingly heavy for its size, titled *The Revolution and Siege of Paris, With the Elections and Entry of the Prussians, in 1870–71*, by an anonymous author referred to simply as "An Eye Witness" (but subsequently identified as Percival J. Brine, a fellow of King's College, Cambridge), which my brother chose for himself after Chimen's death. Detailing the Prussian occupation of Paris that followed the Franco-Prussian War, Brine noted that "The streets were only too tristes. The fortifications were entirely deserted in those parts of the city allotted to the Prussians. The houses, shops, cafes, hermetically closed all day and night, not a soul at the windows, not a thing to be bought for love or money; in fact, it was like a city of the plague, that the people had deserted."

Or ponder the little book, with the dull red cover, that occupied shelf space nearby. Embossed with the gold-lettered title *Paris During the Commune, 1871*, it was a blow-by-blow eyewitness account, by a now-forgotten Victorian Methodist minister named William Gibson, of the great revolutionary upheaval that, for a few weeks during the heady spring of 1871, delivered Paris to a workers' revolutionary committee after the French military defeat in the Franco-Prussian War, and which, quickly and brutally, was obliterated by the army. "This day (Saturday)," he wrote in one of the letters to the *Watchman and Wesleyan Advertiser* that was collected in this volume, "has been a day of great excitement in Paris. Having occasion to go to the Northern Railway Station at six o'clock this morning, I heard the National Guards in all directions being [sic] the rappel, and knew something must be brewing." Gibson matter-of-factly reported that there were bodies lying in the street, and that the injured were being dragged away by their comrades. "11 p.m.," the letter concludes, "we hear the roll of cannon, but hope, nevertheless, to sleep in peace."

———

Almost as important as the words were the ways the books felt and smelled. In turning the thick pages of old books, in heavy, cracked, cardboard covers or vellum bindings, or the crumbling, flaky pages of other volumes, one could imagine what Marx might have felt as he held a particular tome in his hands while researching his great tracts in the Reading Room of the British Museum. In the cloying smells released when ancient volumes were opened up, one could sniff out hints of lost printing techniques and paper-making methods, of inks manufactured centuries ago. In the vellum-bound author's manuscript of Morris's *News from Nowhere*, its handcrafted, thick, cream-colored pages made visible by a loosening of the gold ribbon that bound them, one could see the artistry of Morris's woodblock illustrations. This was a book, set in a utopian, postrevolutionary future, in the year 2102, intended to fire up not just the mental faculties but the senses as well. It was a detailed description of an imagined society after years of violent upheaval and revolution, following which the state had realized Marx and Engel's prediction and magically "withered away," a world where "people live and act according to the measure of their own faculties."

In this future, private property and money did not exist. People worked not because they had to but for the intrinsic satisfaction of a job well done—like-minded workers voluntarily joined together not in factories but in "banded-workshops." There were no schools, but learning was universal. Prisons were no more, their echo but a distant memory from barbaric and, thankfully, long-gone days. Formal marriages, and by extension divorces, were relics from a benighted past. Perhaps most important, since everyone lived in harmony there was no need for politics or legislatures, no need for the old charade in which, on the one hand, elected representatives strove "to see that the interests of the Upper Classes took no hurt," and on the other they worked "to delude the people into supposing that they had some share in the management of their own affairs." Parliament was, Morris wrote, now a "dung market," a magnificent building housing not politicians but manure for the fields of a newly pastoral London. It was the sort of aside that Chimen would have particularly appreciated.

Reading Morris's own manuscript of *News from Nowhere*, holding it, feeling it, was a deeply visual and tactile experience. Its protagonist's house, "the old house by the Thames," which was modeled on Morris's home at Kelmscott Manor, came alive in these pages. It was a house outside of time, in spirit not too dissimilar to Hillway.

Woodcut from William Morris, *News from Nowhere* (1890). The author's manuscript was one of Chimen's most treasured possessions.

Chimen spent his earliest years in Byelorussia, which was a part of the Russian Empire when he was born, became briefly independent after the revolution, and was incorporated into the Soviet Union when Chimen was still a young child; today, it is the independent state of Belarus. He was born during the Great War, in September 1916, and spent his first few years surrounded by the civil wars and famines unleashed in the aftermath of Lenin's revolution. Infant and childhood mortality soared in these years, in part because of the prevalence of diseases such as typhus —which presumably explains why, in early photographs, the heads of

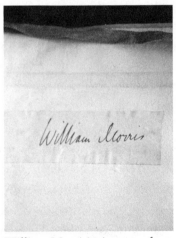

William Morris's signature from his original, bound version of *News from Nowhere*.

Chimen and his brothers are shorn, to counter the typhus-carrying lice. Isaac Bashevis Singer, who was a few years older than Chimen, and like Chimen was brought up in a devout household—though in Poland and, in contrast to Chimen's upbringing, in a home dominated by a Hasidic father—recalled having his sidelocks and head hair shaved off for this reason during the First World War. "Mother and I went off with a policeman," he wrote in his essay "The Book." "Mother carrying the few things she had been permitted to pack. In a strange house full of male and female guards another boy and I had our hair cut. I saw my red sidelocks fall and I knew this was the end of them. I had wanted to get rid of them for a long time."

Family lore had it that the famine accounted for my grandfather's diminutive stature—his father was five foot eight, his brothers were taller; but Chimen, a toddler at a time when there was almost no food to be had, was barely five foot one. The Revolution, the Civil War, the famine, and the years of chaos, violence, and transformation that followed, left their mark on Chimen quite literally. More than three-quarters of a century later, he could still remember the hysteria on the streets of Slutsk when Lenin died in 1924; the family had moved there a year earlier, the latest stopping point in Yehezkel's itinerant wanderings through the Pale of Settlement, which had begun when he became a teenage wunderkind rabbi. And he could recall the fear his family felt after they moved to Moscow in 1929, to be nearer the government agencies they needed to petition in order to secure Rabbi Abramsky an exit visa for the United States or Palestine; Yehezkel had been offered the rabbinate in the Palestinian town of Petah Tikva, but the Soviet authorities had repeatedly rebuffed his requests to be allowed to leave.

In Moscow, Yehezkel had, at least temporarily, managed to convince the Soviet authorities to let him publish religious commentaries —this was the period when the Soviets were expounding the virtues of secular Yiddish culture. But then, not long after the family had settled in, he was arrested and imprisoned. With each rebuff, each example of harassment, each humiliation, Chimen had witnessed the noose tightening on his father. Yet, no longer able to believe in the religion of his ancestors, and heavily influenced by the life of the Soviet Union in which, despite his parents' best efforts, he felt immersed, the pull of Marxism continued to draw him in. He must have felt he was living a horrendous lie: the son of an imprisoned rabbi, he no longer believed in God; the heir to one of the world's great rabbinic dynasties, he was increasingly obsessed with secular revolution.

—

Yehezkel Abramsky was a strong man who had built up his reputation during unfathomably difficult times. During the civil war years, the area of White Russia in which the family lived repeatedly changed hands among troops loyal to the old tsarist regime, Polish nationalists, and Bolsheviks. Yehezkel had been widely written about in the European and American Jewish press after he fought back against *pogromisti* who killed some Jews and attempted to shave off the beards of others, an act that was widely regarded as a peculiarly vicious insult, a desecration, since the Torah and several passages in the Talmud specifically prohibited the shaving of beards. Yehezkel had not only managed to preserve his beard but, according to reports in American Yiddish newspapers, he had even convinced a local Polish commander to sign a proclamation protecting the integrity of Rabbi Abramsky's facial hair. This was the first time the international press paid attention to my great-grandfather.

Then, in Moscow in 1929, Yehezkel, along with a rabbinic colleague named Shlomo Yosef Zevin, was arrested in the wake of his co-editing a Hebrew journal of Torah commentary titled *Yagdil*

Torah (bound volumes of which Chimen kept all his life) and for refusing to tell an American human rights mission that life for religious Jews in the Soviet Union was entirely satisfactory. Yehezkel, then in his early forties, was seized on the street one evening by the secret police, while he and Raizl were taking an evening walk. He was interrogated in the notorious Lubyanka prison and then in Butirki, the city's central jail. During those interrogations, he was beaten, screamed at, and threatened with unspeakable torture in attempts to get him to confess to having conspired to overthrow the Soviet government. He refused. Finally, he was sentenced to five years' hard labor in Siberia—a sentence the severity of which was mitigated in the family's mind only by the knowledge that he could easily have been executed. In fact, he *had* been sentenced to death initially, but the punishment had been commuted, probably because even then Yehezkel was known internationally among religious Jews, and men such as the writer Maxim Gorky and the poet Chaim Nachman Bialik (who had been born a little more than a decade before Yehezkel, and who had studied in many of the same yeshivas, before becoming the first renowned modern Hebrew poet) had urged Stalin's judges to show mercy on their illustrious victim.

In Siberia, Yehezkel recalled later in life, he was forced to run barefoot in minus forty degree temperatures; he was fed near-starvation rations, only occasionally enhanced by care packages sent to him by Raizl; and he was made to sleep on a bed that was no more than a wooden plank, on which shivering bodies lay huddled next to one another. There, his guards made him thread frozen fish onto iron spits in the bitter cold—a torment so painful that he recited prayers for the dying every day before work, assuming there was a better than even chance he would not live to see the morrow. He began his prayers with the Shema, the declaration of faith, muttering in Hebrew "Hear, O Israel: the LORD is our God, the LORD is one," before setting out into the inhuman cold of the Siberian winter dawn to begin the hours of torment. Wear gloves and it was impossible to thread the fish; take off the gloves and one's hands began to freeze.

But, despite the agony of daily life in Siberia, while in the labor camp he continued to compose his commentaries on the Tosefta. The Mishnah, the first part of the Talmud, set down in writing by Judah the Prince (Juda ha-Nasi) about two hundred years into the Christian era, detailed the religious rules that governed Jewish life in the era of the Temple, which the Romans had razed more than a century earlier, and adapted those rules for a people whose central religious institution was, physically, no longer in existence. The Tosefta, by contrast, according to some scholars, possibly emerged out of an earlier Babylonian school of oral Jewish scholarship. Like the Mishnah it was probably first organized into a coherent body of written work in the later Roman period.

Both the Mishnah and the Tosefta minutely document how Jews should behave: how they should pray, bathe, eat; when they ought to have sexual relations; how they should rest on the Sabbath and so on. Compilations of Halakha, or religious laws, they were worked out over centuries of discourse by the great sages; the rabbis represented in this text are referred to as Tannaim. But the Tosefta is a longer, more involved body of work, filled with explanatory notes and comments, its aphorisms and sayings unedited, its attributions of legal rulings to individual rabbis more complete. It includes material by Tannaim that was not included in the Mishnah. Much of the time, according to religious scholars, its passages agree with those of the Mishnah. Sometimes, however, they contradict them. The Tosefta is a difficult work, its origins clouded in uncertainty, its correspondence to and difference with the Mishnah providing a wealth of material on the development of early Jewish religious law in different population centers and under a variety of political conditions.

As he slaved away in Siberia, Yehezkel developed his interpretation of this body of law, calling on his prodigious memory of religious texts to conjure up images of the passages that he would critique. Over the months, he memorized thousands of lines of his commentary, scribbling them down when he had a chance, late at night or early in the morning, on whatever paper he could find. Usually it was the translucent cigarette papers that the convict laborers could occasionally lay their hands on. Once he had written these additions to his growing commentary, he would carefully hide the papers among his personal effects.

After months of international pressure from Jewish organizations in the United States and Western Europe, Yehezkel was finally released in 1931, and he arrived back at his Moscow apartment on the eve of Yom Kippur. He greeted his family and then, putting all thoughts of celebration aside, immediately began his fast. The family, Chimen recalled three-quarters of a century later, avoided going to synagogue that evening, fearing that if they showed themselves in public his father would once again be arrested. Yehezkel spent the next day teaching his sons the commentaries exploring the significance of the Day of Atonement. Compromise, apparently, was not in his vocabulary.

Given a month to leave the Soviet Union, but with his passport confiscated by the Soviet authorities, Yehezkel traveled to the west, to Riga, Vilna, and Berlin, and arrived in London at the end of 1931. He became a refugee. Raizl and their two youngest sons, Chimen and Menachem, were allowed to follow him out of the country shortly afterward; but their two oldest sons, Moshe and Yaakov David, were kept behind in the Soviet Union as hostages, to deter the rabbi from speaking out too vocally against his erstwhile country. In London, Yehezkel and Raizl fasted twice weekly as an offering for their children's freedom, and rallied an international movement to secure their sons' release. With Europe sliding ever closer to war,

Britain's foreign minister Anthony Eden, who had taken an interest in Yehezkel Abramsky's fate since the international campaign to save the great rabbi's life after his arrest, found time to craft a personal appeal to the Soviets to release the Abramsky boys—Yaakov David, at the time, was in internal exile in Tashkent, in Uzbekistan, where he had married and had a son; Moshe was in Moscow. The appeal worked, and in late 1936 Moshe was allowed to join the rest of his family in London. Yaakov David and his family followed a month later, spending a few months in London, where Yaakov apparently quarreled with Yehezkel and Raizl about his lack of religious belief, before moving on to Palestine. Twelve years later, his son Jonathan, Yehezkel and Raizl's eldest grandson, was shot dead on a Jerusalem street by a Palestinian sniper during the Arab uprising that followed Israel's declaration of independence.

Yehezkel's imprisonment and subsequent exile did not, however, lead Chimen to embrace his religion. To the contrary; in rebellion against his father and the unquestioning, ultra-Orthodox religious world that Rabbi Abramsky represented, Chimen started imbibing Bolshevik ideas in Russia while working as an apprentice to an artisanal suitcase maker to support his mother and his brothers during these dark years. He had, at the age of fourteen, begun attending Communist clubs frequented by well-known figures in Moscow's Yiddish cultural scene. By the time

Chimen as a teenager in Moscow, circa 1929.

he was sixteen—a lonely exile living in London's Jewish East End, in an apartment at 1a St Mark Street, Aldgate, which was owned by an immigrant boot maker named Nathan Mitzelmacher; and with two older brothers still stuck in the Soviet Union, to whom Yehezkel sent money each week so that they would not starve—he was writing in Hebrew to his cousin Shimon Berlin, whose family lived in Palestine, declaring that he was a Marxist. "I live here alone, lonely, unable to associate with such people," he reported to his cousin in describing his surroundings. "I read 'a lot' in these three languages: Russian, Yiddish, Hebrew, and a little English," he wrote, his words precisely penned, each word equally spaced one from the next. "I read especially historical and political-economy books, written from a Marxist point of view, because I consider myself a Marxist."

As a young man, Chimen wanted, desperately, to stand up and be counted in his own right. Myopic, stunted in height, flat-footed, averse to physical exercise and sports, he knew that he was never destined to be a hero on the battlefield. But he wanted to make up for it in the arena of ideas. By the time he was fifteen or sixteen, while he still kept kosher and, for the sake of family peace, observed the daily rituals of an Orthodox existence, inside his own mind he had rejected the religious strictures that governed every aspect of his parents' lives. Instead he found intellectual stimulation in the great political and philosophical tracts of the Enlightenment and Romantic eras: He had started befriending secular, left-wing intellectuals, and increasingly, despite the horror stories his father had told him about the prisons and labor camps, he had come to see the Soviet Union as representing a new, beneficent force in human history.

Like so many of Europe's young intellectuals during the 1930s, he looked to Communism as a counterpoint to Fascism and also to the values and political systems that had led the Continent's great nations to throw themselves into the slaughter of what was optimistically referred to as the war to end all wars. His, like so many others, was an existential search for moral purpose in a post-God world, a hunt for new ways of organizing human society in the wake of the Great War in which millions had died, and, increasingly in the 1920s, in the face of the impending threat of Fascism. It was a search that brought in its wake one of the twentieth century's greatest paradoxes: How could so many people, believing so passionately in the language of universalism, so quick to latch onto the language of justice in their arguments, make such appalling political choices regarding whom they trusted and what political institutions they supported? How could so many utopians end up supporting Stalin's intolerant and bloodthirsty project?

At least in part, the answer must remain somewhat metaphysical. It was the zeitgeist, the atmosphere of the times, the immediacy of history—a time when history was seen as a living, breathing, pulsating entity, a thing that was pressing in on individuals caught within its vise. It was part of a search for certainty, unfathomable with hindsight but at the time all too easy to fall into. In America, many filmmakers and artists joined the ranks of the Communist Party. In Britain, the Party struck deep roots in London, Glasgow, and other urban centers. For the writer Arthur Koestler, embracing Marxism allowed him to think that "the whole universe falls into a pattern like the stray pieces of a jigsaw puzzle assembled by magic at one stroke.... Faith is a wondrous thing; it is not only capable of moving mountains, but also of making you believe that a herring is a race horse."

Did Chimen sympathize with the tormentors of his father? Highly doubtful. But did he come to think that his father was misguided, that his father's trial represented an aberration rather than the norm, or that the urgency of opposing a rising Fascist wave by aligning oneself with revolutionary workers' politics outweighed all other arguments? Certainly by the late 1930s it seemed that way. Stalin had notoriously argued that one could not make an omelet without breaking eggs, and the young Chimen, to his later bitter shame, entirely accepted the violent implications of this logic. Where Yehezkel, according to his biographer Aaron Sorsky, wrote of a Soviet Union that was "a land of blood that eats its inhabitants," Chimen wrote that it was a place where anti-Semitism had ended and where the workers were freer than anywhere else on earth.

It was a worldview that, by the late 1930s, Miriam Nirenstein well understood. Educated in the primary schools that catered to the children of immigrants in the crowded, poor neighborhoods of London's East End, and then at Clapton County Secondary School for Girls on Laura Place in Hackney, my grandmother and her sisters, Minna and Sara, had grown up kosher, traditional, yet clearly separated from the ways of their ancestors. They spoke an English influenced by the cockney of the East End and interspersed with Yiddish phrases, went out with boys of their own choosing, and while they attended synagogue, their hearts were no longer in the age-old rites.

Unconvinced by the religious enthusiasms of their parents, who were shtetl immigrants from an old, vanished tsarist Russian Empire, first Minna, then Sara and Miriam turned to Marxism for their rituals, their catechisms. Those who remained religious in the face of the challenges and traumas of the modern world were, they felt, "reactionary." By 1937, all three sisters were card-carrying members of the Communist Party of Great Britain. Like so many of their friends, their reasoning was simple. They were young Jewish East Enders, horrified by Oswald Mosley's Fascist Blackshirts marching through their community in imitation of the thuggish Brownshirts of early

Nazi Germany, appalled by the dithering responses to Fascism engaged in by the mediocre English and French leaders of the interwar years, tormented by the images that they saw in cinema newsreels of the Civil War in Spain. They believed that the Communists offered an alternative vision and so they threw themselves into Communist organizing.

Given the way Yehezkel had been treated in Soviet Russia, his third son's conversion to the religion of Bolshevism must have been a bitter blow. Certainly in biographical notes and essays on Yehezkel published in religious journals and encyclopedias, Chimen is described as straying, having chosen to walk away from the light. Chimen and—after they had met during the early months of the Second World War—Mimi, by contrast, cocksure in their assumption that the future lay with a Soviet-style Communism, must, I think, have reasoned somewhat as follows: "Yes, Rabbi Abramsky is a good man, but he's entirely wrong about religion. And if he's wrong about religion, in all likelihood he's politically compromised, too. Yes, he's a good man, a loving father, a caring father-in-law, but maybe the Soviet system had its reasons for arresting him; maybe, without even realizing it, he was endangering the workers' state. The human progress that Marxist revolution represents is too important to be derailed by sentimental stories and personal sympathies." When he came to write his biography for the Communist Party, on March 28, 1950, Chimen, at the time a fervent Soviet apologist, explained that "my parents are very reactionary. For a short time my father was imprisoned in Russia." The way it was structured, the first sentence seemed intended to justify the content of the second: "He was imprisoned because he was reactionary." Later in that same paragraph, he continued that he had been educated at home "owing to my father's reactionary views." Chimen wrote that he had begun to "rebel" against his parents' conservatism in 1934, when he started attending the Marx House Library and spending time with Communist students at the London School of Economics. In other internal Communist Party documents, Chimen went further; his conversion to Marxism, he averred in one handwritten testimonial, had begun in Moscow, during his father's Siberian imprisonment, when, seeking relief from the claustrophobic environs of the family's apartment, he "became a regular visitor to the Moscow Park of Culture and Rest, and the Jewish Communist Club." There, he recalled, the "famous Communist Yiddish writer" Beryl Dishansky had befriended him. "Unfortunately," the text continues, "I left the Soviet Union soon after, but both these places made a great impression on me and were my steps on the road to Marxism. The seeds sown in Moscow began to bear fruit in England. I began to read Marxist literature in earnest....In 1933–34, I became a member at Marx House....By then, I was completely 'left' in my outlook."

Not for the first time in my research, as I read this letter I am stunned. There is nothing in it of the gentleness that I knew in the older, grandfatherly Chimen. Nothing in it of the grief that he later felt when thinking back on Yehezkel's experiences in Siberia. I understand why Chimen, later in his life, tried to erase all traces of this most dogmatic individual, why he attempted to destroy all copies of these documents, why he refused to discuss how he had once viewed his father's imprisonment. When I read it again, I realize that this six-page missive is written in someone else's hand, with Chimen's signature formulaically added at the bottom. It is twice as long as the biography that Chimen did indeed write for the Party archives, and contains little that was not in the original—but is that much more jargonistic, that much more in the tone of a Party apparatchik. I am sure that Chimen believed in its contents, but it is at least mildly comforting to know the words might not all have been his. Of course, when I look at the handwriting more carefully, I realize, to my shock, that it is my grandmother's.

Later in life, Chimen lectured on the Byelorussian-born Hebrew novelist and journalist Peretz Smolenskin, who believed strongly in a Jewish national identity, yet in the mid-nineteenth century, after migrating to Vienna and modifying his first name to Peter, argued fervently against the role of the rabbinate in Jewish life. Smolenskin, Chimen explained to his students, believed that "yes, we have to campaign against the rabbis in Russia and Poland, who are against education, who are against enlightenment, against teaching Jews skills. They are remnants of an obscurantist age. We have to combat them." In his musings on Smolenskin, I hear echoes of my grandfather's own complicated feelings.

In 1937, while still studying at the Hebrew University, Chimen had been elected general secretary of the Students Federation of Palestine, where he organized a strike against increased tuition fees

Chimen as a student in Jerusalem, late 1930s.

at the university and agitated on behalf of the International Brigade in Spain. Over the next two years, he defied the British authorities in Palestine by organizing May Day parades, despite a ban on such left-wing demonstrations, during the last of which his marchers shouted what he described as "anti-Chamberlain, anti-Munich" slogans at the façade of the German embassy. And he led a series of classes on Marxism for left-wing students at the university. He also spoke at a meeting organized by the outlawed Communist Party of Palestine, justifying the show trials that were under way in the Soviet Union at the time. "The meeting caused a great deal of discussion," he wrote in one of the 1950 biographies, "and we were the subject of an attack by the official Labour leadership." As I read these lines, in Chimen's familiar handwriting, I feel as if I have caught my grandfather in a filthy act; I wish my eyes had been averted. I wish I had not opened the manila envelope containing photocopies of the documents.

But despite his enthusiasm, once Chimen returned to England and was marooned in London by the outbreak of war, he did not immediately join the party. It was not, apparently, for want of trying. Rather, he ran up against a paradox. Until 1941, the Communist Party of Great Britain, while espousing the necessity of internationalism, did not accept foreign nationals as members. As soon as the Party's policy changed, Chimen joined his local branch. For the next seventeen years, he was a committed member, taking part in organizing drives and pamphleteering; and he became a central figure in the National Jewish Committee. To be in the Party was to be a fully fledged devotee; one could not join by half measures. For both Chimen and Mimi, shorn of the religion of their childhoods, it served as much as an expression of faith as of political intent.

In the National Jewish Committee, Chimen quickly acquired a reputation as a top theorist. "Abramsky and Zaidman," wrote the historian Henry Felix Srebrnik, explaining Chimen's place in a revolution that never happened, "who had lived in the Soviet Union and Romania, respectively, and were fluent in a number of languages, seem to have been its [the National Jewish Committee's] chief theoreticians." Behind the scenes, he worked to convert Stepney and the surrounding East End neighborhoods to Communism—work that would pay off in 1945, when the area elected a Communist, Phil Piratin, as its member of Parliament. The committee members became experts on the status of Palestine and on the challenges presented by the competing claims of Arabs and Jews to the disputed land. Increasingly, as the Communist Party looked to stamp its mark on the postwar landscape, at the urging of R. Palme Dutt—an Oxford-educated loner and the author of the book *Fascism and Social Revolution*, who served for decades as the Party's leading theoretician—they expanded their analysis to include the whole Middle East, speculating about what would happen to British colonies in the region after the war ended. "Enemy number one was British imperialism," Chimen told an audience decades later, as he talked about the early postwar years and the Party's policies during this time. "The task of communists was to fight against the British Empire and for the liberation of the colonies." As such, they made contact with left-wing organizers in Persia, Iraq, Syria, Egypt, Lebanon, and even Sudan. A woman from Iraq smuggled in Communist literature from her homeland, sewn into the hem of her coat; British customs officials found other literature in her suitcase, though, and she was swiftly deported. Later, she would become a senior political figure; later still, she disappeared. Chimen believed she had been executed in the aftermath of the Ba'athist coup that brought Saddam Hussein to power.

The Party's Middle East team, and, in the background, the startlingly intense figure of Dutt, became acknowledged experts on the region, looked to for policy advice by left-wing groups throughout Europe; ultimately, Chimen later said, with a mixture of pride and

contrition, Soviet Russia even gave a nod to the expertise of the English Communists when shaping its Middle East policy. Taking this
knowledge of what was still Palestine, and of the countries surrounding it, Chimen and his team set about evangelizing the Jews of East
London, to convince them that their future, as well as that of the
Jews of the Middle East, lay with Marxism. "These theoreticians,"
wrote Srebrnik, "some of them unassimilated immigrants, did not
themselves run for public office, but acted as mentors to the formally
non-Jewish Stepney Communist Party."

There is something clandestine in this description. Something
slightly furtive. In my head, I see Chimen, racing off to a Party meeting, Socialist pamphlets crammed under his arm, weighty Marxist
tomes filling his battered leather briefcase. When he wrote articles
for Communist Party publications, more often than not he used a
pseudonym: C. Allen, or sometimes simply A. Chimen. He must have
suspected that the intelligence services were monitoring him (although, in fact, MI5 does not appear to have a Chimen Abramsky
file in its archives); his friend Hymie Fagan, in his unpublished memoirs, recollected that from the time of the 1926 General Strike on,
each senior Party figure would be tailed by a special forces officer,
many of whom they came to recognize on the streets after a while.
And, like all good Communists during these years, Chimen probably
took steps to avoid compromising himself and his friends. I see him,
a small figure in a rumpled, untailored dark suit and a tie with an
overly large knot, a hat pulled down on his head. I see him taking the
London Underground, the stations and abandoned tunnels of which
sheltered thousands of men and women when the blitzkrieg was at its
height, and emerging in the bombed-out East End, picking his way
through the rubble, making his way in the primordial dark of the
blackout to the all-important Party meeting. It is not too much of a
leap from this scene to another of my favorite images of Chimen: In

the mid-1950s, he somehow acquired parts of the library of Karl Marx's daughter Eleanor. This accession included six draft pages from Marx's *Theories of Surplus Value*; a long, handwritten letter, in English, from Marx to a Dr. Kauffmann in 1875; and two pages of notes for an article on Poland that Marx had composed in 1860. It was, in all likelihood, from that same Marx family collection that Chimen ended up with a stash of intimate Marx family letters, including one the political philosopher had written to his daughter and signed, mischievously, as "Dr. Crankey," and another he had written about his wife's declining health, which he had signed "Old Nick." Having scouted around for a buyer for the papers, Chimen discovered that Mao's government in China was interested. The story passed down in family lore is impossibly vague, but it involves Chimen in

Paris waiting at the base of the Eiffel Tower with bags of precious Marx documents. There, he exchanged them for a briefcase full of cash. Somehow, the image reeks of the Cold War, of upturned collars and shadows falling over cobblestone streets.

Shelves containing Communist histories, including Chimen and Henry Collins's book on Marx. This bookcase was just to the right of the bed.

All of that mid-century Marxist devotional intensity was concentrated in Mimi and Chimen's bedroom. There were Socialist and Communist books in Russian, German, Yiddish, French, English, Hebrew. There were old pamphlets so yellowed by time that one risked their disintegration simply by touching them. When Chimen and his close friend Henry Collins, who had collaborated on a number of articles about Marx beginning in the early 1950s—they had met through the Historians' Group of the Communist Party—decided to write their book *Karl Marx and the British Labour Movement: Years of the First International*, the books and documents in Chimen and Mimi's bedroom provided the nucleus for their research. It was, as Chimen had always intended it to be, a working library.

The book took Chimen and Collins nearly a decade to research. Chimen found it hard to know when to stop researching and when to start writing. One or the other of them would write whole sections and then Chimen would read it again and send a note to Collins telling him that it needed to be entirely rewritten. It could, occasionally, be frustrating for Henry. "Chim, you old lobus!" one letter from him, dated March 6, 1963, began. "What about your promised draft...? I think we should celebrate the final completion of the work." The book was eventually published by Macmillan in 1965, and was widely and favorably reviewed, not only in the left-wing press, such as the *Daily Worker*, but also in a number of mainstream and—surprisingly, given the topic—even conservative journals in Britain and America. *The Economist*, assuredly no friend of Socialism, printed an essay on the book, in which Marx was referred to as undoubtedly the greatest intellectual figure of his age. *The Times* reviewed it. In America, *The New York Times* praised it. A year after it came out, my grandfather wrote a note to his publishers letting them know that the "leading Soviet historical journal, *Voprosy Istorii K.P.S.S.* has devoted a 6 page article to our book, and though it is critical on quite a number of points it also admits that it is a very scholarly work." Chimen, who had left the Communist Party eight years earlier, and who believed himself to be on a Soviet blacklist, was gratified by the attention. He ended on what I hope was an ironic note. "It is quite unprecedented, to my knowledge, that a Soviet historical journal has devoted so much space to a book that is not for sale in the Soviet Union."

Chimen had always wanted to write the definitive English-language biography of Marx. As early as 1964, Collins and he had approached publishers with their idea. In September of that year, they had signed a contract to start work on the volume. Now, with the first book out of the way, painstakingly they began accumulating the materials they would need for this vast project. Chimen's library was their starting point again; they also used the British Library, the archives at the Marx House in London, the Social History Institute in Amsterdam, and an array of other libraries. But the biography did not materialize. A few years into the project, Collins fell ill with cancer and not long afterward, in 1969, he died. Chimen was devastated. Throughout the funeral, he sobbed uncontrollably.

Despite Chimen's occasional talk about continuing with the project alone, the biography gradually faded away. A large part of the book-writer in Chimen died with Collins. To their friends it seemed that Henry had been the stabilizing influence in the partnership, the Engels to Chimen's Marx, the man who could marshal a vast amount of information into something resembling a coherent narrative. Take Collins out of the equation, and there was nobody left to shape Chimen's thoughts on Marx's life into a readable story. A great compiler of facts, a historian-detective of the first rank, Chimen struggled, both in conversation and on the printed page, to humanize his subjects. While he understood every detail of Marx's life, he could not write the biography of the Moor (as Marx was known to his friends) without Collins's help; decades later, he would find it equally impossible to craft his own autobiography. Chimen continued to peruse his tomes on Marx, searching for someone else to share his passion for the life of this extraordinary character. He never quite found a replacement for Henry Collins.

———

In a corner of my grandparents' bedroom—between the treasure trove of Marx volumes and another wall crammed from floor to ceiling with myriad other rare books, as well as a couple of hardback copies of his and Collins's volume on Marx and a set of Isaiah Berlin's books generously dedicated to my grandfather—was a little cupboard. My grandmother stored her few dresses there. In it, too, was a shelf stocked with bottles of spirits, to be taken downstairs for special occasions, and a ceremonial gown that had been given to Chimen long ago by an Iraqi Communist friend. I believe that little cupboard is also where Chimen kept a heavy, gnarled, dark wooden walking stick with a silver handle and tip, a family heirloom passed down from father to son from the eighteenth century. Chimen had inherited it from his father upon the rabbi's death in 1976. When he wanted to entertain one of the grandchildren, he would disappear upstairs and return a few moments later with the impressive cane. Then, his eyes filled with mirth, he would balance it on the tip of the forefinger of his right hand and carefully walk around the dining room, his legs slightly bowed, feet turned out, a sudden Charlie Chaplin vulnerability to his appearance.

Somewhere in that cubbyhole, too, were kept the crumbling pages of the Second World War–era Yiddish journal *Eyropë*, published in London, which Chimen had co-edited. His friend Helen Beer, an Oxford scholar who specialized in Yiddish, believed it was the only extant copy of the volume; all the others had been destroyed in the London Blitz. Or, at least, that was the story he told her. To his friend Dovid Katz, he confided over a glass of whiskey that after he left the

Communist Party and lost his sympathy for left-wing Yiddish culture, he tried to destroy all remaining copies of the journal. Katz had looked at him and responded that, surely, he had kept one copy, that the one left behind would always be "an open question," a link to a past he could never bring himself to bury fully. Chimen had not denied it. And, sure enough, as Beer discovered, he had indeed preserved just one copy in his collection, hidden away in the cupboard in his bedroom.

Incongruously, on the inner wall of that same cupboard was a poster with a photo of their old friend the mathematician Abraham Robinson and some of his mathematical formulae. Robinson and the historian Jacob Talmon (then still known by his original name, Jacob Fleischer), friends of Chimen's at the Hebrew University, had moved to Paris and had managed to flee France just ahead of the Nazi armies. They ended up in London, shortly after the May 1940 decision to intern all "enemy aliens," and were promptly placed under lock and key at a school for the deaf and dumb, which had been temporarily requisitioned as a refugee-processing center.

Three days after Mimi and Chimen's marriage in June 1940, the newlyweds received a letter, sent via Rabbi Abramsky, at the Beth Din in Whitechapel, asking for help in getting Robinson and Talmon released. They quickly made their way to the school, Mimi, characteristically, with a basket of food. Soon afterward, the two young men were released; they spent the rest of the war in England and frequently visited Mimi and Chimen to share what little food there was and to talk about philosophy and politics. Continuing their great conversations from the Jerusalem days, Chimen, Robinson, and Talmon would launch into debates about the merits of Kant's ideas as opposed to Hegel's. They would discuss the relevance of Maimonides's theories to the modern world. They would dissect the Hebrew poems of Bialik and the German poems of Goethe. Sometimes,

Chimen recalled in a conversation with Robinson's biographer, as the bombs fell on London, they would talk right through the night. After all, he noted, during the Blitz each day of life seemed like a miracle, something so precious it ought not to be wasted on sleep. It was, in many ways, the same conclusion that Chimen's father had reached in the labor camp, while slaving away in the frigid cold of a Siberian winter in 1930. Yehezkel had, he told an audience later, gained a true understanding of Deuteronomy 28:66 in the camp: "And thy life shall hang in doubt before thee, and thou shalt fear day and night and shalt have none assurance of thy life."

By this time, Talmon was already well on his way to breaking with the radical left, having become convinced that the revolutionary spirit that had descended down the generations since Rousseau expounded his theory of the "general will" had unleashed the horrors of what Talmon would come to term "totalitarian democracy" and "political messianism." With Chimen a devout Stalinist and Talmon a committed anti-Communist, their through-the-night conversations would have been limned not just by the sense of urgency accompanying the Blitz but also by the urgency of friends in dispute, each convinced that the other was on a fundamentally wrong course, each sure that the other had sold his political soul to the devil.

Robinson was long dead by the time I acquired my own memories of the bedroom—he died of pancreatic cancer in 1974—but his wife, Renée, was a regular visitor to the house. Her high-pitched, Swiss-accented exclamations—eruptions of noise that seemed to unnerve my grandfather almost as much as they did us—about our appearances were a constant source of both amusement and annoyance to the grandchildren. Mimi had known Renée, a beautiful, stylish refugee from Vienna, in the late 1930s, before she met Chimen, and would get upset when we mocked Renée's accent. In private, however, Chimen would show his amusement, chuckling gently before telling us to stop being *chochems*. In Hebrew, *chacham* means a "wise person." In Yiddish, however, in a twist on the original phrase, *chochem* can also mean, when used sarcastically, "a simpleton, a dunce, a sort of court jester." Chimen used it on his grandchildren with infinite affection.

But back to the bedroom. It was a dark, low-ceilinged room, measuring twelve feet by twelve feet, with little natural light and one low-wattage bulb encased in a cream-colored spherical paper lampshade. In the center of all the unfathomable clutter was the bed, a small, boxy old mattress with a headboard that probably had not budged from its little spot against the wall since Mimi and Chimen had first bought the house, at a knockdown price, in 1944, during the dark years of the war. Chimen did not spend much time in the bed; he rarely slept more than four or five hours a night. Most mornings he was up by five o'clock, writing letters, perusing catalogs; most evenings he stayed awake past midnight. When you lay down on that bed in the center of the room, all you could see were books and papers—and the tiny, sooty window that let in just about enough of London's inky night light to make those books look scary.

This was Mimi and Chimen's bedroom, though if truth be told, by the time I came on the scene it did not really make sense to call it a bedroom. Years earlier, it might have been defined by its nocturnal occupants, by their marital relations, by their nightclothes and wardrobes. It might even have exuded romance, back when my grandmother, as a young woman, still sported long, wavy brown hair and a gentle smile that made her look, in some particularly fortunate sepia photos, like the film star Ingrid Bergman. By the 1970s, it was the reserve room of a great and infinitely mysterious library. It was there that the gems in Chimen's collection were held. The bed in which my grandparents slept every night and the few items of clothing begrudgingly allowed space to hang amid the books were, clearly, interlopers.

———

For an adult, to be invited into Chimen's bedroom signified not romantic interest, nor coy flirtation, but academic trust. You had to earn your way in, show knowledge of or love for Socialism and its lost worlds or, at the very least, the esoteric universe of rare-manuscript and book collecting. You had to appreciate the sensation of touching a book that Marx had owned and commented on; or a document on which Lenin had scribbled marginal notes; or a book that Trotsky had carried with him into exile. You had to have the capacity to comprehend the absurdly low probability of Marx's membership card for the First International not only surviving for more than a hundred years but finding its way to Hillway. Or of scrip, printed by the nineteenth-century utopian Socialist Robert Owen as an alternative currency, ending up in this room. There was, recalled one friend, "a touch of the impresario" to Chimen, "a magician's delight in surprising you. He'd trot off to a room and return with something and enjoy your reaction." A cousin recalled first being shown the room in 1978, about twenty years after he had first visited the house, and Chimen wistfully asking him where he thought these books would be in a hundred years. "He wasn't so much talking about where the books would be physically. He was talking about where the ideas would be."

But the grandchildren did not have to earn entry to this citadel. It was simply where we slept at Hillway when we were too young and scared to sleep alone. It smelled old and musty, and I was never quite sure whether that was the smell of the books or of my grandparents.

Later on, I would sleep in the small room that was kitty-corner to their bedroom, a little room with a twin bed, and a set of cabinets that still contained some of my aunt's bric-a-brac from when she lived with her parents, bracketed to the wall over the far side of the bed. By the windows was a cupboard, in which were stacked mountains of catalogs and other research materials that Chimen would use when evaluating rare books and manuscripts for Sotheby's. For more than thirty years he was their behind-the-scenes expert on Hebraica. It was he who had cataloged the extraordinary manuscript and incunabula collection of David Sassoon, the sale of which, in a series of auctions in London and Zurich in the 1970s, essentially jump-started the modern global market in rare Hebrew materials. "Before Sassoon sale Hebrew books were in the doldrums. Few buyers; books sold very cheaply," Chimen wrote in the notes he prepared for a lecture that he gave on the sale when he was eighty-four years old. "Remarkable change with first sale of Sassoon....The sale was a sensation."

Not only did the Sassoon auction massively increase the value of Hebrew manuscripts and early printed books but it also secured Chimen's career as a sought-after evaluator of such items. "You might be amused to learn that I have now added up the catalogues which I compiled, or wrote, since 1961," he informed the young bibliographer Brad Sabin Hill, who had apprenticed himself to my grandfather, in a letter dated June 8, 1988, "and they are nearly fifty.... And nearly all without my name (except for two)."

———

Sandwiched between the cupboard and the bedroom door in this little spare room hung the two low-grade copies of Marc Chagall paintings. When I stayed there overnight as a teenager, I would wake up and look at those paintings in the early-morning light. And then, at a leisurely pace, I would get out of bed, brush my teeth, shower in the impossibly weak stream of water from the handheld nozzle in the bathroom that had not been updated since the Second World War, and head downstairs. Above the bend in the staircase hung the huge (but still only one-third the size of the original), ghoulish, mass-produced black-and-white reproduction of *Guernica*, the mutilated, howling bodies and faces of the Spanish city's experience with aerial bombardment standing as somber testament to the horrors of the modern world. It was those horrors that had convinced my grandmother to cast her lot with the Communist Party.

I would hurry past the painting, down the moth-eaten carpet on the stairs, as fast as possible. At the bottom, I would execute a U-turn by swinging around the banister's angular knob and head down the hallway toward the kitchen. There, I knew, my grandmother would be standing by the stove, a pan full of eggy pancakes waiting for me, a cup of hot tea ready to be gulped down, a pot of warmed honey, for dripping on the pancakes, on the table near my seat.

"Hello, love," she would say. "I made you some breakfast."

———

Thirty-five years after I had been stranded in my grandparents' strange bedroom by fog, I lay in another room, thousands of miles away, dreaming about the House of Books. The first anniversary of Chimen's death was approaching, and I couldn't stop thinking about his terrible final months. I fell asleep and dreamed that I was on holiday with my family, and that Chimen was with us. He was very old, as frail as the most antiquated of his books, but he was intellectually vigorous. We were talking about his books.

Suddenly I realized that we had buried him a year earlier. I couldn't understand it. I took my mum aside to ask her for an expla-

nation, and she started to tell me, in a low whisper, how everyone had thought he was dying, and so they planned the funeral, and then somehow he had lived. (In reality Chimen had, twice in his last year, beaten the odds and survived sicknesses his doctors judged to be fatal.) My conversation with my mother was interrupted. But later I managed to take my dad aside and ask him the same question. "It's all right," he answered. "We were convinced that he was dying, so we arranged the funeral, and we couldn't disinvite everybody, so we held it anyway. We hid Chimen away in the attic and held the funeral." "But the coffin I mourned at?" I asked in disbelief. "Empty."

And then I had an utterly devastating realization. "But the books are all gone. The shelves are empty. Chimen's living like a ghost in a house with no books." The idea of it was intolerable, the sheer agony my grandfather must be suffering in the empty house unendurable.

I woke up screaming.

THE HALLWAY:
AN EXTRAORDINARY PORTAL

I did not write half of what I saw, for I knew I would not be believed.
> —Marco Polo, reputed deathbed statement, 1324

EVEN YEARS AFTER most of the central characters from Hillway had died, I still regularly dreamed about them.

Hillway is part of a small community just off of Hampstead Heath, known as the Holly Lodge Estate. The estate was originally owned by a Victorian banking family, and when it was subsequently sold off and developed as housing the streets remained in private ownership, largely outside of the purview of the local council. That a large number of Communists chose to buy property in this private little enclave was something of an irony. By the time I was a child, however, the only visible signs that it

The exterior of 5 Hillway.

remained an "estate" were the never-closed gate at the bottom of the hill, through which one turned onto the street from Swain's Lane, and the propensity of the traffic wardens to issue tickets to any car whose owner had the temerity to park on the street without either a resident's sticker or a guest permit. Every so often, someone from the estate board of management would send Chimen a sniffy letter, addressed curtly to "Abramsky," alerting him to the fact that he was grievously underpaying the "voluntary" dues leveled on residents each year. As they were voluntary, however, Chimen did not feel compelled to part with more cash.

On one of the streets just off the estate is the overgrown cemetery in which Karl Marx is buried, as is the theorist of electromagnetism Michael Faraday and the social Darwinist Herbert Spencer. Playing on the name of the retail chain, wags would regularly joke about the proximity of Marx and Spencer in their final resting place. Several times during my childhood, Chimen took me up the hill to that cemetery to ponder the massive monument, commissioned by the Communist Party of Great Britain in 1955, atop Marx's remains. He never told me whether he had played a role in the monument's genesis, but given that he was still an active Party member at the time it is certainly possible. On another street, higher up, above the heath, is the Spaniards Inn, an ancient pub in which, so legend had it, Dick Turpin, the eighteenth-century highwayman, had drunk his fill.

From the top of Hillway, all London could be seen, right down to the Thames. Emerging from the huge bomb shelters under Hampstead Heath during the war, had they climbed that hill my grandparents would have witnessed the vast conflagrations that razed so much of London. When the V1 flying bombs and the V2 rockets fell randomly over the city from June 1944 until the end of the war, they would have seen their own new neighborhood pocked by debris-filled lots where houses, shops, and businesses once had stood. A direct hit by a V2 could level an entire block. Londoners attempted to hide from the carnage below ground: The nearby Underground stations of Hampstead, Highgate, and Belsize Park, all deep below street level, were used as shelters by many thousands of bomb-dazed inhabitants. (The future American talk-show host Jerry Springer was born in Highgate Station during a bombing raid in 1944.) Usually the Underground stations provided a safe haven; on occasion, though, a direct hit resulted in terrible loss of life. On October 14, 1940, for example, a huge bomb penetrated the earth above Balham Station in South London, exploding just above two platforms used by shelterers. Sixty-six people died as a result of the explosion, some killed by the blast itself, some apparently drowned by water released from burst pipes, and others suffocated by gas from damaged pipelines.

When I passed my driving test at the age of seventeen, I drove to Hillway so many times that the route became permanently etched into my memory. And even though my grandparents' house was only three doors up from the foot of the hill, I almost always made a detour to the top to take in the view. It was spectacular. As I descended Hillway, the vistas changed. The dome of Christopher Wren's masterpiece, Saint Paul's Cathedral—just north of the sprawling riverfront private school that I attended from the age of eleven to eighteen, which was opposite the abandoned power station that would become the Tate Modern gallery—could be seen from one spot, the British Telecom tower from another. From the top, as I spun my parents' car around the little roundabout and headed back down, I could glimpse the river; later on, when the London Eye Ferris wheel was built to celebrate the millennium, that, too, entered the picture. It was like a moving diorama of all that was best in London architecture (along with a lot that was not), viewable in miniature, as the car slowly rolled down Hillway, back toward Swain's Lane and the bottom of the hill. My grandparents' house was just around the corner from a little supermarket, a couple of cafés, Cavour's delicatessen, and a small hardware store, all on Swain's Lane, and a few steps away from a mechanic's garage that occupied one of the spaces left empty by a bomb blast during the war.

Mimi and Chimen seemed to know half the residents of these streets. Several members of the family lived within walking distance: Jenny, her husband, Al, and their children, Rob and Maia; Mimi's cousin Phyllis Hillel, who moved into the area when she was widowed in the 1980s, her son Peter, his wife, Vavi, and their children, Emma and Nick; and Mimi's niece Julia, who lived in the house that decades earlier had been owned and occupied by Mimi's mother. Then there was Fred Barber, an elegant old doctor who had fled Prague after the Munich Agreement in effect handed Czechoslovakia to the Nazis. Almost daily—until he was well into his nineties and debilitated by old age—he would walk over to Hillway for a cup of tea and a chat, always perfectly attired in a suit and tie, his few thin wisps of white hair trailing off the back of an otherwise denuded, liver-spotted, shiny pate. For some reason, while Mimi always called him "Fred," Chimen never called him anything but "Barber" or "Dr. Barber." There was an elderly academic and former Indian ambassador to the Soviet Union, Krishnarao Shelvankar, and his very proper wife, Mary. No matter what the weather, he always wore sandals—as a result of which, while I cannot at all these years' remove conjure up an image of his face, I can, quite clearly, see his toes. They were long, the nails slightly browned. Mary, without fail, encouraged me to play the piano and, sipping tea in the kitchen with Mimi, complimented my halfhearted efforts—Beethoven sonatas, Chopin études, some Gershwin, a bit of Scott Joplin—when I did. Listening to the pair of them talk about my musical abilities, one would have thought I was destined to win the International Tchaikovsky Competition. In reality, I was lucky if I could play three or four bars without hitting a clunker. For half the year, an Israeli couple, Mike and Ora Ardon, longtime friends of Mimi and Chimen, lived a one-minute walk from Hillway. Old ex–Communist Party comrades and academic colleagues dotted the Holly Lodge Estate or visited from nearby neighborhoods. A host of other regular visitors lived an easy car or bus ride away: Mimi's sister Sara, and her husband, Steve Corrin; their daughter Eve—Julia's sister—and her son, Tom; Chimen's cousin Golda Zimmerman; Mimi's cousins Lily and Martin Mitchell (Lily was the younger sister of Phyllis; their father and several siblings had been killed on the very first night of the London Blitz); and numerous others.

Each relative who entered the house, especially the children, merited their own particular greeting from Chimen: there was "Meester Rob"; for a while, as he went through a period of teenage indecisiveness, my brother, Kolya, became "Meester Maybe"; my sister, Tanya, and cousin Maia were Tweedle Dum and Tweedle Dee—though today, neither can agree on which was which.

———

The person I most associate with the doorway at Hillway, with the ritual of entry, was not, however, a relative. Instead, she was my grandmother's best friend, a dentist named Rose Uren. At least once a day at Hillway, I would hear a growling, roaring sound coming nearer from the street. That would be my cue; I would run to open the door, and there, standing outside, was Rose, her moped driven all the way up the plant-lined pathway to the little concrete-covered patch by the three steps that led to the red front door. Rose would be standing before me, her helmet still on, as often as not with bags of smoked salmon, black bread, and other essentials that Mimi had asked her to buy on her way in. She looked like something out of a 1950s B movie.

"A-lloooh Sasha," she would say, in an extraordinarily thick French accent. And then, in mock surprise, "No-buddie told me you vuhd be here! I vuhdn't 'ave come eef I'd known." Then she'd look past me at my grandmother, standing over the stove in the kitchen. "Mee-mee! Vye didn't you tell me 'ee'd be 'ere?!" And before I could escape, she would grab me and, her breath smelling of strong cheese, plunk a kiss on each cheek. It was an awful smell—and I loved it.

Rose had fled over the Pyrenees into Spain when France fell to the Nazis; she had been interned by Franco's forces and then somehow had made her way back to France to join the Resistance. After the war, she had moved to England. There was not a religious bone in Rose's body, but in some ways she was as Old World as one could get, a perfect shtetl bargainer, always hunting for the best deal, always willing to catapult insults at merchants she felt were not dealing with her fairly. Perhaps that was why Mimi would send her out food shopping for Hillway. "Gangs of women crowd around the peasants who have brought their farm produce for sale, jostling each other in the attempt to get first choice," Mark Zborowski and Elizabeth Herzog wrote of Eastern European Jewish markets, in their 1952 book on the mores of the shtetl, *Life Is with People*. "Bargaining is raised to a fine art. The acquisition of a Sabbath fish may take on all the suspense of a pitched battle, with onlookers cheering and participants thoroughly enjoying the mutual barrage of insults and exhortations." That Rose was shopping at the Cash 'n' Carry rather than in a shtetl market did not negate her enthusiasm for such theatrics.

I adored Rose. She was as over the top—*ungapatchka* was the Yiddish term—as anyone I knew. An ex-Communist, she had firmly joined the ranks of the bourgeoisie, regularly attending the opera at Covent Garden and counting among her dental patients some of the country's leading politicians. Even better, she was a tennis fanatic, and enjoyed nothing more than sitting down with me and talking about Wimbledon or the French Open. Like me, she loved John McEnroe and loathed Ivan Lendl. And when she loathed someone, curses flew out of her mouth that could make the blood run cold. It was Rose who polished my teeth twice a year and, her mouth positively jangling with her own silver fillings, berated me for not brushing longer each day. It was Rose who worked hardest to get me to stop biting my nails and picking my nose when I was a small boy. And it was Rose who, a decade later, put in the most hours teaching me to drive.

For Rose, whose own granddaughter lived thousands of miles away, Mimi and Chimen's five grandchildren served as local substitutes. At times, she could be remarkably territorial. When my cousin Rob brought home a girlfriend from college, Rose rang my aunt and uncle's doorbell with her customary double ring. Entering the house, she shouted, "Let me see zee gurrrl who has stolen my Rob from me!" She was carrying opera binoculars with her for better viewing. When my cousin's somewhat surprised friend showed her face, Rose grabbed her and, with faux-solemnity, took out a dentist's magnifying glass: "Leh-t me see your tee-th!"

Over the years, I met thousands of people at Hillway, and in my imagination decades later, I situate different people in different rooms. Some people, like my grandmother's gossipy Liverpudlian friend Rachel (who always arrived with thick pancake makeup on her cheeks) or her cousin Phyllis—a wonderful cockney character who, for the main part of her meals, ate nothing more adventurous than bread or potatoes, but who routinely baked and brought over the best apple strudel I have ever tasted—I imagine as denizens of the kitchen. Perched on uncomfortable wooden chairs, they sat there with Mimi, drinking cup after cup of tea and exchanging tidbits of community news and family tidings. As they got older, they all grew deafer, and, year by year, the volume of these conversations grew louder. Others have established themselves in my daydreams as dining-room acquaintances. For some reason, however, many of my fondest memories are of hallway people. Of course, they were not really hallway people; like all the others who visited, they simply walked through the book-lined entrance hall on the way to the rest of the house, but my recollections of them are of their entrance, their announcement that they were present, and the way in which they were greeted.

I think of my great-aunt Sara and her husband, Steve, as hallway people. They spent decades collecting children's stories from all over the world and editing them into a wonderful series of volumes titled *Stories for Five-Year-Olds*, *Stories for Six-Year-Olds*, and so on. Every time she came to the house, Sara, who like her older sister believed that all social situations demanded the bringing of food, was laden with cakes and other goodies that she had made in her dimly lit house before coming over to Hillway. Steve always came equipped with new jokes, pithy comments—almost aphorisms—on world affairs, and news clippings neatly folded and secreted away in one or another of his brown tweed or gray sports jacket pockets, which he would ceremoniously pull out to share with me or with Chimen almost before he had stepped through the door. Tubercular in his youth, Steve remained rake-thin for the rest of his life, his presence a bundle of nervous energy, his sharp eyes watching and interpreting everything and everyone around him. They came frequently, but, when Steve was with Sara, often for only a few minutes. Steve seemed to tire easily. He would head into the dining room to perch on the edge of an armchair while quickly, nervously, nipping at a small brandy. Once his jokes had been told and his news clippings shared, he frequently sank into a morose silence, his darting eyes doing most of his communicating. They would leave a few minutes later.

When the daily caravan of visitors climbed the dull red brick steps leading to the front door, their hands resting on the rickety wooden railing alongside, and entered the house at Hillway, it was the books in the hallway that first would catch their attention. The thin paperback biographies of Great Men. The specialist, weighty Socialist encyclopedias. The miscellaneous early-edition histories and novels. If they had stopped in the hallway long enough to take books off of the shelves, they would have discovered an entire second row of books hidden behind those visible in front. On those shelves were many books on the failed European revolutions of 1848—the year that Marx and Engels published *The Communist Manifesto*—including one by Alexandre-Auguste Ledru-Rollin, one of the leaders of the uprising in France; there were also volumes about the 1871 Paris Commune; some rare first editions on Austrian social democracy; and books by Karl Kautsky, who before the First World War had been widely regarded as one of the leading Marxist theoreticians of his age, but who had spoken out passionately against the Bolshevik Revolution after 1917. He had died an old, broken exile in Amsterdam in 1938; his wife perished a few years later in Auschwitz.

Also in the hallway was a complete set of the proceedings of the Congress of the Communist Party of the Soviet Union; too tall to stand on the shelves, they were placed horizontally. There were first editions, in Russian, of works by Georgi Valentinovich Plekhanov, the founder of Russia's first overtly Marxist political party, the original translator of Marx's works into Russian, and a man who later, in the final years of his life, bitterly criticized Lenin's bloodthirsty methods of achieving revolution. The final part of the Marxist collection in this room was a modern version of the complete works of Marx and Engels in English, four dozen large hardback volumes covering several yards of shelf space. In addition, there were many mass-produced paperbacks, including little biographies of famous philosophers and politicians; histories by friends of Chimen's such as James Joll; and writings on the American Communist Party.

To the left of the door, across from the start of the shelves, there was a small cupboard, in which hung Mimi and Chimen's coats and a couple of large umbrellas. But it was so dusty, and so crowded with miscellaneous papers, rolled up posters, and piles of books, that as a cupboard it was all but unusable. Usually visitors simply draped their coats and scarves over the newel post at the foot of the stairs. Between the cupboard and the bottom of the staircase was a little table on which sat, well into the 1990s, a red rotary telephone, the dial of which seemed to be weighted so as to rotate agonizingly slowly. Perched next to the phone was my grandmother's oversize address book, her large scrawl covering page after page with names, phone numbers, and addresses, its scale a study in contrasts to Chimen's miniscule address books and his almost microscopic entries.

In a tiny corner just to the right of the front door was a space where the bookshelves ended and the cracked, wine-red paintwork was exposed. There hung a rather austere-looking oil painting of Mimi's father, Jacob Nirenstein. He had a heavy, drooping mustache, the kind favored by civil servants or other functionaries in Edwardian England, and was wearing a jacket and formal tie, his hair neatly parted; he looked as if he meted out his smiles sparingly. Yet behind this dolorous exterior I knew a passionate heart was beating. In an era of arranged marriages and carefully choreographed matches, Jacob had married his childhood sweetheart, Fanny Nirenstein, later known to everyone as Bellafeigel ("beautiful bird"). What made the story rather discomfiting in the retelling—my mother, in particular, loved to recount this family lore—was that Jacob and Bellafeigel were uncle and niece, an arrangement legal under Jewish law (although an aunt marrying her nephew is not) but illegal in England. He was the youngest of several children, born in 1882; she the oldest, born in 1885, the generational difference obliterated by the size of their families. Growing up together as children in the small shtetl of Multch, near the Pripet Marshes, a vast wetland that encompassed swathes of Byelorussia and Ukraine, they had fallen in love, secretly promised each other they would marry when they came of age, and, true to their word, had migrated to London where they married in Whitechapel in 1908 and started their family in the East End.

They bought a musty old Victorian Jewish bookshop in Spitalfields, at 81 Wentworth Street, named Shapiro, Valentine & Co. They had, early in their marriage, lived above the shop with the Widow Shapiro before buying her out and starting off in business on their own. Through this enterprise, they made a meager living buying and selling Jewish books, prayer books, and religious holiday paraphernalia. It was a well-respected shop, quite possibly the best Jewish bookshop in London, and it allowed Jacob to keep his growing family housed and clad. The family lived just around the corner from the shop, at 9 Commercial Street, a throughway that bustled with fruit and vegetable stalls; nearby, penny doss-houses provided bedbug-riddled beds for the homeless. In Toynbee Hall, well-meaning social workers helped immigrant children assimilate to the broader English culture. Fishmongers crowded Petticoat Lane. Merchants sold live chickens, which would then be ritually slaughtered in a kosher manner nearby. There were bakers such as Goide's, selling bagels and challah. There were kosher butchers such as Barnett's. On May Day, the Communist Party organizer Hymie Fagan (who also ended up living near Hillway) wrote decades later in an unpublished memoir, the local children of radical Russian Jewish émigré families would parade through the streets "dressed in their poor best, but washed, groomed, combed and beribboned," dancing around maypoles pulled on carts, and singing songs of revolution.

When I was a child, as the story of Jacob and Bellafeigel's slightly awkward romance was revealed, laughingly, to yet another friend, I would feel a nervous rush of adrenalin and, at least figuratively, would start squirming in my seat. But to my great-grandparents, it was not really a cause for anxiety. Admittedly, on official documents—passports, their children's birth certificates, and their own marriage certificate—to avoid aspersions on the legality of their marriage, they used a false name for Bellafeigel; she became Fanny (or Fenny) Sherashevsky, taking her mother's maiden name for her own surname. In

The Nirenstein family.
From left to right:
Sara, Bellafeigel, Minna,
Jacob, and Miriam.
London, circa 1922.

Jacob Nirenstein in front
of the shop that became
Shapiro, Valentine & Co., on
Wentworth Street, London.
Date unknown.

fact, legalities aside, theirs was not such an unusual situation. Cousins routinely married each other in the shtetl, and young uncles marrying their oldest nieces, whatever the official laws of the land might say about it, really was not considered unacceptable. To Jacob's and Bellafeigel's parents, innkeepers and fisherfolk in the marshes around Multch, whose own ancestors had migrated to the marshes from the Russian village of Olshevi in the early decades of the nineteenth century, what would have been far more unacceptable than their kinship was the fact that it was a love match. That, in many ways, was a revolutionary rejection of parental authority, almost as far-reaching in its implications as a denial of the revelatory truth of the religion itself. In the classic musical *Fiddler on the Roof*, Tevye the milkman wrestles with just such a dilemma when his eldest daughter announces that she is in love with the tailor Motel Kamsol. It is, he says, "unheard of." But then he reflects. "Love, it's a new style," he finally says, as he reconciles himself to the inconvenient state of affairs. Perhaps not coincidentally, *Fiddler* was one of Mimi's favorite films, the Technicolor scenes of unfolding family drama as guaranteed to produce tears as were the onions that she would cut up in her kitchen to burn, deliberately, for flavor and spread over her lamb chops.

But however much Jacob and Bellafeigel's affair of the heart hurt their parents, they followed through, got married, and ensured that that part of the family tree would become a bemusing tangle for future genealogists to pore over. Two generations later, that tangle became almost impossible to unknot: Bellafeigel and Jacob's grandson Jack Abramsky married Lenore Levine, the granddaughter of Bellafeigel's sister Sophie. Sophie had migrated to the United States when her sister left for England; her daughter Miriam, known as Mim, moved to Los Angeles in the late 1930s; and Mim's daughter Lenore had come on a visit to London in 1966, where she met her cousin Jack, fell in love, and decided she would stay in London. My grandmothers, both Miriams, both presumably named after the same ancestor, were first cousins; my parents, Jack and Lenore, are second cousins; I am my own third cousin. That also made me third cousin to my brother and sister. Maybe, at some level, it was the bizarreness of these kinship relationships created by her marriage that led my mum to choose genetic counseling as a career when she went back to work in 1981, two years after my sister, Tanya, was born.

In 1926, when Mimi was nine years old, Jacob dropped dead from a heart attack in his early forties, not long after the family had gone on their one foreign trip together: They had traveled east across Europe, back to the Pale of Settlement communities out of which they had emerged a generation earlier. Jacob's funeral was held, with little fanfare, in a small Jewish cemetery in North London. His death shattered the upwardly mobile aspirations of his wife and children, leaving Bellafeigel struggling to raise three daughters and keep the bookshop going. For the oldest Nirenstein daughter, Minna, the upheaval was particularly hard to bear. A talented musician and composer, she was enrolled at the Royal Academy of Music at the time of her father's death, but as the family's finances imploded, the expense of her studies became harder to justify. In 1929, at the age of twenty, she had to give up her dreams and return to the East End to work in the bookshop. It must have been a desperately claustrophobic transformation for her. Only decades later—years into her second marriage and now known as Minna Keal—in her seventies, was she able to return to music, eventually composing, in the garage at the back of her house, a powerful, often angry symphony. It premiered in the Albert Hall as a part of the 1989 London Proms series to considerable acclaim. She followed it up with several chamber pieces, and eventually a documentary was made about her, tellingly titled *A Life in Reverse*. For the two much younger Nirenstein sisters, Jacob's premature death meant a childhood of at times desperate poverty in the impoverished neighborhood of Stepney. Mimi later remembered that she had only one small rag doll in her entire childhood, and that even the acquisition of such a small gift was something she treasured, given how little spare money her mother had.

But while Jacob's passing fractured his daughters' world, it was also the catalyst for a political shift. Without the religious strictures of their father, as Europe navigated the cataclysmic aftermath of world war, revolution, and economic collapse, in the decade following Jacob's death all three Nirenstein sisters shed their religious beliefs and veered instead toward a new political faith: Communism. In the early 1930s, with the Labour prime minister Ramsay MacDonald presiding over cuts to unemployment benefits and public-sector salaries, it was the Communist Party of Great Britain, founded in 1920 to promote a Bolshevik-style revolution, which organized the unemployed to demonstrate; coordinated a series of hunger marches through London; and put together the Workers' Charter movement, modeled on the Chartists of nearly a century earlier, to demand a seven-hour working day, increases in unemployment benefits, and political rights for members of the armed forces. Its leader, Harry Pollitt, toured the country, giving speeches in Manchester, Leeds, Liverpool, Newcastle, and London touting the benefits of the movement's platform. A popular Communist song from the era urged:

If you want to fight wage cuts,
Fight for the Workers' Charter.
Stand and show you've got some guts,
You won't be beaten down forever.
Now's the time to make a move
Forward with the Charter.
And together we will prove
That the workers' fight will win the day.

Of course, it was this same Communist Party that engaged in bitter purges of purported Trotskyists among its own members, and resolutely refused to countenance the stories emanating out of Russia, which told of wholesale imprisonment and the execution of dissidents, some of these tales recounted by Westerners who had gone to the Soviet Union to witness the creation of a promised land and returned deeply cynical about the project.

In the early 1930s, however, Mimi did not want to see the downside. Instead, she and her sisters, like so many other idealistic young people during these years, saw the Communists in action on the streets of her beloved East End and were seduced. During the years of appeasement, when one German and Italian outrage after another was tolerated by the British and French political leaderships, it was the Communists who fought back most forcefully against Fascism. It was the Communists who intervened in an ill-starred attempt to save the Spanish Republic. And it was the Communists who took the lead in many labor conflicts during years of mass unemployment and plummeting wages. In hindsight, Mimi and many others came to resent the Party deeply for the way in which it had manipulated grand causes for its own narrow aims: It used noble human aspirations and dreams as currency; with this currency it purchased the support of a generation of idealists. And that support helped to maintain a nightmare in the Soviet Union. At the time, however, it felt deeply liberating.

Mimi's first boyfriend was a card-carrying member of the Party, and when the Spanish Civil War broke out, he quickly volunteered for the International Brigade. The Communists were not just active overseas, however. Seeking to counter the rise of Oswald Mosley's British Union of Fascists and its appeal to working-class Londoners, they mobilized their members in an all-out effort to win the hearts and minds of East Enders and ultimately to secure political control of the neighborhoods in which those East Enders lived. Mosley planned a provocative march of his Blackshirts through the Jewish enclaves of the East End on March 4, 1936. In response, the Party organized a huge protest, which Mimi and her sisters joined, along with tens of thousands of men and women shouting out the Spanish partisans' mantra: "They shall not pass." They stood firm at barricades coordinated by the local Communist organizer and future member of Parliament Phil Piratin, as roughly six thousand police officers attempted to clear a path down Cable Street along which Mosley's marchers could parade. The confrontation was rapidly converted into folklore as the Battle of Cable Street, and those barricades, a journalist for the *New Statesman* wrote later that month, were "the best thing that has happened for some time." Writing of the local populace deciding to bar Mosley's marchers, he noted that "the common people banned it by so filling the streets that even police charges could not clear the way for Sir Oswald's army."

A few years later, when a young man named Chimen Abramsky was hired to work at Shapiro, Valentine & Co. a couple of months after the outbreak of the Second World War, it was the common bond of Marxism and the shared utopian language of an anticipated revolution that initially drew the new employee and the boss's daughter together. Miriam Nirenstein was, Chimen wrote more than sixty years later, "strikingly good looking, with a delicate chiseled face, beautiful warm brown eyes, sparkling, with a wonderful sense of

One of the marches for jobs organized by the Communist Party, London, mid-1930s. Mimi is at the front, holding the rope for the banner.

Chimen and Mimi at the time of their
marriage. London, June 1940.

humor. Her face captivated me instantly." On walks through a London darkened by the blackout, from the shop to the Underground station, she filled him in on the details of her life. "I learned from her that she was originally a Zionist, but through the civil war in Spain... joined the Communist Party. The rise and spread of fascism strengthened her determination and beliefs. During the day she ran the family business, and in the evenings she delivered party leaflets." My grandparents fell head over heels in love.

And yet, despite the fact that Mimi and her sisters had joined the Communist Party largely as a way to fight the rise of Fascism, largely because they realized the savage danger that Nazism posed to the world, when Hitler and Stalin signed an opportunistic nonaggression pact on August 23, 1939—after years of appeasement of the Fascist powers by Britain and France, years in which the possibility of a Soviet-British-French alliance was frittered away—somehow they convinced themselves to follow the Party line in opposing a war which the Party deemed "imperialist." Of course, Mimi, Sara, Minna, and Chimen (who was not yet a Party member or a presence in my grandmother's life) knew the extent of Fascism's horrors. They knew—but at the same time they also now convinced themselves that the Nazi–Soviet Nonaggression Pact was a necessary tactical maneuver intended to buy Russia time while Britain and France dithered and

Germany expanded into Austria, Czechoslovakia, and who knew where else.

What it meant in practice was that after Britain finally declared war on September 3, 1939, British Communists stood back and repeated Party platitudes, while Nazi Germany and Stalinist Russia carved up Poland, the Baltic States, and Finland between them. Some Communist agitators in the United Kingdom, in the early months of the war, plastered posters on walls decrying the war as an imperialist charade; in the aftermath of this, many Communist publications were banned and some Communists were even interned. It was, to say the least, a deeply disingenuous political position, born of a context in which ideological rigidity and undeviating adherence to the Party line was seen as the primary measure of a comrade's worth.

The sloganizing extended beyond politics and, to one degree or another, made its way into the personal realm too. As Mimi and Chimen's relationship blossomed in early 1940, they worried, in their quickly penned love letters, how their parents would take the news that they wanted to marry. Neither was convinced that the other's family would approve. Chimen was particularly afraid of what Yehezkel would say; and both were concerned that Barnett Samuel, Minna's husband at the time and, as such, the male head of the Nirenstein clan, would object to the match since, being a very religious man, he had already made it known, sniffily, to Mrs. Nirenstein, that he was not sure Chimen was *frum* (pious) enough to work in the bookshop. However, when Chimen screwed up his courage in the spring of 1940 to tell his mother that he intended to marry Mimi, he reported, with evident relief, that Raizl was overjoyed. Now the challenge was to convince "such a reactionary as my father" that the match was good. "My dear little Chimen," my twenty-three-year-old future grandmother wrote back, on hearing the news, "I'm glad to hear that you've told my mother-in-law and made her happy. I hope my reactionary

Mimi in London, probably in the late 1940s or early 1950s.

father-in-law will react with similar joy." As it turns out, Yehezkel was equally enthusiastic and, on June 20, 1940, in an East End nervously waiting for the Luftwaffe to turn its attention to England after Germany had overrun Belgium, Holland, and France, the wedding took place unhindered.

Afterward, my grandparents quickly returned to their political activism. Of course, in June 1941, when the Nazis launched Operation Barbarossa against their erstwhile Soviet allies—somehow surprising Stalin, despite urgent memos from Churchill and Roosevelt detailing the intelligence that led them to believe the attack was imminent—Communist cadres in the West performed a quick volteface and became enthusiastic backers of what they now saw as a vital conflict. The instincts that had led people like Mimi to barricade Cable Street against the Fascists were let loose once more. Now they urged the necessity of a "second front" to siphon Nazi military energies away from the Soviet Union; they urged total war; they praised the heroism of the Soviet Union and its foot soldiers. When Churchill's government decided to release the Fascist leader Oswald Mosley from Holloway prison in late 1943, judging that he was no longer a threat to social order, Chimen helped the Communist Party formulate its response. Angered that the Jewish Board of Deputies, with which Chimen's father closely worked, was insufficiently vocal in its criticism of the decision, Chimen penned an angry letter to *The Jew-*

ish Chronicle. "This cowardice," he wrote, "shames all Jews fighting heroically against Fascism. This backwardness, this lagging behind the democratic forces, is a blot on our names."

———

Chimen and Mimi bought the house on Hillway (which had been empty since sometime in 1942, according to post office records from the period) for £2,000 in the spring of 1944, the mortgage held solely by Mimi, since Chimen was still a stateless nonnational. The hallway shelves, made of varnished planks of low-grade pine, would have been filled first, with books Chimen had scavenged from the shop and from sellers in the bomb-battered East End. Many of these, in keeping with my grandparents' politics at the time, were works of propaganda intended to extol the joys of Bolshevik Russia. They were volumes that accompanied Chimen and Mimi throughout the war. They would have occupied shelves in Mimi and Chimen's first home, a small flat near Regent's Park. The flat was too close to London Zoo for comfort: Mimi was terrified that a bomb would hit the zoo and demolish the cages, and that she would come home late one night and be chased down the street by a liberated lion. It was not an entirely irrational fear. The zoo *was* bombed several times, but at the outset of the war many of the zoo's larger animals had been evacuated to facilities outside of the city and, with authorities worried that the zoo's poisonous snakes might escape among the already edgy populace, the unlucky reptiles were killed. And so neither big cats, nor large snakes, escaped to roam and slither through London's blackout-darkened streets. As the war intensified, many other strange sites were also hit: Two years into the conflict, the London Necropolis Railway Station at Waterloo, a Victorian terminus used to transport the bodies of the dead out of London to Brookwood Cemetery, was heavily damaged in a bombing raid. As their numbers multiplied, and multiplied again, no longer could the dead be sent to genteel resting spots in the Surrey countryside.

During the eight months of the Blitz, according to the Bomb Sight online map depicting where the bombs fell in London, well over fifty large bombs fell on the streets surrounding the home on Hillway that Mimi and Chimen would ultimately buy. Expand the search parameters by just a few streets in each direction, and the number of bombs rises to several hundred. Bombs fell on Hampstead Heath, on Highgate Cemetery, on the Whittington Hospital, on at least one local school, and on numerous homes and businesses. In the East End, around Shapiro, Valentine & Co., almost every street experienced at least one bomb strike; many were hit multiple times. Some streets were entirely obliterated; others were left standing in a patchwork quilt of destruction interspersed with improbable examples of architectural survival. As the wheel of chance spun and spun again, somehow the little bookshop remained intact.

The number of casualties was huge. Between September 1940 and May 1941, well over twenty thousand Londoners were killed, three thousand of them on May 10 alone. Four of them were Mimi's cousins. London had become a charnel house. Somehow, Chimen and Mimi managed to preserve at least a veneer of normality: she kept the accounts and made sure the shop could function; he continued to collect his precious books even as the fires from the previous night's bombing raids still burned. One day a customer rushed into the shop to tell Chimen that the Beth Din, the ecclesiastical court of the United Synagogue, which had immense influence over the religious lives of Orthodox Jews in Britain and over which Yehezkel had presided since the mid-1930s when he had turned down an offer to become the chief rabbi of Palestine, had been hit by a bomb. Chimen, terrified that his father had been killed, ran out of the shop toward the religious court. He arrived just in time to see Yehezkel, his gabardine coat caked with dust, stagger out of the rubble. As Chimen ran toward him, Yehezkel rushed off in the other direction, toward the home he shared with Raizl, to tell her that he had survived the attack.

Six months into the Blitz, my grandparents made the decision to evacuate. Taking Chimen's books with them, they decamped to Bedford, some fifty miles north of London, in February 1941, to distance themselves from the fury. Mimi was trying to get pregnant. Jack (my father) was born in January 1942. They lived at 194 Foster Hill Road, a large house they shared with fourteen people, among whom were several of Mimi's cousins. Chimen commuted into London by train six days a week to run the shop. He continued, amid the wreckage of war, to buy books.

In some of these early additions to his collection, my grandfather signed his name "Shimen," elsewhere he wrote "Shimon," in others "S. Abramsky," and in still others "C. Abramsky." He was, it seemed, still experimenting with the best way to spell his Hebrew name using the English alphabet; later, in a 1967 letter to Isaiah Berlin, in which he gave his friend permission to address him by his first name after a ten-year correspondence, he wrote that the nonphonetic construction of his name was due to the idiosyncratic spelling used by Soviet authorities. When he began writing for the Communist Party, he added aliases to the mix and "C. Allen" came into being. Perhaps, in the many ways in which he spelled his name (and in the variety of birth dates he claimed, ranging from September 1916 through to March 1917), he was still trying to work out who he was, who he wanted to be.

Finally, as the reach of the bombs spread and Bedford no longer seemed to offer real sanctuary, Chimen and Mimi returned to London and, despite the fact that V2 rockets were raining down on the city, bought their house on Hillway. It was, perhaps, their way of

staking a claim to the future. When the attacks became too fero-
cious, Mimi would take my terrified father, then two years old, to a
large bomb shelter under the Hampstead Heath victory gardens.
There they would huddle with other refugees from the fiery world
above, the explosions shaking their fragile lair. My father's earliest
memories are of that hideaway. Well into adulthood he would have
nightmares about the bombs.

Throughout these dark years, Chimen continued to work at Shapiro, Valentine & Co. and to build his collection of Marxist literature.
In the evenings, while the German bombers unloaded their deadly
cargoes over London, he was a fire-spotter with the Metropolitan
Borough of St. Pancras Fire Guard. He would stand on rooftops,
scanning the blacked-out city below, looking for flames, and phoning
in locations to the fire brigades. The next morning, he would see the
full effect of those fires. One day, he wrote in the notes for his never-
finished autobiography, "there was a shattering, violent explosion.
We went out to have a look. London was on fire, burning from four
sides. It was hellishly frightening."

In my mind's eye I can see him coming out of Aldgate East tube
station the day after a bombing raid and carefully navigating through
the rubble, past the narrow old Huguenot houses, some still standing, others destroyed, as he made his way from Whitechapel High
Street over to Commercial Street and then along Wentworth Street to
his shop. He might, perhaps, in the strangeness of the rubble, have
paused for a moment to orient himself; quite possibly, the soaring
early eighteenth-century spire of Christ Church, Spitalfields, designed by the architect Nicholas Hawksmoor, helped to set his path.
On a clear day, the calm blue sky would have brutally contrasted
with the smoldering ruins, the noise of the East Enders attempting to
get on with their lives dissonant against the silence of the dead. The

ruins would have stunk of burning wires and rubber and all the other detritus of destroyed buildings.

Chimen would have trudged among the ruins, aghast at the horrors unleashed on his adopted city, yet thinking about what that city would look like, and how it would be run, once the war ended. For by the time he, Mimi, and their toddler son relocated back to London, it was clear that at some point soon the Nazis would be defeated. What was also increasingly clear was that Chimen, no longer viewed with suspicion as a newcomer, was now the effective head of his wife's extended family. It was the bookshop that he ran that would provide employment to relatives in need of work; and it was, increasingly, his and Mimi's words that would count in family dramas and conflicts.

———

For the first decade after the war ended, until she became too old and sick to live alone, Bellafeigel lived around the corner from Hillway. In the 1950s, when my father and aunt were children, she and her brother Leibl, Leibl's wife and daughter, and sometimes other relatives would rent a house at the seaside every summer, and Mimi and Chimen would dutifully drive down with the children for day trips. At first, they went to Southend-on-Sea in Essex and later on to Bournemouth, which was noted for its kosher hotels.

Chimen had, to his considerable pride, learned to drive in 1952; his enthusiasm was only slightly dampened by the fact that he'd had to spend several months after he passed his test dealing with mechanical problems in his old Morris (a car of prewar vintage with a crank-handle starter) and insurance claims for minor accidents. Mimi waited to learn to drive until 1956, not far short of her fortieth birthday. And so, in the early 1950s, when my grandparents and their two children would head to the coast, it was Chimen who was behind the wheel. Mimi loved to swim—in fact, she found the waters so pleasing that in early 1940, shortly after they had secretly pledged to marry each other, Mimi had sent her "Dear little Chimen" a coquettish, passionate letter, urging him to find an excuse to leave the bookshop for a couple of days and take a train to join her in Cardiff; she was, she told him, longing to show him the sea. As a token of her love, she had recently written an "autobiography" to him, in which she detailed the previous loves of her life. Chimen, in his reply, wrote that, upon reflection, he preferred to share his own amorous stories orally rather than in writing.

Unlike Mimi, Chimen did not love the sea. In fact, he had never learned to swim. At the beach he would sit in a deck chair or on the ground, his legs splayed in front of him, as often as not wearing a suit, with a handkerchief, its four corners knotted, atop his balding head, his eyes protected by dark glasses, reading Marxist history. As a concession to the summer, on a particularly hot day he would take off his jacket. British summers being generally on the tepid side, however, the jacket usually stayed on. In the late 1950s, after the Morris finally packed it in, Mimi and Chimen bought a small, secondhand Hillman Minx. From then on, Chimen would drive from Hillway to Wentworth Street. His back was starting to bother him—at times he could only sleep by lying flat on the wood floor—and the car, which he would park behind Shapiro, Valentine & Co., made the lugging of books to and from the shop that much easier.

Inside the claustrophobic dark confines of 81 Wentworth Street, its façade still looking the same as it had in the Edwardian period, Chimen would always wear either a velvet velour hat or a cloth cap. He did so not because his head was cold but, I suspect, because he did not want his religious clients and the friends of his parents who came to the shop to see that he was not wearing a yarmulke. He had stopped wearing a yarmulke as he went about his daily business years earlier, but he would still put one on when visiting his father. Even though he told his Party comrades that his parents were "reactionary," he went out of his way to avoid offending them gratuitously. His parents knew that he was not a believer; but that did not mean that their friends had to know as well.

When it came to people who wavered in their faith or who sought to assimilate into the secular culture, Yehezkel could be scathing in his criticism. In 1934, when he was appointed the head of the rabbinic court of the London Beth Din, *The Jewish Chronicle* had editorialized that Anglo-Jewry was being "hijacked" by religious extremists from afar, by men who spoke little or no English, cared little or nothing about the broader culture, and sought only to impose rigid rituals on their brethren. One commentator wrote that men like Yehezkel Abramsky were promoting an "alien dogma, custom and superstition which had never before been any part of Judaism except in dark corners deep inside the ghettoes of Eastern Europe." The rabbi responded: "My aim is to strengthen *Yiddishkeit* both in the practice and knowledge of Judaism." He was, noted the Oxford historian Miri Freud-Kandel in 2006, a polarizing force in British Jewry.

Much as the U.S. Constitution is continuously held up to interpretation by succeeding generations of legal scholars as a way to decide everything from the legitimacy of gay marriage to the right to bear arms, for religious Jews, the Talmud sets a theoretical framework within which later texts—the Shulhan Arukh and other codes—can be read, to lay down the rules for contemporary modes of conduct. For the Orthodox of London, many of the practices of everyday life—from the rituals of birth, marriage, and death, to the food that they ate—were filtered through the rulings of the Beth Din. And thus its leading interpreters of the Talmud, and the various commentaries on it written over the millennia, acquired tremendous influence. Ye-hezkel had, for his Orthodox followers, a status similar to that of the Supreme Court Justice Oliver Wendell Holmes among students of the Constitution in the United States. He had the power to make or break the country's chief rabbi, his approval being a necessary prerequisite for anyone wanting the job; his word could, and on occasion did, destroy the careers of young rabbis with whose interpretations of Torah he disagreed. In 1948, almost three years after the long-serv-ing chief rabbi J. H. Hertz died, Yehezkel helped install Israel Brodie in the job, but only after Brodie had "unequivocally relinquished au-thority over religious matters to Dayan Abramsky," wrote Freud-Kandel. Chief rabbis were convenient figureheads, but as Freud-Kandel explained, it was Yehezkel Abramsky who would shape how the community interpreted religious law. He was, she concluded, an ex-traordinarily effective political manipulator, but all his machinations were to two ends only: to increase the religiosity of Britain's Jewish population and the influence of conservative religious authority fig-ures over them.

So Chimen had good reasons to avoid having his parents' friends report back to Yehezkel that their third son was flaunting his atheism in public. He did not want his father's private disapproval of his and Mimi's worldview to be expressed in public. It was a double life that Chimen would keep up for decades. The Beth Din offices were on Hanbury Street, three blocks away from the shop; and the Machzikei Hadath synagogue, where Yehezkel had been the rabbi before be-coming head of the Beth Din, was even closer, on the corner of Brick Lane and Fournier Street. When Yehezkel or one of his rabbinic friends visited the shop, Chimen would immediately be able to launch into a conversation about the Talmud. When his Communist Party friends, such as the local tailor Mick Mindel, dropped by, he was equally at his ease talking about Marx's dialectic over a cup of tea.

During the run-up to the great religious festivals, Shapiro, Valentine & Co. bustled with shoppers looking to purchase Haggadot (books used at the Passover Seder), Jewish calendars, almanacs, prayer books, or the lemon-like etrog fruit and palm fronds to be used in the rituals of Sukkot (the Feast of Tabernacles). In the days leading up to Rosh Hashanah (the Jewish New Year) and to Yom Kippur (the Day of Atonement), the whole extended family would be brought in to help cater to the rush of customers buying New Year's cards and the religious equipment associated with the holidays. When the store closed at the end of a long day, Jenny, a young child at the time, would be entrusted with counting the money brought in since that morning.

On Friday afternoon, the shop's doors were shut and locked, and its customers disappeared into their homes to prepare for the Sabbath meal and then, on Saturday, to attend synagogue. On Sunday, however, those doors opened once more, with people drawn to the area not only by the goods on offer inside Shapiro, Valentine & Co. and the other shops lining Wentworth Street but also by the stalls of the Petticoat Lane street market, which ran along the center of Wentworth Street, literally past the front door of the old bookshop. On market days, well into the 1960s, the area became as noisy, vibrant, and crowded as the great London markets and fairs of an earlier era. In those years, a now firmly middle-aged Mimi would leave the bookshop and head off with her bags into the maelstrom of Petticoat Lane to shop for her week's supply of fruit and vegetables. She would make a point of asking where the produce was from, and if a stallkeeper was rash enough to mention South Africa, Mimi would simply stalk away; her refusal to put money into buying food grown in the apartheid state probably earned her the undying enmity of the stallkeepers, but in the years after her Communist faith was utterly destroyed, supporting the boycott movement launched against apartheid South

Africa in 1959 made her feel that she was still on the side of the (secular) angels.

At lunchtime, Chimen would slip out to Ostwind's, a nearby workers' café–cum–Jewish deli on Wentworth Street just the other side of Commercial Street from the bookshop, for a change of pace. All around the neighborhood, decades after the war ended, on Wentworth Street itself, on Commercial Street, on Middlesex Street, on Toynbee Street (home to the nineteenth-century center of social reform, Toynbee Hall), were craters left by the bombs that had fallen on the area during the Blitz.

One day these streets would be rebuilt, and like so much of the East End, its character would shift: The buildings would look different, the businesses that had made the district their home for generations would die off, the old immigrant groupings would be replaced by new ones. Walking through Chimen and Mimi's old neighborhood in 2013, I found that where Shapiro, Valentine & Co. had stood, a four-story brick block of flats, the upper-floor windows sporting small balconies with green-painted railings and colorful flowers in pots, had taken its place. Next door, Goide's bakery had been replaced by a Turkish-Lebanese restaurant. The synagogue at which Yehezkel had been rabbi was now the Brick Lane Jamme Masjid mosque. And along the nearby side streets halal butchers had replaced kosher ones, and Bangladeshi and Pakistani restaurants had opened in place of the old Jewish delis. Only a few scattered mementos of the Jewish East End were left for the eye to see: the building façade on Brune Street announcing the presence of a soup kitchen "for the Jewish poor"; a small Star of David visible under the black paint on a gutter coming down from the steepled roof of what was now a Church of England school; a historic shop front with the lettering "S. Schwartz." The scars of the war had largely vanished, the holes in the fabric of the streets patched with boutique cafés, fashionable restaurants, and expensive new residential dwellings.

In the meantime, though, as Chimen navigated the complicated religious and political terrain of the Jewish East End, Ostwind's served a surprisingly good fried egg sandwich with chips and beans; and, while the noise inside mirrored the kaleidoscopic chaos of the East End markets outside, it let Chimen escape the cares of his business for a few minutes each day.

When Chimen turned the lock on the shop door early on Sunday afternoon, the family would decamp to Golders Green, to visit Chimen's older, Orthodox brother Moshe, who was working at that time as a supervisor in a kosher slaughterhouse, and his wife, Chaya Sara, and their two young children. Chimen and Moshe, both at the house and over the phone, would natter away in Yiddish, talking for hours about politics, gossiping about mutual friends. Chimen would perennially disparage the gossip as "rubbish," while at the same time filing it away in his mind for subsequent retelling and, quite likely, embellishment. Later on Sunday afternoon, the family would make the short hop across Golders Green for a midafternoon tea with Mimi's sister Sara and her family. Finally, they would return home in time for Mimi to cook Sunday dinner for Chimen's first cousin Golda Zimmerman, a successful journalist who had helped Chimen find work at the bookshop back in the early days of the war and who was thus considered to have brought my grandparents together; Mimi felt she owed it to her cousin-in-law, who as she aged became a somewhat isolated lady, to invite her to Hillway at least weekly.

Despite their break with formal religion, theirs was, in many ways, a world bound by ritual and the densely woven fabric of family ties.

All the while, Chimen obsessively hunted for books. Shelf by shelf, he began creating his House of Books.

Walking from the front door at 5 Hillway into the house, you saw the hallway and its contents reflected back at you from an oval mirror hanging next to the staircase. It added a modicum of light, an illusion of scale, to what was otherwise a dark, narrow passage. Here, in this overcrowded hallway, was the evidence of Chimen's fascination with the arcane disputes and almost Talmudic reasoning of the late nineteenth- and early twentieth-century revolutionaries. The sprawling political and philosophical battles in which these book-writing men and women had immersed themselves in the years before he was born were not abstract arguments for Chimen; it was by these disputes, by their earnestly footnoted essays and manifestos, that my grandfather measured much of his life. He had done so since he was a teenager.

After arriving in London, Chimen learned English at Pitman Central College and later, while on holiday from his studies in Jerusalem, he worked for the publisher Bela Horovitz on the East and West Library, a series devoted to Jewish philosophy. For his labor, he was paid in books instead of cash. He was as determined to imbibe the written word as Yehezkel had been ten years before the First World War, when as a penniless yeshiva student in Vilna, Lithuania, he would wander into bookshops and spend hours in a corner reading from cover to cover volumes which he could not afford to buy. And increasingly the written words that Chimen cared most about were on Socialism. From the family's first days in London, while his father was at the synagogue on Brick Lane, Chimen had begun surreptitiously attending classes at Marx House, the home of the Marx Memorial Library and Workers' School in Clerkenwell. When his landlord's son walked in on him in his attic bedroom one evening, he found Chimen absorbed in Marxist literature. Guiltily, as if he had been caught reading smut, the teenager hid the book and quickly replaced it with a more respectable religious text.

Stuffed into many of the volumes in the hallway were letters between Chimen and some of the country's leading left-wing scholars, written and received as his fascination with Marxism grew. Of greatest interest to my grandfather as he aged was his correspondence with Piero Sraffa. Eighteen years Chimen's senior, the Italian-born Sraffa had ended up on Mussolini's wrong side in 1927 and had fled to England, where a few years later he was befriended by John Maynard Keynes. By the time the Second World War broke out, he was a fellow at Trinity College, Cambridge, and had made a reputation as one of the country's top economists. He was also busily building up a collection of Socialist literature that would have been unparalleled had Chimen not also been on the scene. In the postwar decades, Sraffa was the only other collector in England with a similar love for and knowledge of the arcane Socialist volumes that the rabbi's son so cherished.

Over the decades, they swapped rare books and shared with each other the joy of the hunt, the unspeakable pleasure—that only a fellow connoisseur could understand—of finding a particular edition of a particular book or pamphlet, and of procuring it for a lower-than-anticipated price. Chimen visited Sraffa at Trinity College numerous times, dining with him in the long hall, at the north end of which was an oil painting of the college founder, King Henry VIII, attributed to Hans Holbein or one of his disciples. In turn, Sraffa was frequently pressed upon by his friend to dine at Hillway. The art was less illustrious; I am fairly certain, however, that the cuisine at my grandparents' house was somewhat more adventurous. Many of Chimen's most valuable books were documented in this correspondence with Sraffa, which might well have been why he obsessed over this particular collection as he aged, repeatedly asking my brother or me to show him the letters, as if he were pinching himself, making sure that both he, and the world of books that he had so painstakingly created around him, were still alive.

In these letters, for example, was discussion of an early edition of *Das Kapital*, signed by Marx himself and dedicated to the German Workers' Association in London. Chimen had bought it in the late 1950s and sold it to Sraffa for the then-staggering sum of £750—£600 of which was paid in cash, the remainder in kind: Chimen wanted another Marx volume that was in Sraffa's possession. The total amount the book sold for was roughly the annual salary for a junior-level civil servant at the time, according to annual salary estimates produced by the country's Ministry of Labour in 1960. (The *Das Kapital* volume was subsequently stolen, turning up only decades later, in Switzerland, whence Trinity College ransomed it back.) Here also were references to letters by Marx; to original Lenin pamphlets and newspaper writings; to a first edition of Malthus on overpopulation, which Chimen bought and promptly sold to Sraffa for £15. Here were intimations of letters he bought and sold from Russian authors such as Ivan Turgenev (Chimen was scornful of the Soviet government's decision not to bid a decent amount for the Turgenev manuscripts, which thus allowed him to pick up more than thirty of the author's handwritten missives); and of negotiations conducted with the Soviet government in Moscow for the purchase of rare Marx documents in Chimen's possession. He explained in gleeful detail how he had acquired Marx's membership card of the First International (which Sraffa had put up for sale) and a signed letter by Marx as part of a Marx collection sold at Sotheby's, for what he regarded as the knockdown price of £110 in early April 1960. He would, he acknowledged after the fact—gently teasing his friend that he could have received more money for his treasures—have been quite willing to go as high as £250. And he played Sraffa off against the Soviet government, using the Soviets' interest in materials that he owned to encourage his friend to make a counteroffer. "Moscow has offered me for the two Marx pamphlets on Palmerston [the mid-nineteenth-century British statesman] one hundred and fifty pounds in cash," he wrote, in a note quickly scribbled on cheap lined paper on June 20, 1960 (which was, incidentally, his and Mimi's twentieth wedding anniversary). "If you are willing to give a bit more you can have them. I want one hundred and seventy-five pounds."

To another correspondent, Leo Friedman, in Boston, Massachusetts, to whom he periodically sold books and other documents, he wrote of acquiring a two-page letter that the poet, essayist, and journalist Heinrich Heine had written from Paris in 1844 to the editor of the *Augsburger Allgemeine Zeitung.* "This letter has never been published before and is of the utmost historical interest regarding Heine," he opined, "and his attitude to the radicals of the time."

It was in these letters that Chimen the intellectual, rather than Chimen the propagandist, came out. In the 1940s and early 1950s, his public writing, often written under aliases, was more propaganda than scholarship. He had contact with the Communist Historians' Group for a time and, when he could come up with the annual dues, was a member; but he was not a regular attendee. He wrote the occasional historical paper for them, but most of his Communist writing was either leaflets aimed at the Jews of London's East End or articles and editorials published in the Party's *Daily Worker,* the *Jewish Clarion,* and other journals and newspapers. More often than not, the articles were predictable and filled with jargon. A ten-point leaflet, from the late 1940s, entitled "Why Jews Should Vote Communist" was a typical example. Point Six patiently explained that the "Communist Party denies that the standard of the life of the working class must be lowered merely to meet the greed of American dollar financiers." In 1946, when writing critically about the growing pressure for the creation of a Jewish state in Israel, as "C. Chimen" he wrote that the "unhampered defeatist propaganda, which avers that there is no future in Europe for the Jews, has helped considerably to make the displaced Jews a catspaw of imperialism." Only in Chimen's private correspondence did he allow the panoramic range of his interests to clear a path through this fog of jargon. He wrote to Harold Laski on the workings of parliamentary democracy. He penned notes to Isaiah Berlin discussing whether or not Machiavelli had influenced Marx. He wrote letters on Jewish history and pages of musings on the great philosophers. He bounced from current affairs to medieval political dramas.

For Chimen, letters were his great intellectual safety valve, the genre in which he could most freely and fluently express himself. He subscribed to the notion that Alexander Herzen had proclaimed in 1862, when writing to his friend Turgenev: "It is for the sake of digression and parentheses that I prefer writing in the form of letters to friends; one can then write without embarrassment whatever comes into one's head." Over the decades, Chimen wrote tens of thousands of letters, making carbon copies for posterity, or when he had no access to carbon paper, simply rewriting his missives before sending off the signed originals and then filing the duplicates. They ranged in length from one- or-two-line notes setting up meetings, to multipage treatises on the great political thinkers, philosophers, historians, artists, and musicians of the last millennia. Some were about arranging fellowships for needy students, others about the great political events of the day. With friends such as Sraffa and Isaiah Berlin—he had been introduced to the famous philosopher in 1958 by the Oxford Slavonic scholar and librarian John Simmons, and had, the following year, sold him roughly £150 worth of Russian literature by Pushkin and others—he covered a vast intellectual terrain. "You are," wrote Berlin to his friend in June 1979, "an exceptionally honest, penetrating and sensitive man and scholar; and the fact that you think me to be some good, fills me with much needed confidence." Chimen called these missives *megile*, a Yiddish term roughly translated as "a lengthy, detailed explanation or account." Elsewhere, he described them as *megilah*, a Hebrew word meaning "scroll." Thousands of these letters still remain in the archives of University College London. In a storage unit that my father rented after Hillway was cleared out, there were several large cardboard boxes full of correspondence. Elsewhere were kept

Letter from Chimen to Isaiah Berlin, June 6, 1969. One of several hundred letters from a correspondence that lasted for nearly forty years.

twenty-four more folio boxes, each containing hundreds of letters written and received by Chimen.

When Chimen died, my aunt and my father found, in a hidden compartment in the back of the huge rolltop desk in his bedroom, a collection of letters, many of them handwritten, addressed to Harold Laski of the London School of Economics. They were from such luminaries as Prime Minister Stanley Baldwin; the philosopher Bertrand Russell; the owner and editor of the *Manchester Guardian*, C. P. Scott; and the Fabians Sidney and Beatrice Webb—the latter of whom, in a sloppy, at times almost illegible scrawl, exhibited a surprising infatuation with Mussolini's Fascists in correspondence to Laski from the mid-1920s. In another pile was a fading handwritten letter from Turgenev, written in English interspersed with Russian and signed in Cyrillic script, from Bougival, France, in 1881, to an unknown friend, the only one of the trove of Turgenev letters that Chimen ended up keeping for himself. "I am staying here alone with a tremendous grippe, and shall not go back to Paris before the end of next week," the great author wrote. "Believe me. Yours very truly, Iv. Turgenev." Chimen reported to Sraffa that he had resold almost all of the Turgenev manuscripts, including four pages of an unpublished Turgenev story. There was, however, one other exception: correspondence between Berlin and Chimen indicates that he gave one of the letters to Berlin in June 1984, on the occasion of his seventy-fifth birthday. Turgenev was, wrote Chimen in explanation of his gift, a man "whom we both admire and on whom you wrote so brilliantly."

A handwritten, signed letter from the Zionist leader Chaim Weizmann, who would one day become Israel's first president, to the Liverpool-based Rabbi Isaiah Raffalovich, dated June 21, 1917, was also found in the desk. "Our enemies will not rest and try and devise means to hurt us mortally," Weizmann wrote. "We must watch things and be on the alert and before all organize and organize an all Jewish congress, which would definitely consolidate our position." In a handwritten list of some of his more important possessions, which he wrote late in his life, Chimen referred to an original letter by Voltaire, on the topic of Europe's Jews. The letter was not found when his house was emptied out. Like the Laski correspondence, he had probably secreted it away somewhere and simply neglected, or forgotten, to tell anyone else where it was. Maybe it was in a hidden drawer, the lock of which could have been opened by one of the dozens of tiny unlabeled keys also found in his great desk. In all likelihood it accidentally ended up in one of the hundreds of rubbish bags that were filled with all the printed matter that Chimen himself could never throw away: old receipt forms from Shapiro, Valentine & Co.; utility bills dating back half a century; bank statements from decades past. But maybe it did not. Perhaps, somehow, the letter escaped. Perhaps, one day, generations from now, someone will buy the old desk in a junk shop in some nondescript place or another and discover the Voltaire letter, a time capsule inside a time capsule from the past. Whomever that person might be, I hope they recognize the exquisite beauty of what is resting in their hands.

Farther down the hallway, in between the doors to the living room and the dining room, opposite a little closet with a toilet and sink, was another set of images: black-and-white photos, taken by my cousin Rob, as part of a school photography project. The space where they hung had been grudgingly saved from books, probably because the hallway was so narrow that had bookshelves been placed opposite the toilet, there would have been no easy way to use that necessary room. The images showed Chimen in action, and also included one photo of Mimi and Jenny, "the two women of his life," as Rob put it. There, on that wall, was a close-up of Chimen in a wool hat; another of his hat resting on a bookshelf; Chimen hunched over a chessboard, deep in concentration. Sometimes there would be a person on the other side of the chessboard—myself, or one of the other grandchildren; other days, Chimen would simply re-create a grand master's game he had read about in that morning's edition of *The Times*, carefully poring over the moves, studying them as he would the text of a rare book. "Chess was his sport," Rob noted, as he explained his choice of photographic imagery. "Like so much of his life, the muscle he liked to exercise was his mind." In 1995, when he was nearly eighty years old, Chimen wrote the foreword to Victor Keats's book *Chess in Jewish History and Hebrew Literature*. There was, apparently, almost nothing about Jewish life upon which Chimen could not expound.

It was at the end of the hallway, where the passage branched off either to the dining room or the kitchen, that I recall frequently standing and watching as my older cousin Raph would enter the house, walking deliberately slowly, his hands in the pockets of a light brown suede jacket. I would feel a shiver of excitement at Raph's entry, fueled by my half knowledge that he and Chimen had been feuding for years, with an intensity born of deep love and extraordinary intellectual competition: both were leading historians of their generation; both were book collectors of remarkable importance; both were fascinated by Socialism; and both felt rather proprietary about the movements they chronicled. Some of that I knew, some of it I intuited. But what was clear to me, even as a young child, was that when Raph came through the doorway, the atmosphere at Hillway would change: Mimi would almost cry for joy that her beloved nephew was visiting her, but then she would glance at Chimen to see how he was reacting. And every time a tension would descend, Chimen's blood pressure would increase visibly, voices would soon be raised. It was predictable, but it was, nevertheless, often spectacular.

Through it all, Raph would keep up his insouciant expression, his sort of deliberate cool-intellectual appearance. He had wispy hair, falling forward chaotically onto his forehead; round glasses perched atop his thin nose; that wonderful, tattered suede jacket. There was about him the permanent smell of cigarettes; his voice was desperately gentle, slightly nasal, and as full of passion as any voice I had ever encountered; and there was an almost beatific expression in his eyes. And yet, for all the otherworldly qualities that Raph exuded, when he got into arguments with Chimen over Israel or the activities of left-wing trade union leaders or the validity of direct action protests, there was something steely about those eyes and that voice. Chimen knew it, and it bothered him—at least in part, I came to think, because it reminded him of who he had once been. I loved the anticipation. I loved being a spectator to and, as I got older, a participant in these epic verbal jousting contests.

Raphael Samuel and Chimen at Chimen and Mimi's 50th wedding anniversary party, 1990.

The hallway, I knew, was somewhere special. Not just a narrow stretch of carpeted terrain from portal to kitchen, but a carefully constructed gateway to debate and conversation, to a magic realm. "This world is like a hallway before the world to come," Rabbi Yaakov was quoted as saying in *Pirkei Avot*, a tractate from the Mishnah written nearly two thousand years ago: "Prepare yourself in the hallway so you may enter the banquet hall."

Chimen reflected in his hallway mirror.

THE KITCHEN:

SALT, SUGAR, AND A DASH OF LOVE

Love is a symbol of eternity. It wipes out all sense of time, destroying all memory of a beginning and all fear of an end.
—attributed to Madame de Staël

HILLWAY WAS A unique salon because the two obsessions of two obsessive people gelled there in a most unusual way: Chimen's passion for his books and the ideas they contained, Mimi's for nurturing and nourishing an endless stream of people. Left to his own devices, Chimen would quite probably have collected books and ideas in his house, and done his socializing in more public places—cafés around Shapiro, Valentine & Co.; university dining rooms; and academic conferences. As a child, he would sometimes recall, he had been desperately lonely. He and his elder brothers were educated at home because his father was anxious to avoid his sons coming into contact with the world around them: Yehezkel had repeatedly sought an exit visa from the Soviet Union, in large part because he was so nervous about his sons becoming contaminated by Bolshevism. As a result of this enforced isolation, Chimen had been unable to develop friendships with other children. It was, my grandfather said sadly, the single biggest regret of his youth. He claimed that once, with little else to do, over a period of several weeks he had counted aloud to one million, breaking into his task only to sleep and eat. Had anyone else told me that, I would have dismissed it as exaggeration; Chimen, however, I was inclined to believe.

To be sure, the apartment in Moscow to which Yehezkel had moved his family, so that he could daily petition government bureaucrats to grant them an exit visa from the country, had housed many guests, mainly Torah scholars seeking illicit intellectual solace in a Soviet Union that Yehezkel had taken to calling a "house of bondage." At times, guests, who were fed the few potatoes that could be bought in the shops by Raizl, had slept on, and even under, the table. There is a sense of a gathering of the doomed in the descriptions of the apartment that eventually made their way into Yehezkel's biography, of individuals waiting to be arrested, to be sent to labor camps in Siberia or executed. In that tableau, there were no children in whom Chimen could confide or with whom he could make friends. The experience left him craving human interaction; but at the same time it also left him strangely unable to communicate on a mundane level about the little things, the nuances that cumulatively make up the fabric of most people's lives.

Had Chimen's life taken some different turns—had he not found Mimi, had he not been given an opportunity to let his gregarious nature run free at home—he might well have evolved into one of those lonely, eccentric, somewhat contrary antiquarians who inhabit so many of Dickens's pages. Taken to an extreme, had that gregariousness not been allowed to take root and flourish, as he aged he might eventually have become like the character in Elias Canetti's *Auto-da-Fé* who literally walled himself up in a house of books, able only to relate to the printed page. But Chimen was not left to his own devices. Collecting people was as important to Mimi as collecting books was to Chimen. She simply always *had* to be a hostess, and once she had invited you into her *Yiddish hoyz*, she had to feed you. "She is the one who tends, cares for and above all feeds the family," Zborowski and Herzog wrote of Jewish wives in Eastern Europe, in *Life Is with People*. "When she offers food, she is offering her love, and she offers it constantly. When her food is refused it is as if her love were rejected." At the end-of-week dinner, which celebrates the Sabbath, a Jewish table is filled with good food, ritual wine is drunk, prayers are said, and, of course, strangers are welcomed and hosted. Around that table, community is renewed. At 5 Hillway, almost every day was a Sabbath.

For Mimi, food was a vicarious pleasure. Even in childhood, her health had been fragile. When she was in primary school, in the East End of London, she had almost died of an infection; for the rest of her life, she bore a long, curving scar on the side of her neck as a reminder of the emergency surgery that she'd had to undergo to drain the site of pus. A diabetic who failed dismally to adhere to her no-sugar, low-salt diet, from middle age onward she was beset by health problems. Increasingly overweight, she accumulated pills that she had to take daily to keep her blood pressure in check, her heart in order, her kidneys functioning. After she had a few awful falls, one of them down a flight of concrete steps while traveling in Israel, her legs became increasingly unreliable, crisscrossed like a street map with varicose veins, her thighs prone to unsightly bruising at the slightest knock. However, when people asked her about her health, she would pooh-pooh their concerns, tell them that "we don't need to talk about such things," and quickly change the subject. While feeding thick, creamy sauces and rich, delicious desserts to her myriad guests—roulades, trifles, cakes she had decided her grandchildren liked and therefore had to be served repeatedly and in copious quantities—Mimi could snack illicitly without feeling that she was utterly ignoring her doctors. These were her improbable masterpieces;

I might even say they were her culinary versions of the deaf Beethoven's symphonies. And so, whenever you entered the house, you were greeted by a rush of competing aromas: the smell of ducks roasting, the fat bubbling off them as the oven heated up; the gorgeous aroma of chicken soup, so saturated in salt, in my cousin Maia's recollection, that "it was just like the Dead Sea"; chocolate cakes baking; thick rye bread cut into slices; and the tart odor of herrings sitting in brine in their glass jars. My grandmother's guests would eat a lot; she would eat a little—and everybody would feel sated.

Over the decades, Mimi acquired layer upon layer of friends, one generation atop the next, who regarded 5 Hillway as their second home and Mimi as an extra mother, a supplement to their biological family. During the final year of the war, a number of refugees found safe haven at Hillway. Later, a succession of lodgers became honorary members of the family. Minna's son, Raph, spent more time at Hillway than in the home of his recently divorced mother, coming to view my grandparents as his surrogate parents. He brought future academic and journalistic luminaries such as Gareth Stedman Jones, Stuart Hall, Perry Anderson, and Peter Sedgwick to the house. Henry Collins, Chimen's urbane literary collaborator, practically lived in the downstairs front room at times. One night, when he was exhausted and could not convince the other guests to vacate his quarters and let him sleep, he simply took off his clothes and climbed into bed in front of the surprised guests. Whether that did the trick, or whether they continued debating Marxist theory over Collins's snoring, was not recorded.

Several young French cousins, whose families had been partially destroyed in the Nazi death camps, spent months at a time living there. My father's best friends from school all camped out at the house. There they engaged in furious chess competitions and equally frenetic games of table tennis on a table my dad had jerry-rigged in his bedroom. My aunt, five years younger than her brother and less enamored of the chaos, was more reluctant to bring her friends around. Later on, a young girl named Elisabetta Bianconi, whose parents, Margaret (a colleague and close friend of Mimi's) and Roberto, had both died in a car accident, became a part of the inner circle. Chimen's best friend, Shmuel Ettinger and his wife, Rina, visited several times a year from Israel. Left-wing English historians such as Eric Hobsbawm, James Joll, and E. P. Thompson came through the house and were drawn, irresistibly, to Mimi's table. So too were economists, including (of course) Piero Sraffa; Communist world travelers such as Freda Cook, a correspondent for the *Morning Star* who had moved to Hanoi to express her political solidarity with Ho Chi Minh; some leading character actors; a businessman named Danny Nahum, who corresponded with Chimen on expensive, embossed letterhead paper, and who, during the good times, would arrive at Hillway in a Rolls-Royce and during bad ones would arrive bedraggled and looking for one of Mimi's meals to tide him over; and innumerable others. Artists and musicians made their way to the house, as did rabbis and philosophers. For a time, an American entomologist studying butterflies was a staple of the salon. A Canadian government official and his wife also flew in on a semi-regular basis to visit. Claudia Roden, the renowned author of well-received cookbooks on Jewish and Middle Eastern food, came to the kitchen to discuss food with Mimi and history with Chimen. Each visitor was what was called in Yiddish an *oyrekh*, a guest, to be hosted, fed, and cared for as etiquette and tradition dictated.

I doubt that anyone ever attempted to calculate how many visitors tramped through Hillway over the years, though it would have made for an entertaining school math project. Certainly it was in the thousands, quite possibly in the tens of thousands. It is entirely possible that the number of people for whom Mimi cooked meals over the decades rivaled the number of books that Chimen accumulated. It was through her hospitality and the energy and wisdom that she put into making Hillway a gathering place that Mimi sought to manifest the ideal virtues of Jewish women described in the book of Proverbs. She had much in common with Rahel Levin, Henriette Herz, or Fanny von Arnstein, Jewish women who held salons in eighteenth- and early nineteenth-century Berlin and Vienna. These *salonnières*, wrote Emily Bilski and Emily Braun in *Jewish Women and Their Salons*, "presented an ideal of social interaction free of considerations of social rank." Levin, in particular, they wrote, was renowned for "her intelligence, wit, depth of understanding and gift for friendship."

———

It was in the kitchen that the true melting-pot nature of Hillway unfolded. Sleepy-eyed guests, who had bedded down on sofas, spare beds, even chairs when the house was particularly busy, would wander into the kitchen in the morning, only to find other temporary residents or passersby who had not been there the night before. My cousin Elliott recalled, when he was over from America for a short stay at Hillway, once meeting the playwright Harold Pinter in the kitchen over breakfast. My father and aunt did not think that was likely—to their knowledge Mimi and Chimen did not know Pinter. Yet nor was it entirely implausible, since 5 Hillway was, after all, one of London's crossroads. Frequently it seemed more like a hostel than a midsize suburban home, replete with the stale air that accompanies too many people confined in too small a space, and the babble of many different tongues.

It was, at times, overwhelming. You could come into the house, tell Mimi that you had just had a five-course meal at a restaurant, and within minutes she would be placing bowls of soup and plates of steaming chicken or duck or lamb in front of you. Often, she would get all her "children" confused: "Have some more chicken, Raph," she would urge me. Then, realizing her mistake, she would try to make amends. "Kolya, Rob, I mean Sasha!," and she would laugh. "Oye yoy yoy!" Chimen would exclaim in mock horror, "Mir-ri, it's our oldest grandson. It's Meester Sasha." When I was younger, it frustrated me. As I grew up, however, I realized that the confusion grew not out of carelessness but an excess of love. She knew who we all were; but she cared so much for each of us that we occasionally blended in her mind into one great mass of people for whom she bore responsibility for feeding.

Whenever I stayed the night at Hillway, I could be sure that in the morning I would be greeted by the sight and the aroma of Mimi cooking potato pancakes or quickly putting together a heaping plate of her regular pancakes, always covered with lemon juice and sugar, and rolled tight into a cigar-shape. It was from the kitchen—extended into the back garden by a few feet when I was a young child, so as to provide more room for Mimi's cooking—that the grandchildren would go into the still-spacious grassy expanse on Guy Fawkes night, when our fathers would set off all the fireworks that we had bought with money raised by the old custom of asking for a "penny for the Guy"; Mimi would venture through the glass sliding doors to the garden, plates of kosher mini–hot dogs in her hands, to feed her guests as the explosions rocked the night sky.

It was while my brother and I were eating plates of Mimi's pancakes in the kitchen one morning in the early 1990s, when she was already very old and very ill, that Chimen got a call from Sotheby's suggesting he come in to see a copy of Stalin's death mask that had mysteriously been deposited at the auction house the night before. In high excitement, Chimen told us to hurry up and finish our pancakes; and then the three of us dashed off to Sotheby's. There was the mask, a ghastly portrait of the dictator in his final pose before eternity. There was something hideous about it, something vastly awful about touching the mask that had lain on the inert face of a man responsible for the deaths of millions. For Chimen, now in endless flight from the politics of his younger and middle years, it must have been particularly macabre.

———

Mimi's urge to hospitality seemed, occasionally, to border on the pathological. She simply could not endure the thought of an empty, quiet house. Nor, as someone who had grown up as a sickly child in the impoverished, war-torn East End, and who had reared her own children during the grim years of another world war and food rationing that continued long after hostilities had ceased, could she countenance her guests not eating: After all, it was not until 1954, when my father was twelve years old, that the rationing of meat and other foodstuffs finally ended. The consumption of sweets and chocolate had also been severely restricted for many years (the ration was as low as two ounces per person per week in 1942), as had the usage of butter, sugar, eggs, and most other staple foods. For a couple of years after the war, with wheat crops hit by appalling weather, even bread, that most basic part of the British diet, had been rationed. So it was not surprising that, when Chimen left Britain for the first time in nine years, in 1948, on a mission to buy and sell books in an America untroubled by rationing and food shortages, Mimi's daily letters to him were full of descriptions of the food parcels he should send home.

Chimen, traveling on his newly issued British passport (for his official photograph he chose to wear a pinstripe suit, a dark tie, and a white striped shirt), sailed for New York on the Cunard liner the *Mauretania* on November 6, 1948. His passage in a shared berth on the overbooked vessel was secured by the intervention of Yehezkel with the head of the shipping company. Mimi worried that Chimen—who, as documented on the form from the British tax office stapled into the back of his passport, had journeyed to America with £510 sterling, as well as rare texts to sell by the French revolutionary, Marat, and the founder of Zionism, Theodor Herzl—would develop a paunch when he was let loose on American restaurants. (Decades later, one of his New York cousins remembered how the little man from England had wolfed down enormous Reuben sandwiches, one after the other, in the city's delis.) My father, then six years old, ran around the kitchen when he received Chimen's first letter, shouting, "Hurrah, hurrah, Daddy is in New York." He was, Mimi reported, beside himself with excitement at the prospect of chewing gum finally arriving at Hillway. Meanwhile, Mimi's sister Minna teased Chimen about the beautiful women he was likely to meet overseas. The sisters would, she wrote, have to start jitterbugging for him once he returned from his extended trip. But for Mimi more prosaic concerns predominated. On December 28, ten days before Chimen was due to set sail home, my grandmother wrote, "as far as food goes— eggs, tinned fruit, wurst, salmon, tinned chicken etc." Presumably, the wurst, or sausage, she was referring to was of the non-pork variety because, despite their lack of religious sentiment, my grandparents, throughout the more than half a century of their marriage, kept a strictly kosher kitchen.

In the delicate balancing act that made the salon work, Mimi owned the kitchen. But Chimen staked out a presence at the Formica-topped table; he frequently played chess or Russian dominoes with his grandchildren there, and often he brought back to the house people with whom he had been speaking and with whom he hoped to continue in conversation over a mug of tea or a small, delicate cup of coffee in the kitchen, its contents carefully measured out by Chimen.

So, too, he controlled the portable radio, increasingly ancient-looking as the years progressed, its telescopic antenna extended as high as it could go, which was always tuned to either classical music on Radio 3 or the news on Radio 4. Most days, he would hush his visitors and ceremoniously turn on *The World at One* or *Today*: both were programs that his daughter, Jenny, would edit as she rose up the ranks of the BBC. While the headlines were being read, he enforced strict silence on his guests.

When I think about the kitchen now, it strikes me that it was a place of initiation. A guest would first come for a cup of tea, perhaps to grill Chimen on his knowledge about a historical topic and ask him for references for which, inevitably, he could conjure up the exact page (and go on to locate the book on his shelves to prove his point); and then, inexorably, and assuming Chimen did not find fault with the visitor's approach to the world of ideas, the guest would be invited to dinner. Tea in the kitchen was a testing ground for the salon. To the intellectually agile, witty, and cultured, the doors were thrown open in succession: first to the kitchen, then the dining room, then the front sitting room—where it was entirely likely that the conversation, begun over a cup of tea in the kitchen early that afternoon, would continue well into the small hours of the night. That was how Chimen's Oxford friend, the historian Harold Shukman, was initiated; introduced to Chimen by Shmuel Ettinger in the late 1950s on the steps of the British Museum, Shukman wandered the streets of Bloomsbury with his new acquaintance for two hours, discussing early twentieth-century Russian Socialist movements. Soon thereafter, he received an invitation back to the house for tea. And after that, Mimi started feeding him.

Despite the part that the kitchen played in Chimen's routines, I had the impression that, barring his dish-washing duties, after the guests had left, he was allowed into this room mostly on sufferance. In tacit recognition of this fact, it was the one part of the house, with the exception of the bathrooms, that Chimen did not invade with his armies of books. Written materials in the kitchen were generally limited to *The Times* and the local *Ham & High* newspaper. On occasion, *The Jewish Chronicle* and *The New York Review of Books* would also find their way onto the table. But that was about the extent of Chimen's printed-word incursions into Mimi's fortress. If he did not like the conversation, if he was bored by the gossip that Mimi and her friends shared, if the presence of nonacademics chatting over a cup of tea with Mimi frustrated him—and she was as likely to brew some tea, over which to engage in conversation, for her elderly cleaning lady, Josie, a Caribbean immigrant who must have worked at Hillway until she was into her eighties, as she was for close friends such as the tiny but feisty Ray Waterman, or her childhood school friend and, more recently, neighbor Wynn Moss—well, Chimen knew where the doors were.

———

This was the casual room, the "drop in for a nice cuppa tea" room, far more Mimi's than Chimen's—and she fought to keep it that way. It was the one room in the house in which Mimi felt that she could command some privacy and for that reason it was, I would guess, in her kitchen that Mimi sat down in early 1965 to write two secret letters to Isaiah Berlin, desperately seeking his help in securing Chimen the job at Oxford that he so craved. And it was in all probability at her kitchen table that she read his dispiriting reply: However brilliant Chimen was, Berlin wrote, it was highly unlikely that he would be able to get a job to meet his talents, because he had no formal qualifications.

Mimi's own career had flourished: When her children were still very young she had trained as a social worker at Walthamstow Polytechnic; then between 1956 and 1959 she studied psychiatric social work at the London School of Economics. She took a job at the National Hospital for Nervous Diseases in Maida Vale before moving to the Royal Free Hospital where, by the time I was born, she had become the head of the Psychiatric Social Work Department.

In addition to being Mimi's culinary fiefdom, the kitchen was also an extension of her professional world: She would hold impromptu therapy sessions there; always on the phone, stirring a soup with one hand, holding the telephone with the other. Often she was talking to psychiatric patients; she felt no compunction about giving out her home number to patients who were sometimes paranoid or schizophrenic. She had been hit or pushed a couple of times by those whom she was trying to help, but none of it seemed to scare her. For Mimi, who believed deeply in the universal principles underlying the National Health Service, this was all in a day's work, knocks that one took without complaining. All her life, from her youthful Communist years to her post-Communist old age, Mimi craved community: If she could not find it in politics or religion, she would re-create it in her own home and in her work. And it would be as expansive and as generous as anything in the wider world beyond. It was this need to belong to a community that made Mimi and Chimen so furious with the Conservative prime minister Margaret Thatcher when I was growing up. Thatcher had famously said that there was no such thing as society. It was a worldview that contradicted their most cherished beliefs, and one that left them, at times, practically sputtering with rage.

———

From as far back as I can remember, Mimi's freezer was always stocked to bursting with whitefish fillets; packages of lox; KitKat bars, kept deliciously crispy by the cold; dubious inventions such as milk lollipops; cardboard containers of orange juice concentrate;

lamb chops; and enormous ducks. To the right of the freezer was a fridge, just as full. It housed fruit, vegetables, great jars of herrings, more lox, whatever meats were scheduled to be cooked that day, and endless little treats: boxes of chocolates, sickly sweet chocolate oranges, cakes, strudels, and any other goodies visitors had brought to Mimi as offerings.

On the other side of the freezer was a chrome bread bin. It always contained challah and dark, heavy, presliced Russian brown bread; often it had pumpernickel and rye as well. On that bread, one would be expected to either slather marmite or pour on sticky honey from a pint-size glass jar, or to heap piles of lox or briny herring. For Chimen in particular, herring and brown bread was a taste of childhood. Next to the bread bin were boxes of cereal, many different brands to appease the various tastes of Mimi's grandchildren. Under the bread bin were two drawers. One was filled with cutlery to be used for meat dishes. The other contained a duplicate set, fashioned slightly differently, to be employed in the eating of dairy dishes. In cupboards above the oven and over the washing machine and dryer were similar duplicate sets of plates and bowls. Crammed into spare spaces in these cupboards was more food: tins filled with biscuits, packages of crunchy and sweet sponge-cake fingers, and boxes of chocolates brought by guests. In more cupboards nearer floor level were the pots and pans, carefully separated by usage so as not to be polluted by the wrong kinds of food.

It was in the kitchen—more than in any other room of the house—that tradition refused to die.

———

That Mimi and Chimen kept a rigidly kosher home, in which they routinely fed militantly nonreligious diners, bespoke the larger issues of the contradictions between the personal and the political, between their cultural Jewish identity and their rejection of religion. Yes, they believed, as Marx had written in *The Communist Manifesto*, that religion was the opiate of the masses; yes, they believed that religious rituals were, generally, hocus-pocus. Furthermore, the one time in his life that Chimen admitted to having been drunk, he'd had to be carried out of a cousin's wedding ceremony in what was then Palestine while serenading his audience with "The Internationale." The poem, composed by a Paris Communard in 1871 and set to a rousing tune by Pierre De Geyter, had become the Communist anthem—indeed, until 1944 it was the anthem of the Soviet Union. The lyrics, translated into many languages, denounced the brutality of capitalism and promised the creation of a new and fairer world in its stead. In the English version, the singers called on the struggling masses to

Arise, ye workers from your slumber
Arise, ye prisoners of want
For reason in revolt now thunders
And at last ends the age of cant!

At the end of each of the three stanzas, the chorus encouraged the listeners:

So comrades, come rally
And the last fight let us face:
The Internationale
Unites the human race.

Mimi would joyously tell the story of Chimen's drunken escapade, and he would sit sheepishly, an impish grin on his face as he listened in mock horror. He was like Étienne Lantier, the Socialist central character in Émile Zola's novel *Germinal*, riveted "by a great beam of sunlight," for whom "justice came down from heaven like a dazzling fairy vision. Since God was no more, it was the turn of justice to bestow happiness upon mankind and usher in the kingdom of equality and brotherhood. As happens in dreams, there grew up a new society in a single day and, shining like a mirage, a great city, in which each citizen lived by his own appointed task and shared in the joys of all." Zola added, with a suitable pinch of cynicism, "And the dream grew ever grander, ever more beautiful, ever more enchanting, as it soared higher and higher into the impossible."

But, if my young grandparents wanted to sweep the past away and create a new world, set on new foundations, at the same time they also believed deeply in family, and in the obligations that generations owed to each other. And for the daughter of religious immigrants who had fled the tsarist pogroms, and for the son of Rabbi Abramsky, onetime prisoner of conscience in the Soviet Union and now the head dayan of the London Beth Din, and thus automatically one of the most senior rabbinic figures in Europe, that meant keeping the kitchen strictly kosher. Moreover, in their heart of hearts—the inner sanctum beyond the reach of ideology—I suspect that they never quite believed their own dogmas when it came to religion.

Quite possibly Chimen felt like one of the characters in Isaac Babel's collection of stories about the Russian Revolution and its aftermath titled *Benya Krik, the Gangster*, which Chimen kept in his office at University College London. "Gedali," I said, "today is Friday and it's already evening. Where can you get a Jewish cookie, a Jewish glass of tea, and in the glass of tea a little taste of that God who has been asked to step down?" "Nowhere," Gedali answered me, hanging the padlock on his little tavern box, "nowhere." In the name of ideology, Chimen and Mimi had retired their God; but for the rest of their lives, He hovered in the background, tempting them to resurrect Him in the rituals and habits of their daily existence. Sigmund Freud had once written of a community of Jewish *Unglaubensgenossen*, roughly translated as "fellow unbelievers." Among the members of such a synagogue, wrote the historian David Biale, would be counted Freud himself, Spinoza, and Heinrich Heine, who had converted to Christianity not on principle but to gain an "entrance card" to European society. Had such a synagogue actually existed, Chimen and Mimi would probably have been loyal members.

Although Mimi and Chimen seemed comfortable with the compromises they made between the demands of adherence to tradition and ritual, and their personal religious and political beliefs, the compromises stretched thin with the younger generation. As his son Jack planned his wedding with Lenore, to be held in the early autumn of 1966, Chimen began what would become a series of unhappy arguments with Lenore about the role of religion in daily life. She had been brought up an atheist and was violently opposed to the idea of being married in a synagogue in a traditional ceremony. Chimen announced that he would rather see Jack and Lenore cohabit than to suffer the indignity of them being married in a civil ceremony. When Lenore, a stylish young woman from California, with the sensibilities of the 1960s generation, chose a chic, imperial purple, sleeveless wedding dress, my grandfather declared that the religious members of the family would be appalled at seeing so much female flesh on display. On both fronts, after weeks of haggling, they reached an awkward—but workable—agreement. They would hold an abbreviated wedding ceremony conducted by a member of the Beth Din, and would then hold two receptions; the whole event would take place in the back garden at Hillway. First, the family members witnessed the marriage ceremony (Lenore in long sleeves) conducted by a rabbi, under the Jewish wedding canopy known as a chuppah; then the religious guests arrived for a short reception. And finally, when they left, Lenore was free to pull off the detachable sleeves to her dress, as the secular guests came to celebrate the same event. It made no sense—except to Chimen, who must have recalled the stories that his parents had told him of their own wedding, in the summer of 1909, when the entire population of the shtetl of Ihomen came out to see the daughter of Rabbi Jerusalimsky, the granddaughter of the famous Rabbi Willowski, marry the up-and-coming religious scholar known to his students as the *Moster Zadik*, and four hundred cheder students with lit torches paraded by as Yehezkel and Raizl were walked up to the chuppah. Chimen and Mimi, by contrast, had been married in Silberstein's, a Jewish restaurant in the East End of London, in a tiny, quick ceremony conducted by Yehezkel and seven of his colleagues, witnessed by Mimi's brother-in-law Samuel Barnett and a civilian registrar for marriages, on June 20, 1940—days after Nazi forces had entered Paris and just before the French government surrendered to Hitler—thirty-one years to the day after Yehezkel and Raizl's wedding. Now, in 1966, eight years out of the Communist Party and desperate to do things right by his parents, Chimen was going to make sure that Jack was married properly. If that meant holding two wedding receptions, one to meet the religious requirements, one to meet his new daughter-in-law's detestation of all things religious, then he would make sure that Hillway hosted two wedding parties.

Chimen's sensitivity to the opinion of the religious Jewish community persisted: On a later occasion, when my parents were being driven somewhere in North London that involved a route through the religious Jewish areas of Golders Green, Chimen begged them to lie down on the floor of the car so that friends of the family would not see them flagrantly violating the Sabbath prohibition on the use of machinery. They refused.

Six years after the wedding rigmarole, another pretense was

concocted: When I was born, my parents had me circumcised in a medical setting rather than by a mohel in the religious ceremony known as a bris. This time, Mimi was as horrified as Chimen. And so, eight days after my birth—the day that my extremity was supposed to have been modified by the mohel—Mimi and Chimen hid out in their home, pretending to their religious relatives that they were at my bris. Thirteen years later, they manufactured a party for me at their house, thus allowing them to tell themselves that I was, to all intents and purposes, bar mitzvahed. It suited me fine—many of my friends had recently been bar mitzvahed, and I liked the idea of a special celebration, complete with fine gifts, in my teenage honor.

When my aunt Jenny married an atheist of Christian background, Chimen never told his nonagenarian father the news. Nor, when Jenny became pregnant, did Chimen inform him. He knew that the old rabbi would not have been able to reconcile himself to such a state of affairs. It was bad enough that Jack had married a Jewish atheist, unfamiliar with the daily rituals of Jewish life. It was a whole circle of hell worse that Jenny was now married to a non-Jewish atheist. Nor did he tell his other Orthodox relatives. Jenny's mother-in-law placed a birth notice in *The Telegraph* when my cousin Rob was born, the February after Yehezkel's death in September 1976; Chimen and Mimi's phone immediately started ringing. Some of his relatives were astounded and furious that he had hidden Jenny's wedding from them; others, as he had feared, were distraught that she had married out of the faith.

And yet Chimen considered himself to be an über-rationalist, a man enlightened by a political vision. It was that side of his personality that allowed him, in time, to come to love both my mother and my uncle dearly. Despite their lack of knowledge about the Jewish traditions that had so shaped his life, he knew they were good people. And he knew they made his children happy.

Eight years after Charles Darwin published *On the Origin of Species* in 1859, laying out his theory of evolution, Karl Marx unveiled the first volume of his grand economic treatise, *Das Kapital*. He would spend much of the remaining sixteen years of his life expanding the theories laid out in this volume—although it was not until after his death that his collaborator, Friedrich Engels, collated his notes and published them as volumes two and three of *Das Kapital*. Marx felt, Engels explained, at his funeral in 1883, that he was the Darwin of the social world, having unlocked the scientific secrets explaining how societies and economies evolved and transformed over time, why some were successful and others withered. For many years, scholars of Marxism believed that Marx had written to Darwin offering to dedicate volume one of *Das Kapital* to him. More recently, however, these specialists have come to realize that it was actually Edward Aveling, the common-law husband of Marx's daughter Eleanor, who at a slightly later period had offered to dedicate one of his tracts to Darwin. In the end, the founder of modern evolutionary theory politely declined Aveling's offer.

Documents from, and about, the correspondence were, not surprisingly, among Chimen's collection. It was not, apparently, that Darwin particularly objected to the Communist economic theory or to the analysis of how modern market economies had evolved, which Marx so carefully laid out, and for which vision Aveling had become a leading advocate by the 1880s; rather, Darwin feared being associated with so notorious a group of atheists. After his work on evolution, he was, he knew, in quite enough trouble already with his devoutly Christian wife.

So it was in Mimi's kitchen. Her religious family members and in-laws were already suspicious of Chimen's and her political leanings (although Chimen never exactly came out and told his father that he was an atheist Communist). The last thing the older generation wanted was to see bacon in the fridge or milky and meaty cutlery all mixed up together at Hillway. It would be, both Chimen and Mimi feared, a bridge too far. And thus, while Mimi occasionally ate pork at restaurants, and while Chimen might sometimes buy lobsters when the family was on holiday on the south coast of England or (later) in Italy, in their home—and in London—my grandparents kept up kosher appearances.

As a result, the kitchen had two sinks, one for kitchen utensils and cutlery that had been used for the preparation of meat dishes, the other for those used with dairy products. Not that anything was ever properly cleaned in that kitchen; everything had a layer of grease on it, and the oven hob always seemed to have the burned remnants of earlier meals sticking obstinately to its surface. After all, Chimen was in charge of washing up, and despite the fastidiousness with which he put on his apron before setting into his task, he never really managed to put his heart into the chore. There was also a dishwasher, in later years, to be used exclusively for meaty cutlery and plates—or was it milky? When I was a child, my mother could never keep them straight, and as a result, when she tried to wash the dishes after a family gathering, Chimen would almost literally chase her out of the kitchen. I have a hunch, looking back on it, that this state of affairs suited her perfectly.

My mother was an American, and as such was tolerated *despite* the circumstances of her birth when she first moved into the Hillway orbit. For in the 1960s, Hillway was gripped by a cultural suspicion of all things Yankee—of jazz and baseball as much as of McCarthyism and racial segregation. It was a hangover from the days of Communism, but it was also redolent of the zeitgeist: In the postwar period, many of the British, struggling to accustom themselves to the United Kingdom's diminished status in the world, were deeply hostile to America, whatever their political persuasion. Americans were, as the sardonic wartime jingle had it, "over-fed, over-sexed and over here," the new imperialists, brash in their assumptions of power, culturally crass, not quite sophisticated enough for the world stage. Or perhaps that was just sour grapes: America's global aspirations were neither more obnoxious than those of Britain during the recently faded glory days of empire nor more all-encompassing. Be that as it may, whether out of political conviction or simple snobbery, Hillway in the immediate postwar decades was as anti-American in sentiment as, say, the conservative Carlton Club, or Jimmy Porter, the nasty, alcoholic protagonist in John Osborne's play *Look Back in Anger*, who bitterly noted that "it's pretty dreary living in the American Age—unless you're an American of course." (Or, for that matter, Chimen's own great-grandfather, the Ridbaz, who had lived in New York for a few years in the late nineteenth century, before returning to Byelorussia in disgust. America, he told anyone who was interested, was *treyfene medine*, an impure land of secularism and assimilation.) In postwar England, anti-Americanism was the acceptable bigotry of the times.

Several years after Chimen left the Communist Party, he wrote to an old Party friend, the journalist and filmmaker (and, it later transpired, Soviet spy) Ivor Montagu, regarding a rare-books deal he was trying to close. "My dear Ivor," he began, "I wonder whether you can help me. Some months ago I offered Jack, for our mutual friends, some very important unpublished letters of Marx, and four pages of his draft for *Das Kapital*. In addition also some exceedingly rare first editions of Lenin and Marx. To the present day I have not heard anything from them. There is an American collector who wishes to purchase them, but I am most unwilling to sell these things to an American capitalist." Montagu replied that he had not been able to get a response from his Party contacts about purchasing the documents. Chimen's response, penned a few days later, practically exploded with misery. "Many thanks for your note," he wrote. "It is a great pity that the Marx letters and manuscript will go to an American capitalist where they will lie hidden and unknown."

Ironically, Mimi, along with her sisters and mother, had traveled to America in 1933 to visit relatives in Connecticut and she'd had a wonderful trip. Likewise, Chimen had thoroughly enjoyed his time in the United States in 1948. But while the endless sandwiches suited his ration-shrunk stomach, and while the many cousins whom he met in New York, Detroit, Connecticut, and elsewhere hosted him like visiting royalty, he remained unconvinced by the culture. He felt far more at home in Western Europe, traveling numerous times to France, Belgium, and Holland over the following years, the pages of visas stamped into his passport testifying to an urge to travel, to see the world, that had been stifled over the preceding decade. Only much later in his life would his passport bear an almost equal number of entry stamps from the other side of the Atlantic.

———

As the occupants of Hillway aged, the kitchen seemed to get inexorably greasier. One year, as my mum, Jenny, and Vavi were preparing the Seder dinner, my cousin Rob came in to help. The saucepans were covered in grease, the plates were a disaster. "How can I help?" Rob asked. He was told to wash the dishes. Rob looked around in amazement. "I thought you did that *after* the meal," he said, and set to work.

In his last years, long after Mimi had died, the kitchen was the room in which Chimen sat, passively, staring out at the plants and the squirrels. It was where his carergivers fed him, sometimes it was where the social workers and nurses came to examine him. And yet, for all the sadness of that room as Chimen began to fade away, because the kitchen was where he sat for most of his waking hours it was also the room where, in the last five years of his life, I had better conversations with him than anywhere else in the house.

THE FRONT ROOM:
THE HASKALAH

And so, covering himself with his shield, and couching his lance, he rushed with Rozinante's utmost speed upon the first windmill he could come at, and, running his lance into the sail, the wind whirled about with such swiftness, that the rapidity of the motion presently broke the lance into shivers, and hurled down both knight and horse along with it, till down he fell, rolling a good way off in the field.
—Miguel Cervantes, *Don Quixote* (1605)

AS MIMI STIRRED her pots of soup and dressed her ducks in the kitchen, gradually the dinner crowd would gather. They would start coming in around six, chat for a while at the kitchen table, and then, when a critical mass for a conversation had arrived, they would migrate into the front room with their cups of tea or, if the hour was late enough, their glasses of wine.

The front room looked out onto Hillway, its round bay windows jutting slightly into the front garden. Under the window was a built-in, angular wooden ledge, its white paint graying with age and flaking with disrepair. The top of this ledge lifted up to reveal a chaotic storage area filled with yarmulkes, Haggadot, and other Seder accoutrements. Sitting on that ledge, in between some heavy potted plants, you had a slight vantage point, to look out over the rest of the crowd. Peering into the room from that window seat, the small fireplace edged with dark green tiles was off to the right. Back when English houses still used coal, it had been a functional fireplace, vital to heating the house during London's cold, dank winters. By the time I came on the scene, however, it had long been abandoned in favor of central heating, and rendered largely inaccessible by an old record player, radio, and tape recorder hi-fi system resting on a table in front of it, and by two more large potted plants with deep green velvetlike leaves which stood sentinel on each flank.

Chimen and Mimi both liked music, but they did not know much about it. When they did listen to a record, their tastes mainly veered toward high culture—Beethoven symphonies, Mozart chamber music, the occasional opera—but at the same time they also enjoyed the Yiddish folk music of their own and an earlier age. Chimen had in his collection many of the original manuscripts of Velvl Zbarzher, a nineteenth-century Galician Jew described in the *Jewish Encyclopedia* as "a real folk-poet," as well as a complete collection of all his published works—it was a trove of Zbarzher material unrivaled by that owned by any other individual or institution in the world, including the Hebrew University in Jerusalem. Zbarzher's real name was Benjamin Wolf Ehrenkranz, but like Robert Zimmerman a century later, he decided his folk music needed a snappier nom de plume. And so what we might, with hindsight, think of as a Galician Bob Dylan was born. Zbarzher wrote Yiddish poems, often recited to music, about love and loss, social injustice and religious intolerance. A follower of the Jewish Enlightenment, he loved poking fun at his Hasidic neighbors, writing mocking lyrics about how they believed they had all the hidden knowledge and that therefore the achievements of science, in an age of technological transformations, were for naught.

Eventually, the Galician troubadour fell in love with a woman known as Malkele the Beautiful and moved to Istanbul, where he died in 1883, the same year as Marx. Zbarzher's story ended only six years after Thomas Edison had invented the phonograph and, to posterity's loss, he did not leave any recordings behind. Had he done so, I am sure they would have found their way into my grandparents' small collection of LPs. After all, Yiddish was the language in which Chimen wept; it was in the *mamaloshen*, the mother tongue, that he read poems of love and loss. It might very well have been the language in which he dreamed.

What *was* in that collection were the recorded songs of Itzik Manger, a larger-than-life twentieth-century Yiddish poet, playwright, and self-proclaimed "folk bard" who had worshipped Zbarzher. Chimen had befriended him shortly after the outbreak of the Second World War, and for a brief time they co-edited the left-wing Yiddish literary journal *Eyropë*. During the war, Manger was the central figure in a group of Yiddish essayists, poets, and playwrights with whom Chimen drank tea and talked in a little café on a side street near the British Library. It was there that they met the journalist and art critic Leo Koenig; quite likely that was also the spot where Chimen would have met another close friend from the period, the Yiddish novelist, playwright, and book collector Scholem Asch. There too he may have befriended the German Yiddish poet A. N. Stencl, an eccentric figure who published the journal *Loshn un lebn* (Language and Life) and who was rumored to have smuggled himself out of Nazi Germany and into England in a coffin. Stencl ran a salon in Whitechapel, known as the Friends of Yiddish, which survived for nearly thirty years after his death in 1983. Manger was, however, the focal point of this group. He spent eleven years living in London, first as an unhappy refugee during the war—by a convoluted path, he had gone from Poland to France to North Africa to Gibraltar, then to

Portugal, and finally to London, in the early months of hostilities—
and subsequently as an unhappy, stateless resident after the war. In
1951 he moved to Israel, where he died in 1969.

Chimen admired Manger and loved speaking Yiddish with him,
but he came to resent his friend's inability to control his tongue.
Manger was a notoriously difficult man, a breathtakingly good poet
who, when he got drunk—which he did all too often—was capable
of saying the most appalling things to those close to him. Many decades later Chimen told his friend the Yiddish scholar Efrat Gal-ed
(who taught at the Heinrich Heine University in Dusseldörf), that
Manger had burned his bridges with him when, sometime after the
war ended, Chimen had spoken at a London gathering to commemorate the lives of two Bundist leaders killed by the Soviet secret police.
Manger had taken offense at Chimen's words and had accused him
of "murdering" the two men all over again. Quite possibly, Chimen,
then in the full bloom of his Stalinism, had indeed said something
offensive—Chimen also feuded so angrily with Koenig during these
years that in a fit of utterly irrational, counterproductive pique he
returned an original piece of art by Chagall that Koenig had given
him—but it was equally likely that Manger had just let his tongue
run rampant against an erstwhile friend.

Despite my grandmother's attempts to smooth things over, Chimen could not forgive the poet. The two men never spoke again. But
Chimen continued to love Manger's poetry and music. Every Seder,
after concluding the serious work of reading the Hagaddah and after
the guests had finished consuming Mimi's feast, Chimen would belt
out a rendition of Manger's whimsical love poem "Rabbeinu Tam,"
complete with the meaningless refrain "Haydl, didl, dam." He would
recite the Yiddish quickly, semi-melodically, pause at the chorus line,
and wait for us all to jump in. Without fail, we did. Over the years,
we learned to sing much of the Yiddish story line too, simply by

memorizing the inchoate sounds of the words. There, in late twenti-eth-century London, Chimen had a table of thirty guests singing Manger's song, in a language most of us did not understand, about events we had no inkling of. Until I researched the song for this book, I had no idea that we were all singing about a lovelorn queen of Tur-key, sending her yearning letters to Rabbi Tam, the missives carried by a golden peacock across the ocean. I had no idea that when Rabbi Tam's wife intercepted the letters she would thwack him with a roll-ing pin. Or that Tam himself would seek refuge from the complexi-ties of his life by talking to a goat in his stables. I can, all these years later, still remember Manger's rhythms, his sounds. I can still almost feel the vibrations of the sonorous, melodramatic basso in which Chimen and Mimi's friend Manny Tuckman (whose wife, Ghisha, was Koenig's daughter) would slowly build up to the final, climactic "Haydl, didl, dam," the last word lingered on, a gradual glissando from major to minor.

Many of Mimi and Chimen's other musical tastes were, however, only comprehensible in the light of their politics. Among the records of symphonies conducted by Otto Klemperer and operas sung by the great Russian bass vocalist Feodor Chaliapin (whom in childhood Chimen's mother had taken him to see) were recordings by the Amer-ican singer Paul Robeson. Robeson's sonorous voice was truly beau-tiful; but the reason the Abramsky family listened to him, rather than to, say, Frank Sinatra, had more to do with the fact that he was a Communist Party sympathizer than that he could hit a perfect low C, and that he spoke out in defense and sang for the supporters of Julius and Ethel Rosenberg, who on June 19, 1953, were executed for passing atomic secrets to the Soviet Union. At the height of the Mc-Carthy purges, the American government confiscated Robeson's pass-port because of his left-wing political activism; in 1958, under pressure from an international campaign, the Supreme Court restored his passport—and immediately afterward, he flew to England to give a series of concerts. Three years later, he sang in a concert at Albert Hall celebrating the *Daily Worker* newspaper's thirty-first birthday. Robeson's records were advertised in Party brochures, and purchasing them was thus roughly akin to a political obligation. So, too, back in the early postwar years, was the playing of Russian Communist airs such as "The Tractor Song" and "Varushka's Sorrow," homages to the Russian workers, toiling to transform their fatherland into a workers' paradise.

There, in suburban North London, Chimen, Mimi, and their Communist comrades would gather to listen to the music of revolt. "The Party," Raph wrote, with the benefit of hindsight, "had some resemblances to a 'gathered' church: a people apart, in the world but not of it. We comported ourselves as an elect, a moral aristocracy, a congregation of true believers." Party members, he observed, "never tired of proclaiming their faith in the masses, even when it seemed that their arguments were spurned."

Anyway, it did not really matter what music Mimi and Chimen had in their collection, or how unsubtle the music's message was. Unless Chimen was traveling (when Mimi would temporarily put the salon on hold, and catch up on her own reading and correspondence and maybe even listen to some of her favorite LPs), when their children were at home and the cares of daily life and work were layered atop the obligations of running a house like 5 Hillway, there was almost never a moment, during waking hours, when the house was quiet enough to really listen to music. Just as, in a city, there is always background noise, so omnipresent that one ceases to be consciously aware of it, so too at Hillway there was a continual hum of animated, multi-accented conversation, the clatter of cooking utensils, and the clamour of people calling from one room to the next. Chimen, in particular, would call out "Mir-ri" from wherever he was and hope she would hear him; whether she could often depended on how loud was the sound of food frying in the kitchen. If she did hear his shouts, she would call back "Yes, Chim!," her voice tinged just slightly with exasperation. "Our guests are getting hungry!" Children would run madly between rooms. A critical mass of adults would gel in small groups, each with their own argument or analysis or joke under way. Then, like a kinetics experiment in a laboratory, the individuals would shift, new groups would form, and then new ones again. The doorbell would ring, or someone would bang the knocker. The roar of a moped coming up the garden path to the steps leading to the front door would signal Rose's imminent arrival.

Above the fireplace was a large reproduction, the colors muted, of the famous Marc Chagall painting of a fiddler on the roof, created by the artist in 1912–13. And on either side of it were shelves: thick, dark, unfinished wooden planks, all the way up to the ceiling. On these shelves were hundreds of books on Jewish history, many of them on eighteenth- and nineteenth-century intellectual movements in Eastern Europe. It was a rich vein to mine. From the late eighteenth century onward, the writings, the friendships, and the political campaigns of the German Jewish religious scholar, philosopher, and literary critic Moses Mendelssohn were the catalyst for a Jewish Enlightenment known as the Haskalah, which made its way east from Germany.

Mendelssohn, who was born in the town of Dessau in 1729 and moved to Berlin as a young man, sought to use the rational principles and language of the Enlightenment to prove the existence of God, the immortality of the soul, and the necessity of the Talmudic code, and at the same time to emancipate Europe's Jews, both from the age-old restrictions imposed on them by the state authorities (limiting what work they could do and where they could live, for example) and also from the self-imposed isolation that separated most Jews from the broader intellectual culture of the time. His theories on the immortality of the soul, developed in his book *Phaedon*, were unconvincing; his commentaries on emancipation were more profound. Preaching a form of separation of church and state, he attempted to bring the Jews of Europe's ghettos into the intellectual mainstream. In his homeland he sought to teach them German in place of the Judeo-German that most of his contemporaries spoke; to have them read the great works of literature and science of his age; to have them engage in the great philosophical debates of the day. In a project that was, in its way, as ambitious as that of the Protestant reformers centuries earlier, who had translated the Christian Bible into vernacular languages, in 1783 Mendelssohn translated the Hebrew Bible into German. It caused consternation among many rabbis, who feared their influence would decline if the populace could actually understand the Holy Book without their mediating power, and who encouraged their rowdier followers to burn the offending volume. But the translation found a ready audience, who rapidly made his effort a best seller. In his book *Jerusalem, or On Religious Power and Judaism*, published in the same year, Mendelssohn made a powerful—albeit ultimately flawed—attempt to reconcile age-old Jewish traditions with the philosophical rationalism espoused by Immanuel Kant that was so in vogue among his contemporaries. Kant had, after all, urged his readers to "dare to use your reason."

Mendelssohn believed the existence of God could be proved through rational argument; the divine revelation of the Ten Commandments to Moses on Mount Sinai, however, he was happy to leave as revelation. In Mendelssohn's world, therefore, the reality of God was akin to a mathematical proof; but God's law, His code of conduct for daily living, had to be taken on faith. And whether one chose to take it or not was, he felt, a matter of individual conscience. Like his Enlightenment peers, he believed the state should not attempt to enforce any form of religious orthodoxy. The promulgators

of the Haskalah thus embraced the great liberal political vision, formulated in Western Europe and America in the decades surrounding
the French Revolution, of a secular state, its umbrella broad enough
to encompass people of all faiths or none (though Mendelssohn himself was harshly critical of atheists), and honed this vision into a sophisticated message aimed specifically at Europe's Jewish population.
The eighteenth- and nineteenth-century men and women who embraced the Haskalah in the wake of Mendelssohn's writings welcomed change and the prospect of civic emancipation, of full political
and economic rights. They did not, however, stop with liberalism.
For many of them, as their involvement with European political
movements deepened, so too did their radicalism.

By the later part of the nineteenth century, large numbers of young
Jews, in reaction to government-supported pogroms in Russia and
violent repression against political activists in countries across the
Continent, were attracted to a more explicitly Socialist vision. It had
first acquired momentum with the wave of revolutions that swept
through Europe in 1848, and then gathered speed in Russia from the
1860s onward. Many sympathized with Alexander Herzen's idea, itself a modified version of the "noble savage" theory espoused by
Rousseau, that the purest incarnation of mankind was the peasant
commune, that the daily life of a peasant was, somehow, more real
than that of the urbanite or the landed gentry. Others adopted the
varieties of Marxism coming to the fore in Russia during the last
decades of the nineteenth century and the first years of the twentieth:
some supported the Mensheviks and their more democratic vision of
Socialism, while others put their faith in Plekhanov and then in Lenin's Bolsheviks and their theory of a small, elite vanguard of urban
revolutionaries laying the groundwork for a broader uprising. In the
dying years of the century, some joined the General Jewish Labour
Bund, a workers' organization in Russia, Lithuania, and Poland,

whose members believed in a Socialist transformation of society. Still others threw in their lot with the Folkspartey, founded in 1904 by the historian Simon Dubnow with the idea of promoting Jewish cultural autonomy within a broader liberal political settlement. They wanted Jews to stay in Russia but to be allowed to nurture their culture without being persecuted. In that regard they stood in opposition to the growing numbers of Zionists who at the time were encouraging Eastern European Jews to leave the pogroms behind and relocate in Palestine—a land they hoped would one day again be known as Israel.

———

It was out of this chaotic political world, this kaleidoscope of endless reconfigurations of radical ideological associations among the Jewish communities of Eastern Europe, that literary figures like the great Yiddish writer Sholem Aleichem emerged. It was in this world, too, that revolutionaries like Lev Bronstein—known to history as Leon Trotsky—came to the fore. But there was also a reaction against these liberal and radical ideas, an Orthodox Jewish equivalent to Joseph de Maistre's opposition to the French Enlightenment nearly a century earlier. The Yeshiva movement in Lithuania, from which as a young man Yehezkel had emerged as a feted religious scholar, destined to be considered among the *gedoylim*—or saintlike religious sages—of the next century, was cast in direct opposition to the liberalizing, secularizing forces of the Haskalah. Students at these yeshivas mocked Haskalah followers, according to Chaim Grade; some of the more outspoken among them even trailed after their secular rivals in the street to hurl insults at them. Theirs was the task of restoring the traditional order to communities caught in the crosshairs of history; of reimposing a timeless vision of the cosmos on a world in flux. Not coincidentally, the Yeshiva movement's scholar-activists were equally opposed to the mystical, ecstatic, religious movement of Hasidism, which had swept Eastern Europe from the eighteenth century onward, created new rabbinic dynasties, and downplayed the importance of the legal texts of Judaism. The Hasids, following the teaching of their founder, the Baal Shem Tov, emphasized the importance of prayer and love; with these two tools, they argued, even an unschooled Jew could reach the spiritual heights. This was a challenge to the strict hierarchies of Talmudic learning; and by the time of the Baal Shem Tov's death in 1760 many thousands had cast their lot with his teachings. They, and their descendants, were considered to be dangerously hostile to authority, bound up in the emotions and sensations of the religious experience, rather than preoccupied by the law and by the word-by-word minutiae of Talmudic debate. The Haskalah students were considered to be too freethinking, too critical of age-old authority. Neither vision augured well for the traditionalists.

Of course, there were limits to how far the Yeshiva movement could roll back the clock. The ideas of the Haskalah, in particular, once let loose in the Jewish communities of Eastern Europe set off a whirlwind of change. They paved the way for a generation of shtetl Jews to gain knowledge and political awareness, to move to big cities, to participate in the intellectual ferment of the nineteenth and early twentieth centuries. The lives and culture of the shtetl Jews were so mysterious and unexplored by historians that, according to Nathaniel Deutsch's book *The Jewish Dark Continent: Life and Death in the Russian Pale of Settlement*, late-tsarist ethnographers planned to circulate a Yiddish questionnaire of roughly two thousand questions, to study the folk traditions of what the ethnographers saw as this strange people. The Haskalah movement took this "dark continent" (the phrase is Dubnow's) and rooted it in history. It gave the Jews of Eastern Europe the ability, the right, to pen their own histories.

In Chimen and Mimi's front room, the debates unleashed within

Judaism by the Haskalah played out keenly—both in the conversations and lives of its residents and among the thousands of books housed from its rickety floor to its paint-flaking ceiling: Zionism versus international Socialism; assimilation in contradistinction to nationalism; religion against secularism; tradition contrasted with modernity; the authority of the rabbis versus the power of the new revolutionaries.

On the shelves in this room there were also many books on the Holocaust and more generally on anti-Semitism. So, too, there were rare, oversize Socialist volumes—collections of essays, policy tracts, and so on—many of them with stamps suggesting they originally were held by the library in Leipzig, a collection Chimen must have purchased shortly after the war ended. And there were first editions of the leading Fabian thinkers on those shelves—Harold Laski, Sidney and Beatrice Webb.

Dotted among the volumes, jewels camouflaged in anonymity, were a few dozen large tomes of varying heights, in which were bound thousands of original color images from the 1870 Franco-Prussian War and the Paris Commune that followed a year later, including English magazine cartoons of the Commune, and full-page French newspaper pages containing various manifestos and calls to arms. This was a collection that Chimen treasured as much as any in the House of Books. The volume covers were black morocco leather, the spines knobbly. Each one had a red rectangle on the spine, and in each rectangle, printed in small gold letters, was *Distractions des deux sièges de Paris 1870–71*, along with the volume number in roman numerals. Inside those tomes were spectacular images: a militia man, gun slung over his shoulder, dragging a weeping woman through the streets; Prussian soldiers, in spiked metal hats, leaving a burning, looted building, a bloodied dead woman spread out on the street before them; an illustration from the barricades, showing the Communards, their bayonets resting against a cannon, a red flag fluttering overhead. On the flag were the words "*La 1871 Commune ou la mort.*" There were political cartoons showing the impotence of Emperor Napoléon III; conservative commentaries from the English press denouncing the atheism, the disrespect for property, and the bloodthirstiness of the revolutionaries (one, by the famous illustrator George Cruikshank, was titled "An Awful Lesson to the World for All Time to Come"); reproductions of a proclamation by Robespierre in 1792 on the "Rights of Man and of Citizens" and of revolutionary manifestos by the Socialist Louis-Auguste Blanqui. Many of the pictures showed skeletons surrounded by pastel-colored floral arrangements, the skulls, intended to symbolize various moribund political movements and social structures, ghoulishly staring out at observers; they were part of an iconographic tradition that spans from Goya's sketches of the Napoleonic Wars in the Iberian peninsula nearly seventy years earlier to Grateful Dead album covers a century later.

À Versailles! A Communard with a red flag proclaiming, "The Commune or Death!" points his cannon toward Versailles, the base of the anti-Commune government. From *L'Actualité*, no. 3, April 1871.

Chimen had bought the collection, already bound, at a Sotheby's auction decades before I arrived on the scene. One of my favorite images, hidden deep in volume twenty-one, was *Les Amis de L'Ordre* (the Friends of Order). It showed a brown-cloaked friar, bald and fat, holding the feet of a prostrate figure of a woman representing the *République*, while the deposed emperor Napoléon III and the duc d'Aumale, pretender to the throne of France, held the Republic's chest. Completing the dreadful scene was a well-dressed assassin, Thiers, the head of the anti-Commune government, his midriff bumping against the Republic's head, prepared to plunge a knife into her heart. It was not subtle, but it conveyed a suitable sense of grotesqueness, of the betrayal of the ideals of the Commune.

In the way in which he stored these precious posters, whether consciously or not, Chimen was emulating the Talmudic students of the

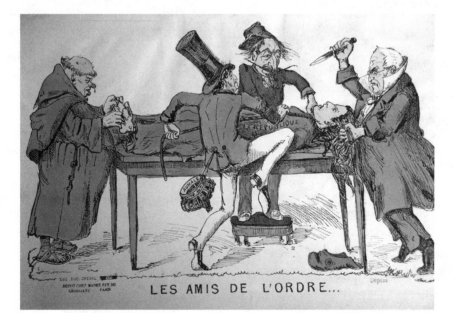

Les Amis de L'Ordre. Anonymous satirical print, 1871, showing the murder of the Republic by the French government led by Thiers.

Volozhin yeshiva in Telz and the other great religious schools that dotted the landscape of his father's youth; there, banned by the rabbis and the *rosh yeshiva* (the school principals) from any literary connection to the dangerous secular world outside, the more daring students subscribed to newspapers and academic journals. Such intellectual adventurism was, wrote the former student Natan Grinblat later in life, an illicit experience like "sipping heady wine." After all, unless a rabbi had certified a Hebrew book with a *haskamah*, which was essentially a stamp of approval testifying that the book contained nothing of a heretical nature, it was out of bounds to the students. The newspapers and journals picked up at the town post offices were passed from hand to hand surreptitiously, in much the same way that samizdat copies of banned books such as *Doctor Zhivago* or *The Gulag Archipelago* were distributed years later in the Soviet Union. Finally, the papers were collected and an entire year's issues from a given magazine were then carefully bound into a single volume and secreted away high up on a bookshelf. As a young man, Yehezkel had read forbidden Haskalah texts. In a surprising act of rebellion he had also gone so far as to familiarize himself with great Russian literature by authors such as Dostoyevsky and Tolstoy; for the rabbis, this was *bittul Torah*, which means, roughly, a royal waste of time, time that could be better spent studying the Talmud. Readers of such books could even be denounced as *apikorsim*, or heretics. But reading books such as *Crime and Punishment* was about as far as Yehezkel's rebellion stretched—that, and becoming an expert swimmer, presumably in the many rivers that crisscrossed the Lithuanian landscape where he had come of age. In a time of grand political upheavals, when Jews were coming to play a huge role in Russia's political protests—by 1905, a third of political arrestees in the Russian Empire were Jewish—Yehezkel stayed aloof from temporal concerns.

In fact, as he grew into maturity, Yehezkel was very much at one with the austere Musar movement of self-abnegation and asceticism that had actively rooted out heretics from the yeshivas of his youth. The modern world was desperately tempting, but precisely for that reason it was, he believed, desperately dangerous. In this, he was a kindred spirit to many of the leading lights of Musar, men of an older generation who in their younger years had dabbled with new ethical and philosophical notions, had been intrigued by new scientific advances, even by great novels and newfangled theories developed by people such as Sigmund Freud, but who had subsequently reverted deep into Orthodoxy. Shaul Stampfer writes that these men often "used vocabulary borrowed from philosophy and psychology," but they would also memorize and repeatedly chant religious texts such as the Mesilat Yesharim, or the "path of the upright," to cast a protective net over the students—both the chanters and also their peers—keeping out corrupting influences from the world beyond. Despite his adherence to the Haskalah, in many ways Chimen remained protected by that net throughout his life. He was a man of modernity who had nonetheless been shaped in myriad ways by the worlds of his father, his maternal grandfather, and his great-grandfather—by that long line of fabled rabbis of which he was the progeny.

In the center of Mimi and Chimen's living room, a woven, tattered, dark purple wool rug covered the uneven, unpolished dark wooden planks that had been put down as a makeshift floor during the war years and never replaced. Two or three rather lumpy, unmatched armchairs and an old rocking chair with a stiff wooden back were crammed into that center space, arranged so they were all facing inward, angled so that the occupant of any of the seats could hold court. Thomas More, imagining an ideal society, a utopia, wrote of

its inhabitants that "of golde and sylver they make commonly cha-
umber pottes, and other vesselles, that serve for moste vile uses. They
marveyle that any men be so folyshe, as to have delite and pleasure in
the doubteful glistering of a lytil tryffelynge stone...so much that a
lympyse blockehedded churle, and whyche hathe no more wytte than
an asse...shall have nevertheless manye wyse and good men in sub-
jection and bondage, only for this, bycause he hath a greate heape of
golde." In his copy, Chimen had underlined this passage in pencil,
one presumes more for the value of its antimaterialist insight than the
creativity of More's spelling.

There was something Musar to this deliberate, austere neglect of
appearance; the planks on the floor were as haphazard, as barely
functional as were the uneven old wooden fence posts that surrounded the three-story brick building that housed the Novaradok
yeshiva that twelve-year-old Yehezkel had entered to such acclaim in
1898. Ironically, there was also something deeply British Communist
to the ramshackle appearance. In the 1980s, Raph Samuel published
a series of articles in the *New Left Review*, reprinted after his death
as a book entitled *The Lost World of British Communism*, in which
he grappled with the Communist Party mind-set and aesthetic that
he had grown up with during the years straddling the Second World
War. The homes of Party members were, he noted, "by contemporary standards drab, visually impoverished, but redeemed by very
well-stocked bookshelves, the spiritual heart of the living space."
Convinced they were fighting for "the way, the truth, and the life,"
the Communists of Raph's youth had little time for mundane, bour-
geois chores such as tidying up their houses, upgrading the plumbing,
or mowing their lawns.

On the other side of the room from the fireplace the wall was
lined from floor to ceiling with two layers of books. On these shelves
were Chimen's sociology texts: volumes by Émile Durkheim and

Max Weber, by American sociologists and cultural critics like C. Wright Mills, Irving Howe, and Daniel Bell. Here was explained the rise of mass man's mentality, as well as the growing reactions against that mentality in the bohemias of the Western world. Like Charlie Chaplin in *Modern Times*, one of his favorite films, Chimen was both a creature of modernity and a man utterly repelled by the mechanization of modern life. In this room were gathered many of the great cultural critics of the twentieth-century human condition, as well as their earlier antecedents, including Rousseau's writings on the origins of political society and the ideal of the noble savage, and the works of the nineteenth-century Romantic philosophers who clustered around Nietzsche.

Halfway up that wall, opposite the fireplace, on a little shelf barely six inches high were the Everyman political classics, my favorite collection in the house. In that collection were many of the great political thinkers of the past two and half millennia, from Plato and Aristotle to Roger Bacon, John Locke, and Thomas Hobbes, from the utopian Thomas More to the theorist of the unification of Italy Giuseppe Mazzini. Included, somewhat surprisingly, in that collection was Marco Polo; he was not a great political thinker, but he was an adventurer—and his travels had, I am sure, intrigued my globe-trotting grandfather. There was something Lilliputian about these books, yet in their conception there was also something wonderfully egalitarian. They were cheaply produced hardbacks, each with its own distinctively colored cover with a canvaslike texture, many of them dating to the Great Depression years when high-quality paper was in short supply; they were books meant to be carried in sports-jacket pockets, to be removed easily and read on the Underground while standing jammed up against other commuters in the rush hour. They were books produced for every man, at a moment when it was quietly assumed that people in England of all classes and all walks of life were interested in bettering themselves intellectually. Each volume carried the motto "Everyman, I will go with thee and be thy guide, in thy most need to go by thy side."

Joseph Dent had begun publishing the Everyman's Library in London in 1906. By the mid-1930s, when Chimen started buying the books as a teenager and annotating their margins with densely scribbled comments in Hebrew and, later, in English, much of the Western political, philosophical, scientific, and literary cannon had been made available, at low cost, as part of the series. There were by then 937 volumes in the catalog; Chimen owned about fifty of them. It was through these books that his political ideas matured. When he read Rousseau's *Social Contract* he underlined the sentence, "The passage from the state of nature to the civil state produces a very remarkable change in man, by substituting justice for instinct in his conduct, and giving his actions the morality they had formerly lacked." In Plato's *Republic*, which he read in Jerusalem in 1937, he marked a passage on tyranny, which "plunders by fraud and force alike the goods of others, sacred and holy things, private and public possessions, and never pettily but always on a grand scale. . . . Men revile injustice, not because they fear to do it, but because they fear to suffer it." And in his copy of Aristotle's *Politics*, bought when he was in his early twenties, Chimen bookmarked several passages with newspaper fragments, and then underlined, in pencil, lines on those pages. "Everywhere inequality is a cause of revolution," the Greek philosopher had written in one of the passages that Chimen marked. "And always it is the desire of equality which rises in rebellion." In another of the underlined sections was the observation that "democracy appears to be safer and less liable to revolution than oligarchy." When, three-quarters of a century later, Chimen's Everyman collection passed into my hands, the newspaper fragments were still there, brown and crumbly with age, the senile ecru of their delicate pages leached into the leaves of the book itself.

Aristotle was a man of extraordinary intellectual versatility: In addition to being a political theorist, he was a mathematician, a natural scientist, an ethicist, and a moral philosopher. Among his most important contributions to the world of ideas was his deep philosophical investigation into first causes—seeking an origin point for the universe, and if the universe was indeed created by God, an origin point for that divine entity. He concluded that there had to be an Unmoved Mover, an incorporeal being who had always existed, whose thought processes themselves made the physical universe possible, made human thought possible, made possible time itself. Since God had always existed, so the universe and time itself had always existed. Aristotle's God thought, therefore everything else was and always had been. For Aristotle, the building blocks of the world had to have always existed.

Fifteen hundred years later, the great twelfth-century Spanish Jewish philosopher Maimonides amended Aristotle's ideas about first causes. He accepted that God had always existed, or rather, had never not existed. But unlike Aristotle, he argued that the physical world itself had a finite starting point, and that prior to the universe coming into being, time itself could not exist, that time and matter were intimately intertwined. According to Maimonides, God exists outside time. Then, somehow, God stirs and the dimensions of space emerge. Then, and only then, time begins. It was an extraordinary intuitive leap, a hint, perhaps, at the world of relativity that Einstein would eventually reveal. But Maimonides's project extended further. It was to reconcile the idea of creation, a single starting point for all living things, governed by a moral code, as outlined in the Hebrew Bible, with the philospher's notion of an eternal world. If the world conjured into being by God will always exist, its structures determined not by man's actions and choices but by a God whose motives cannot be fathomed, what room did that leave for morality, for freedom of will, for concepts of good and evil?

What interested the philosopher was how the Jewish ethical principles guiding everyday life could be reconciled with notions of eternity; how the littleness of mankind's needs and desires could fit into the vastness of the cosmos; how a God that had always existed and would always exist could interact with the hopes and fears of individuals as small and temporary as humans. Here, he made another intuitive leap. It was, he concluded, precisely man's ability to think rationally about these grand questions that gave him a spiritual presence—and it was that, rather than his corporeal body, that made him an image of God. Even if God did not, in reality, care about individual humans, in humans' thoughts about God and in the dream that He did intervene in daily lives was rooted the chance of transcendence, the possibility of becoming something more than a brute animal, the code to morality. For Maimonides, religion thus became strangely pragmatic. Admittedly, the stories of miracles and angels might be little more than fairy tales—or, at best, God's calling cards, reminders He sent out episodically to let people know He was still present in the world; but by believing that the skein of everyday life could be torn by divine intervention, mankind kept alive the possibility of change. And because of the possibility of change, there was an incentive to behave morally—to behave in ways likely to trigger extraordinary events. It was a way of rendering history bearable, of holding out the opportunity of transformation.

From his student days, Chimen found Maimonides's concepts strangely reassuring. But where the medieval scholar—an Arabic-speaking Jew living under Muslim rule in the land that is now Spain —allowed miracles to be seen as reminders of a greater organizing principle behind the vagaries of everyday life, for the young Chimen revolutions served that role. It was those spectacular breaks with the ordinary, those occasional violent convulsions that destroyed the rhythms of the generations, which pointed to the underlying patterns, the deep structures of history. In place of Maimonides's timeless God, Chimen substituted Marx's dialectic, the rules of history that ultimately explained movement from one epoch to the next. In place of Maimonides's ethics, Chimen substituted the Marxist idea of class consciousness.

———

Behind the Everyman volumes were still more books, cheap paperback political texts, worth little monetarily but cumulatively providing an understanding of the day-to-day political debates of the first two-thirds of the twentieth century.

Roaming this world of ideas, especially on the fireplace side of the room, one was increasingly struck by a sense of time warp. This was a story "rent out of Eastern Europe and landed in London," the American historian Steven Zipperstein marveled, when he visited the house from Oxford and, later, from his position at Stanford University, in California. It was, he felt, in many ways a Russian saga from the nineteenth century that was playing itself out decades later in English suburbia, a scene, say, from "HaMatmid," Chaim Nachman Bialik's poem about Talmudic scholarship.

In this room, the different sides of Chimen's intellectual personality most visibly warred for influence: the religious scholar versus the Marxist; the polymath interested in art, philosophy, sociology, in all the great ideas of the Renaissance and the Enlightenment versus the ideological dogmatist; the Zionist against the Socialist internationalist. It was in this cluttered space that the massed ghosts of the pogroms and then of the Holocaust and of the shattered Jewish communities of Eastern Europe most assertively overlooked everything he did and believed. It was here that ancient Jewish teachings met the Renaissance, the Enlightenment, and the Romantic movement. It was here that a specifically Jewish take on modernity could be encountered, one that engaged with liberalism, anarchism, Socialism, and nationalism. There were books on the rise of Zionism, on the quest for a Jewish homeland not just in Palestine but also via the Soviet attempt to create a Jewish, Yiddish-speaking state in the Siberian region of Birobidzhan, and on abortive plans to carve out part of Uganda for displaced Jewish refugees; there were other books on proposals to earmark large swathes of American territory for a Jewish homeland.

It was, in sum, the room where the greatest debates within Eastern European Jewry, during the decades in which Chimen's grandparents, parents, and Chimen himself had come of age, were on display.

Corralled into the Pale of Settlement, Russian Jews had for hundreds of years largely lived their lives outside of the ebb and flow of temporal history. The students in great institutions such as the Volozhin

Bookshelves from the downstairs front room at Hillway. In the photo at right, on the third shelf from the bottom are Chimen's Everyman Classics.

yeshiva—which was shuttered by a tsarist decree in February 1892, but which continued to exert a powerful pull on the imagination of young scholars for many decades—learned Talmud; they learned *responsa* to Halakhic questions engaged in by more than one hundred generations of rabbis and pre-rabbinic scholars over thousands of years. But they did not specialize in secular history. Theirs was a universe, as is that of the Amish today, at least partially insulated from temporal events, at least partially constructed around timeless codes that could withstand the tumult unleashed by modernity. It was a world that Russian anthropologists and imperial ethnographers were starting to study for its folklore, for glimpses into ancient pasts and into behavior patterns that had stood the test of time for many centuries.

Now, with the Haskalah, a bridge to modernity was being built, which would pave the way for a secular Hebrew and Yiddish literature and for young Jews to enter the full ferment of Russian politics as tsarism came under increasing attack; it would also create new institutions of authority (political organizations, cultural clubs, publishing houses, newspapers) that could compete with the rabbinate for the loyalty of Russia's millions of Jews. The Russian-born novelist Yosef Haim Brenner, an early convert to the return-to-Israel cause and one of the first to adapt modern Hebrew to the requirements of fiction writing, described "half-intelligentsia," young Jews, schooled in Orthodoxy and yeshiva methods, who had rebelled against the strictures of religion and set out on an autodidactic quest for knowledge, imbibing anything and everything written in an attempt to find more satisfying answers to the existential questions than those they found in the Talmud.

For the Jews in the Pale of Settlement during the decades around the turn of the century, life carried the perpetual risk of instant, violent death—or, at the very least, of the overturning of all things familiar. In 1881, a series of pogroms had been unleashed, probably with government backing, in the wake of Tsar Alexander II's assassination in St. Petersburg by bomb-throwing members of the anarchist People's Will party. Over the next three years, more than two hundred pogroms occurred in the Russian Empire, some in small villages but others in large cities such as Warsaw, Odessa, and Kiev. If they were to scapegoat Jews as dangerous revolutionaries, the new men of power under Tsar Alexander III believed, they could achieve two goals: distract Russian peasants and workers from their all-too-real grievances, and at the same time denounce radical, often violent, political movements as somehow being a Jewish conspiracy against the state. In turn, revolutionary Russians during these years came to believe that, far from being spontaneous outbreaks of violence, pogroms were carefully orchestrated, designed to consolidate the power of Russia's autocratic rulers and to intimidate reformers and revolutionaries into silence. In neither instance did the strategy really succeed—the tsarist system would totter from crisis to crisis for the remaining few decades of its life—but the price paid in blood and fear was, for the Jews of the Pale, vast.

Even many of the anarchist groups that sympathized with the bomb-throwers who had targeted Alexander II's carriage opportunistically rode the anti-Semitic wave, seeking to marshal support in the countryside by "out-pogroming" the pogromists. As a result, during the period of Yehezkel's childhood and early adulthood Jews in the Russian Empire were caught in an increasingly brutal vise, targeted not just by government propaganda and organized nationalist mobs responding to the drumbeat of hate tapped out by groups with names such as the League of the Russian People (of which Tsar Nicholas II was an honorary member) and the Black Hundreds, but also, frequently, by radical anarchists as well.

In April 1903, a particularly deadly pogrom in Kishinev (now

Chisinau, the capital of Moldova) took the lives of at least forty-five Jews and left many hundreds injured. Hundreds of homes and businesses were looted or burned. The event garnered international attention: A reporter for *The New York Times* wrote that the Jews were "slaughtered like sheep." The anti-Semitic atmosphere worsened. The text of a purported Jewish conspiracy, global in its aspirations, began circulating in Russian nationalist circles. It would become known as *The Protocols of the Elders of Zion*, and its distributors claimed that they were exposing a conspiracy among Zionists, Freemasons, and the British foreign office to sow the seeds of anti-tsarist revolt in Russia. Stories based on the age-old "Blood Libel," the story of Jews killing Christian children, passed from one ear to the next in Kiev and other cities, adding fuel to an already blazing fire. Only years later, after much investigative work, did it emerge that the *Protocols* had been concocted by the Russian secret service. But by then they had become part of the staple anti-Semitic arsenal, quoted to justify suspicion of Jews, quoted to justify atrocities against Jews.

Two years after the Kishinev outrage, more than six hundred Jewish communities were subjected to pogroms in a single lethal week at the end of October and beginning of November 1905. In Odessa alone, according to Chimen's Columbia University historian friend Salo Baron, in his book *The Russian Jew Under Tsars and Soviets*, "no less than 300 victims lost their lives, thousands more were wounded and crippled, while 40,000 were economically ruined. In all, this pogrom wave cost the Russian Jews about 1,000 dead, 7,000 to 8,000 wounded (many of them permanently crippled), and property losses of 62,700,000 rubles (ca. $31,000,000)." Hundreds of thousands of Jews who had escaped the killings left their homes and, uncertain of their welcome, headed west: To England, to South America, and to the United States. They left on foot, by wagon, by train, by boat. They left any way they could, often leaving all their worldly possessions behind. Even as some of his siblings—his younger brother and an older sister—and cousins migrated to America during these violence-filled years, and others left for Palestine, Yehezkel, who was just starting out on what promised to be an extraordinary rabbinic odyssey, chose, for the moment, to stay.

Russia had been riven by revolution since January 1905, when a workers' demonstration was fired on by troops guarding the Winter Palace in St. Petersburg. The pogroms of November 1905 were a product of the unrest, largely nationalist-led, opposed by leftist revolutionaries, and resisted by armed Jews organized into self-defense units. There was a last great spasm of ferocity in 1906; thereafter, the intensity and frequency of the pogroms started to decline dramatically. The anti-Semitic vise that squeezed Jews from both the left and the right of the Russian Empire's political spectrum started to loosen once Marxist revolutionaries, who opposed the pogroms and also opposed the use of religion and nationalism as a way of dividing one man from the next, began to outperform their anarchist rivals in attracting the support of workers and peasants.

In the meantime, however, the twenty-five years of pogroms and reaction in the countryside, of revolution and intellectual ferment in the cities had made it all but impossible for young Jews in Russia who engaged with the secular world to support the status quo. Three responses came to dominate their thinking. First, there was Zionism, either of the literal variety, embracing the idea of migration to Palestine, or in a territorial guise, with supporters advocating setting up some other protected political and territorial space for Jews. The second response was to support organized migration to an assimilationist culture and country, leading to the waves of emigration to the United States and to a lesser extent Britain. The third response was to promote revolution within Russia, sweeping away the old anti-Semitic autocracy and nationalist movements and replacing them with an internationalist-minded revolutionary government. Hence the increasing embrace of Marxism, and of the non-anti-Semitic anarchist groupings, by young Russian secular Jews. It was neither accident nor happenstance; rather, it was a perfectly logical reaction to the events unfolding in Russia. After the Kishinev pogrom, increasing numbers of Jews in Russia armed themselves to fight back against the *pogromchiki*. Others prepared to fight against the tsarist government that they saw as pulling the strings of the mob. They joined the Bolsheviks and other groups calling for the overthrow of the tsar and the creation of a workers' state.

A religious Jew could believe in Eretz Israel (the Land of Israel), or could seek, as did the young Yehezkel, to obliterate the pain and fear of the present by burrowing ever deeper into Talmudic scholarship. Yehezkel—who was discovered as an *illui*, or prodigy, as a young child; anointed a *gaon*, or genius, as a young adult; termed a *gadol*, or great one, as an old man; and posthumously referred to by his biographer, Aaron Sorsky, as a "king" watched over by angels—would routinely spend more than ten hours a day locked in the yeshiva's study room, burning candles late into the night as he read ever more complex Aramaic and Hebrew commentaries. He wanted nothing to do with the secular world: Until the all-consuming fires unleashed by the First World War rendered it impossible, for many years he succeeded in largely shutting out the cacophony around him. He was, after all, a product of the code of discipline that ruled the yeshivas— fines, slaps from the rabbi, even expulsion for such sins as "time-wasting" (playing card games, for example), or reading trivial, nonreligious texts. "Students," wrote Shaul Stampfer, in *Lithuanian Yeshivas of the Nineteenth Century*, "were meant to devote every possible moment to study." Mostly, their studies were unstructured; they attended a few hours a week of *shiurim* (lectures) from the rabbinic scholars in residence, but otherwise they were simply expected to organize their own time. Many, Stampfer found, spent upward of eighteen hours a day working on their understanding of important texts. They were known, simply, as *matmidim*, or perpetual students. Yehezkel, with his ability to memorize extraordinary amounts of text, was just such a figure—a young man utterly absorbed in his studies, disinterested in the transformative political events in the broader world beyond the yeshiva walls.

Nearly a century after these events, Chimen, by then a very old man, remembered the suspicion with which Yehezkel viewed secular education: "For him, science was more or less permissible. What was not permissible was the humanities, because with the humanities you became less religious." When my father got into Trinity College, Cambridge, to study physics, Yehezkel would quiz him on the theory of relativity. But when Chimen himself had traveled to Jerusalem in 1935 to study philosophy and history, Yehezkel had been underwhelmed. "I went as a rebel against his wishes," Chimen remembered. "I went to a university. He was not very happy about that. He wanted people to go to yeshiva. He and I disagreed."

In the yeshivas of his youth, Yehezkel had felt protected from the often-savage realities of life. Many secular Jews, however, who witnessed the pogroms of the late nineteenth and early twentieth centuries, were pushed into political activity. History was, quite simply, a politicizing agent, one that made it ever harder for the Jews of Russia to sit it out on the sidelines. "We demand civil equality and equal submission to general laws as men who, despite everything, are conscious of their human dignity, and as conscientious citizens of a modern state," wrote the authors of the 1905 Declaration of Jewish Citizens, which was signed by six thousand politically active Russian Jews, men and women who had joined a variety of political clubs, parties, and clandestine organizations in the previous few years.

In many ways, those Jews who combined a vigorous intellectualism with revolutionary political beliefs were *matmidim* by another name. Chimen, born in the autumn of 1916, in the dying months of tsarist rule, was just such a figure. His and Mimi's house, by the 1950s, was a sort of secular yeshiva, a place where students came to study great texts; to hear great masters exploring their ideas; but, above all, a place where people would be expected to think about difficult moral and political topics for many hours at a time. Chimen might have been a dyed-in-the-wool Communist at this point in his life—but even then he was an intellectual snob. He valued not status per se but intelligence. And he could be more brutal in his verbal responses to a Communist he considered stupid than he would be to a clever person who happened to be a member of the hated bourgeoisie. For my father's lifelong friend Krishan Kumar, who went on to become a sociologist and an expert on utopias, Hillway, which he started visiting at the age of eleven, with its endless political discussions and its spiraling columns of books, was the greatest university he could have ever attended: "I remember being very struck by the books in the downstairs room. Great fat tomes in the front room where you sat. From the moment you opened the door, it was a house of books. The front room was a room of learning and talk. You'd sit there and everybody was so close to each other. Everybody talked. It was a galaxy of talent."

Opposite the door of the front room coming in from the hallway, on the wall of shelves to the left of the fireplace at about eye level, was a row of books on the Holocaust. Among these was a large volume by the historian Lucy Dawidowicz, titled *The War Against the Jews 1933–1945*. When I was about ten, I began asking Chimen questions about the Holocaust. It was, after all, one of the great elephants in the room at Hillway, an omnipresent reality that would be hinted at in ghastly, sometimes coded references around the dinner table. Periodically, survivors would come to the house for dinner. Frequently, friends who had escaped from continental Europe prior to the Second World War would tell their stories. Fred Barber, the bald, genteel doctor who lived around the corner from Hillway, would drop remarks about life in prewar Czechoslovakia; the cousins from France—Irene and her daughters; Jeanette and Michel and their children -- many of whose family members had been sent to the death camps, would come to visit.

Rather than fob me off with half-truths, modified to dull the scale of the atrocity for my young ears, or try to comfort me with explanations that hid more than they revealed, Chimen, always the historian, took this book—its jacket white at the top, with jagged, burned edges blending into a red bottom, an abstract image redolent of blood and fire and carnage, of ghettos burned and corpses cast into furnaces— off the shelf, gave it to me, and told me to read it. I still remember my horror as Auschwitz was described; and, in case I ever need reminding, I still possess the book. On my own bookshelves, it sits next to Art Spiegelman's *Maus* and just a few tomes along from William Shirer's *The Rise and Fall of the Third Reich*. Its cover, suggestive of burned, ragged paper, looks similar to the sheets of burning paper that fluttered down over Brooklyn, where I was living at the time, from the World Trade Center on September 11, 2001, sheets that I gathered up that horrifying day and put into a beige folder as reminders, however inadequate, of the capacity for evil to rain down suddenly out of a clear blue sky.

Chimen had gone through the book meticulously, underlining passages in pencil that he found particularly powerful. Hitler's Final Solution program, Dawidowicz wrote, "was part of a salvational ideology that envisaged the attainment of Heaven by bringing Hell on earth." "The Devil is loose," Friedrich Reck-Malleczewen noted in his diary on October 30, 1942. The most important event of our time, André Malraux said, was *le retour de Satan,*" citing the German system of terror. Chimen had underlined both the English and French references to the devil. It was, as far as I could tell, the only time he highlighted such allegorical imagery to describe a historical event. And it spoke, I think, to the paucity of words that he felt were available to explain such an epic atrocity. My grandfather, never otherwise at a loss for words, was frequently tongue-tied when it came to discussing the Holocaust. All the tools of the historian's trade, the understanding of Marxist dialectic, the belief that history moved in a generally progressive arc, fell mute before such organized psychopathy. When Chimen watched documentaries on, say, the Warsaw ghetto, I would turn to him and see him silently sobbing.

Chimen's erstwhile friend Itzik Manger wrote, in the opening stanza of his poem "Ballad of the Times":

There's a dead child lying in the road,
A little girl with blond hair.
Five or six weeks more maybe
She'd have reached her seventh year.
Marshal Göring is playing with his child.

It is such a simple image, yet so utterly horrifying—the orchestrators of mass murder sitting back and enjoying their domestic bliss as everyone around them drowned in blood.

In his University College London office, Chimen kept a copy of Hitler's *Mein Kampf.* As carefully as he had with Dawidowicz's text, in *Mein Kampf* too he had underlined key passages in red ink, and had scribbled precise little notes in the margins. "He [the Jew] lacks completely the most essential requirement for a cultured people, the idealistic attitude," Hitler had written; Jews were stateless wanderers who corrupted whatever cultures they inhabited. Chimen wrote on this page that the Nazi leader's idea was that "the Jews had never had a territorial limit and were worse than nomads." Forcing himself to carefully read the bile-filled screed, the historian had underlined Hitler's description of the Jews as parasites and bacilli, of Marxism as a Jewish idea, of Germany's defeat in the First World War as caused by Jews. In a letter that he wrote to Dr. John P. Fox in 1978, as Fox prepared a BBC lecture on the Jewish Councils in occupied Europe, Chimen made reference to that passage: "Hitler, in his *Mein Kampf*, portrays the Jews as a dangerous bacillus—a parasite in the body politic of Germany, which must be destroyed to save the German nation. Whether this finally led to the Final Solution is a separate question, but there is little doubt that the germ of the extermination of the Jews is contained already in *Mein Kampf*."

Over coffee once, when I visited the house from university, Chimen mentioned that after the war his family had found out that his own grandmother—Raizl's mother, Leah, daughter of Rabbi David Willowski—who was very elderly by then, had been shot dead during the Einsatzgruppen actions in Byelorussia, either in one of the ghettos or in the killing fields in the forests outside of town, or perhaps gassed in one of the early mobile gas units that were so lethally utilized in Byelorussia. Chimen, from a distance of sixty years, could not tell me how my great-great-grandmother had died; but he knew that she had been murdered by the Nazis. It was the only time I ever heard him discuss the personal losses he had endured during the Holocaust; and he mentioned it quickly, reluctantly, with few additional details. It was as if the event, for Chimen, was too vast—and the people lost within it were too small to be mourned individually, their deaths too easily swamped by other, bigger horrors: by destructions of entire populations; by industrial, methodical killings that numbered in the millions; by the complete loss of communities that had survived in Eastern Europe for centuries. Never a social historian—unlike his nephew Raph Samuel, who specialized in telling the stories of individuals and bringing their lives out of anonymity—Chimen was always more comfortable in exploring the impact of historical events on countries and economic systems than he was in detailing the lives of individuals trapped within that historical web.

And yet, those individual stories did, at some deeply personal level, affect him enormously. Not until after he died did I find out that Chimen had been instrumental in bringing to London more than fifteen hundred Torah scrolls from the Czech provinces of Bohemia and Moravia. They had been collected both by Jews, hoping to salvage at least some artifacts from their world before it was consumed by the genocide, and, bizarrely, by Nazi ethnographers, eager to add loot to the macabre museum they hoped to create in Prague as an epilogue to the story of an extinct race. During the war, the scrolls and thousands of other fragments from vanished Jewish homes and communities were put on display in Prague's Jewish museum and a handful of local synagogues, the exhibits curated by Jewish librarians and scholars, cataloged and tagged by Nazi clerks, and viewable only by a select few SS officers. During those years, the Jewish populations of Bohemia and Moravia were systematically destroyed, most of their members shipped first to the "model" camp of Terezin (known in German as Theresienstadt), and then on to Auschwitz and the other extermination centers. A population of nearly one hundred thousand was reduced to barely seven thousand. After the war, the scrolls lay unused and forgotten, stored in a tiny synagogue in the suburbs of Prague, wrapped in polythene, many of them covered with a fine veneer of mold.

There they stayed for more than eighteen years, until 1963, when a London gallery owner named Eric Estorick, who specialized in

Eastern European art, heard about them from a Czech government official and arranged for Chimen to travel to Prague to evaluate them. Chimen's initial task was to determine which were kosher (undamaged, and thus fit for use in a synagogue), which were *pasul* (desecrated or torn, moldy or water-damaged, and thus unfit for religious use), and which fell somewhere in between (damaged, yet in the hands of skilled scribes and scholars, salvageable). Chimen, normally so meticulous about writing down even the most mundane of appointments in the tiny cloth-covered diaries that he carried around with him in his jacket pocket, left no record of this trip; no airplane number jotted down in his little maroon-colored year planner, no note saying something to the effect of "leaving for Prague." He was, by then, fearful to the point of paranoia of any written connections to the Eastern bloc. The trip must, however, have taken place in late October, as there is a little more than a week of empty space in his diary for that period.

He spent that time in a dreary Prague, followed by KGB agents, he subsequently told those connected with the venture, continually terrified that he would be arrested and shipped back to Moscow. There was nothing to do but work; the shops were so empty that he could not even find a present to bring back to Mimi. He returned, shattered by his discovery of the massive Torah collection, with tales of how some of the scrolls had had SOS messages tucked into their folds, with notes such as "Please God help us in these troubled times." He then proceeded to work with Estorick, along with a wealthy businessman named Ralph Yablon and the liberal rabbi Harold Reinhart, the founder of the Westminster Synagogue, to negotiate the purchase of the entire collection. In late 1963, a few cryptic notes appear to that effect in his diary: "5 pm Rabbi Reinhart," says one such notation, on December 10, the first evening of Hanukkah. Nothing else. No details. No mention of the project at hand.

What he had found haunted him. "The agony of the work remains with Chimen Abramsky to this day," wrote Philippa Bernard in her 2005 book, *Out of the Midst of the Fire*. "Some of the Torahs were burned when the synagogues were torched, and he recalled the Rabbinical tradition that if a Torah is burned the words are sent up to Heaven. Some were blood-stained, many lacking binders to hold the two rolls together, were tied with *talleisim* [prayer shawls], or even in one case with a child's mackintosh belt. Two were held together with pieces of a woman's corset. The human misery embodied in that tragic collection was a palpable reminder of what had befallen the Jewish race." By February 1964, when the scrolls arrived in a chilly central London, delivered by a fleet of trucks, Chimen had been a fervent anti-Communist for six years. He stood in the crowd and wept: for the horrors of the Holocaust and for the sheer callous neglect that the scrolls, these extraordinary memento mori, had experienced under Communist rule in the decades afterward.

As I root around my childhood memories of the books in that front room, it seems to me that the texts on the Holocaust also provide hints as to why Chimen remained so ferociously pro-Soviet during the war years and their immediate aftermath. For, despite their many other crimes, before and during the Second World War the Soviets were not actively anti-Semitic: Their imprisonment of religious proselytizers such as Yehezkel in the 1920s and '30s had been antireligious, not anti-Semitic per se. They did not tar all Jews as enemies nor, as had the Nazis, declare that the Jewish race as a whole was inherently foreign, inherently apart from the broader society. Wholesale, across-the-board hostility to Jews was not part of Stalin's calculus until the postwar period, when opposition to the State of Israel (which had been welcomed initially by the Soviets, who were eager to take potshots at the crumbling British Empire) morphed into a more explicit anti-Jewish rhetoric and then a series of lethal actions against the Jewish intelligentsia in the Soviet Union.

During the war, the British Communist Party, with Chimen's Jewish Affairs Committee playing a vital role, compiled a huge dossier of evidence on the unfolding Holocaust, with testimony from those few who had managed to escape the death camps and join up with partisans in the surrounding forests, and providing information on the mass shootings and then on the gas chambers. As early as June 1942, they had gathered a body of material, provided to them by the Polish National Council, on the makeshift extermination campaign that had begun in what was still known as Eastern Galicia in the summer of 1941, on the use of mobile gas-chamber trucks in Chelmno, on the shootings carried out by the SS Einsatzgruppen death squads, as well as the systematic slaughter inside the death camps. The British Communists helped to organize some of the earliest public events to discuss and denounce the unprecedented massacres. And it was at least in part as a result of their actions that, years before the defeat of Nazism, British parliamentarians, including the foreign secretary Anthony Eden, began to talk about war crimes trials for the architects of the Holocaust. By the summer of 1942, the British Labour Party and the Trades Union Congress had passed resolutions condemning these unprecedented atrocities. The Communist Party was publishing pamphlets documenting the destruction of Eastern European Jewry. And at a huge meeting convened in London at Caxton Hall on September 2 of that year, representatives of governments in exile from the countries of occupied Europe, as well as members of Socialist groups from around the world, met to speak out against the killings and to urge the Allied governments to hold Germany's leaders accountable for their crimes after the war ended. The dossier on the unfolding genocide, put together by Chimen and others in the

Communist Party, sits now, long forgotten, in a filing cabinet in the People's History Museum in Manchester.

After Hitler unleashed his vast armies against the Soviet Union in 1941, the fight to defeat him became intertwined with the fight to protect Stalin's Soviet Union. If the Soviet Union could withstand the German onslaught, in the long run Hitler's empire was doomed. In 1941, the year Chimen officially joined the organization, membership of the Communist Party of Great Britain nearly tripled, reaching a peak at just short of 60,000 members. In some so-called "little Moscow" enclaves—in the mining communities of Fife in Scotland and in South Wales, in Chimen and Mimi's East London neighborhood of Stepney—the Party came temporarily to dominate the local political scene. Chimen was a close friend of the Scottish Communist MP William Gallacher, even going so far as to help Gallacher write his autobiography. Raph Samuel, who was reputedly quite capable of holding his own in a theoretical conversation about Marxism from around the age of seven, a Communist child prodigy, an *illui* of revolutionary theory, wrote that Party members obsessively followed news about fighting on the Russian front, and busily worked on putting up stickers on lampposts: "Second Front NOW!" They went to see Soviet films in undamaged cinemas and busied themselves every May Day by going on demonstrations on behalf of the workers of the world. "The Lenin Album was my bible at this time," Raph continued. "A sumptuously produced volume of facsimile reproductions, photographs and pictures. There were only five copies in the country, I was told, and my uncle was the proud possessor of one of them. It introduced me to the idea of clandestinity and persecution, revolution and counter-revolution, barricades and strikes."

No matter that from the summer of 1939 until Operation Barbarossa sent German soldiers streaming east in June 1941 Stalin had been an uneasy ally of the Führer's, carving up Poland with the Nazis, occupying Finland, devouring the Baltic States; no matter that in 1939 there had been a schism in the British Communist Party over the decision of its leadership to toe the line on the Nazi–Soviet Non-aggression Pact, with Party theoreticians arguing that good Communists should fight against the "imperialist" war and seek to replace the leadership of Chamberlain and then of Churchill with a "people's government." Now that the fight was joined, now that Soviet Russia was fighting for its very survival, no rhetoric was to be spared in urging the successful prosecution of the war. In the early 1990s, newly opened Soviet archives revealed the extent to which British Communists chose to follow edicts from Moscow during those crucial early days of the war. "Direct your fire against capitulationist anti-Soviet elements," the executive committee of the Comintern had ordered its British comrades, *New Statesman* journalists Paul Anderson and Kevin Davey reported in an article dated February 4, 1994, on the revelations contained in the archives. Support a "united national front around the Churchill government," the Comintern urged. Opposing that government, the Moscow scribblers wrote, now would "bring grist to the mill of pro-Hitlerite elements in England."

In May 1943, twenty-six-year-old Chimen edited a pamphlet on behalf of the Jewish Fund for Soviet Russia. Titled *Calling All Jews to Action!*, it issued a stirring decree: "Fellow Jews of Great Britain, America and the other countries, if you want to prevent Hitler from exterminating us, if you want to save your own lives...help the great heroic Red Army." In February 1944, in a pamphlet also published by the Jewish Fund for Soviet Russia (a rare copy of which is now housed in a special collection in the University of Sheffield's library), the United Kingdom's chief rabbi, Joseph Hertz, saluted the Soviet Union for saving "so many of our brethren from bestial torture and fiendish annihilation." A year earlier, in another Jewish Fund publication, Hertz had called on all people of faith on Red Army Day to

pray for a Soviet victory. The president of the Federation of Synagogues wrote, in a letter published as part of a collection of tributes
by the fund, of "the brilliant victories of the Russian armies against
the German sadistic hordes."

———

Further cementing Chimen's belief that the Soviets had the interest of
Jewish communities at heart, immediately after the war ended, Russian writers such as Vasily Grossman—nowadays best known as the
author of the magnificent, sprawling *Life and Fate*—were instrumental in bringing to light the horrors of the Holocaust and what they
termed, with careful precision, the "annihilation camps." Grossman
and his colleague Ilya Ehrenburg had toured the liberated camps,
detailing the conditions, interviewing the skeletal survivors, documenting the Nazi's bookkeeping on the number of Jews who had
been sent to each camp, calculating how many had been killed and
how. Grossman and Ehrenburg had detailed their findings in *The
Black Book: The Ruthless Murder of Jews by German-Fascist In-
vaders*. It was the earliest published comprehensive overview of the
slaughter, and it created shock waves around the world. (Not that
that did Grossman any good; as Stalin became more anti-Semitic,
Grossman fell into official disfavor, and for many decades his books
were unavailable to Soviet readers.)

The Black Book carefully detailed the way the Holocaust had
been implemented, including in Minsk and Slutsk, the towns of Chimen's childhood, both of them in a region controlled by the sadistic
Hauptsturmführer Friedrich Wilhelm Ribbe, and both of which,
even by the monstrous criteria of the Holocaust, witnessed extraordinary outbreaks of creative violence, a horror show that took peculiarly twisted imaginations to organize and reserves of stamina to

implement. Pretty much every kind of torture designed by man was unleashed in the ghettos of these towns between 1941 and 1943. By the end of 1943, the Minsk ghetto—which at one time had housed between 75,000 and 100,000 Jews—was no more. Over a two year period all but the few thousand who had escaped to join partisan units in the surrounding forests had been killed. (Minsk was, as documented by the historian Barbara Epstein, in her book *The Minsk Ghetto 1941–1943*, one of the few ghettos where Communist partisans outside the ghetto and resistance inside managed to successfully coordinate their actions.) They were murdered either inside the ghetto or shot into mass graves dug at Tuchinka and other villages outside of Minsk. Even before Auschwitz and the other annihilation camps were fully "functional," the Jewish communities in Byelorussia which Chimen had been born into had been destroyed. The people were slaughtered; grenades were lobbed into hideouts, and the buildings were razed to the ground so as to bury any survivors who might have successfully hidden during the mass killings. Gallows lined the town squares, and the Jewish population was progressively culled; its members hung, gassed in mobile killing units, shot, or stabbed.

Regarding the massacres in Slutsk, Ehrenburg found a letter from a young woman by the name of Manya Temchina who had managed to escape the slaughter by jumping off a truck that was transporting her to the murder grounds: "On Monday, February 6, 1943, the entire area was surrounded, and they began to load people onto trucks. Pinkhos was taken first. Then they took Mamma and the children. That was at 9:00 a.m. They took me at one in the afternoon. I can still hear the screams of our little sisters as they were taken to be shot." In towns like Minsk, contemporary writers who lived through the savagery, and who were grasping for a language to describe what had been unleashed, wrote of "pogroms." They wrote of wave after wave of pogroms, on a scale unimaginable even by those who had survived Kishinev and the other atrocities during the last decades of tsarism, pogroms conducted by local policemen as well as by Einsatzgruppen killers from the Waffen SS, which would take the lives of thousands of people, sometimes tens of thousands, in a couple of days of uncontained savagery. But the word could not do justice to the totality of the crime. Within a few years, a new term would have entered the lexicon: Holocaust, or, in Hebrew, *Shoah*.

For Chimen and his fellow Jewish Affairs Committee theoreticians, during the war years and well into the postwar period, the answers to the grotesque questions raised by the Holocaust were simple, even if they often seemed contorted to outsiders. In their ten-point typed-out list explaining to a British audience "why Jews should vote Communist" in the aftermath of the Nazi's defeat and at the onset of the Cold War, they wrote: "The Communist Party knows that the days of pogroms and anti-Semitism in Russia are gone, and Jews there stand free and equal with other Soviet citizens. It is against this that European and American capitalists are arming, and that a new Nazi revival is being encouraged. They are all becoming fascist-minded."

And again I return in my mind to my grandfather's determination to identify a safe haven for the people and the culture out of which he had come, for a place not riven by murderous attacks on Jews. His embrace of the Soviet Union in his youth came, at least in part, out of that search. After all, while the USSR was only too quick to persecute religious leaders, it had declared, in writing, anti-Semitism to be a serious crime. And in the late 1920s, and more particularly from 1934 onward, it had promoted a form of internal Zionism, by setting up the Jewish Autonomous Region of Birobidzhan in Siberia and encouraging the migration of Jews to this place where Yiddish culture would, supposedly, be allowed to flourish. In 1944, community leaders in Birobidzhan apparently marshaled 72,000 signatures on a document they sent Stalin praising him for his war leadership, for his role as "the wise and capable strategist of the all-conquering strength of progress, whose services to history and humanity are as innumerable as the stars in the heavens, and the sands on the sea-shore!" It was a somewhat startling number given that, according to a 1941 report by the New York City–based Institute of Jewish Affairs, at its height no more than 60,000 Jews had relocated to the territory. Then again, the exaggerated number was, perhaps, a lesser sin than the literary nonsense that accompanied it. Like so much else about Eastern European Jewry, like the Jewish East End in which Shapiro, Valentine & Co. was situated, Birobidzhan was simply another echo, a ghostly, ethereal presence from the past, by the time I was old enough to rummage through Chimen's books, its Jewish identity attenuated in the purges of 1936 and 1948–52. It still exists, but largely in name only, the ideal of a Yiddish-speaking homeland, a self-contained community-within-a-country long-shattered.

Shortly after I read Dawidowicz's work, I told Chimen that Hitler must have been crazy. I remember my grandfather, his eyes fiery with passion, becoming furious with me; such a diagnosis, he told me, his accent even heavier than usual, his index finger wagging in my face, gave Hitler and the Germans a free pass, it somehow negated the enormity of their crimes. He believed that to understand the Holocaust, you had to explore the gigantic systems—political, economic, bureaucratic—that underpinned it. These systems did not, could not explain why the Holocaust had been unleashed; but they did help to explain why Germany had slipped into the sort of chaos that had paved the way for a monster like Hitler to assume power, and why, once in power, he was able to use Germany's formidable bureaucratic institutions to turn Europe into an abattoir. The mechanisms of the Holocaust were, Chimen felt, rationalism turned in on itself, science perverted, philosophy hijacked. The *results* were madness, Dantean in their vision of cruelty, but they sprang from a self-contained, bureaucratic logic of evil. An evil that carefully categorized Jews into workers and the unemployed, specialists and nonspecialists, healthy and sick; that gave people in some categories jobs and food and immediately killed the others. An evil that assigned individuals not just color-coded badges but also individual numbers. An evil that methodically and minutely tracked who would die now and who would be set aside to be killed later. "The German people," Chimen wrote to a friend, forty years after the end of the war, "spewed the Jews out, killed them, looked for the final solution." Barbarous it most certainly was, but crazy? Not by Chimen's reckoning. To reduce it all to the psychotic tics of a few insane leaders was, Chimen felt, an insult to the memory of the individuals who had died and the communities that had been wiped off the face of the earth, and, as important, it was an underestimation of the ever-present human capacity to inflict evil, to obey heinous commands.

Victor Gollancz, the founder of the Left Book Club, wrote in his pamphlet *What Buchenwald Really Means*, published in April 1945, just weeks before the Third Reich's final defeat, that the Holocaust was a "sin against humanity—this sin so great that even to speak of it, even to think of it, makes one ashamed to be a man." How, Gollancz wanted to know, could so many people have turned a blind eye, despite years of evidence of the scope and depravity of the unfolding genocide? "And now ask yourself, reader—what did you do about it? Nothing? Why? Because you didn't care enough? Because it was none of your business? Because you couldn't bear to think about it, and so averted your eyes? Or because—because—'well, what on earth could I, an ordinary, powerless individual do anyhow?' They are all poor answers, all those. They say little for your citizenship, for your humanity, for your active belief in the brotherhood of man." Gollancz's cri de coeur represented well Chimen's thinking on the Shoah. It was so monstrous, so vile, that for the rest of his life it would hover over him, haunt him.

In the 1940s, Chimen still believed that Communism could offer a way out for humanity, a way to prevent such horrors from recurring. "In the Soviet Union, where no threat of extermination exists," Chimen and his National Jewish Committee comrades wrote in 1944, "where there is no national discrimination, and where the fullest democratic freedom is enjoyed by the whole people, there is no Jewish question." The "Jewish question" they believed, could only exist when and where anti-Semitism flourished. Abolish anti-Semitism, and the question itself disappeared. "A new world will follow the defeat and extermination of fascism together with its oppression of the Jews and other peoples: a world of freedom brought into being by the united efforts of all decent mankind and guaranteed by the presence of the USSR, the proven champion of all oppressed peoples."

During the latter years of the war, in keeping with this hope, when Chimen and his fellow National Jewish Committee theoreticians were hard at work turning the Jewish East End Red, leading Communist figures frequently visited Chimen and Mimi's various homes. In November 1943, the Soviet Jewish poet Itzik Feffer and Schloyme Mikhoels, the director of the Moscow State Yiddish Theater, came to Britain to rally support for the Russian effort against the Nazis and to call for the swift creation of a second front in the west. Thousands of men, women, and children showed up to hear them talk in Manchester, Glasgow, and London. Invitations to receptions at which the duo would speak were sent out on small off-white calling cards by the Jewish Fund for Soviet Russia. Prominent Jewish figures were invited to write letters to Soviet Jewry expressing solidarity with their struggle. In early November, after a huge gathering, Feffer and Mikhoels met the chief rabbi and his colleagues—which probably included Chimen's father, Yehezkel. Then, according to the historian Henry Felix Srebrnik, in *London Jews and British Communism, 1935–1945*, they stayed up until three in the morning meeting with Chimen and his fellow National Jewish Committee members: Lazar Zaidman (a Romanian Jew who had been blinded in one eye by his captors during years of incarceration for his political activities in Romania in the 1920s), the Imperial College mathematician Hyman Levy, Jacob Sonntag, and Alec Waterman. Their strategy was blunt: to use the organizing powers of the Communist Party, and in particular its Jewish committee, to rally the British and American public to the Soviet fight. Chimen told his young friend David Mazower sixty years later that they talked several times that week at the Hyde Park Hotel, where the Soviet pair had been accommodated.

———

Chimen's fears about the vulnerability of Jews to extraordinary violence did not end with the Allies' victory over the Nazis. Immediately after the German capitulation on May 8, 1945, while the war with Japan was ongoing, shadowy publications such as *The Patriot* and *The Vanguard* started circulating in English towns, blaming a Jewish conspiracy for Hitler's defeat, and warning England to expect its own demise as Jewish financiers and radicals sought to gain control. In Parliament soon after the war ended, while the revelations of the scale of the Holocaust against the Jews of Europe were still fresh in everybody's mind, the virulently anti-Semitic Conservative MP Captain Archibald Ramsay proposed reenacting the Statute of Jewry of 1275. (Among other things the code contained was a requirement that Jews wear identity badges, precursors of the yellow Star of David enforced by the Nazis.) In December 1945, Oswald Mosley, whose British Union of Fascists had marched through the East End before the war, took Fascist salutes from his followers at a gathering in the Royal Hotel in London. A year later, several Fascist groups decided to unite under the auspices of a National Front. Meanwhile, yet another of the would-be dictators, a Fascist leader named Victor Burgess, responded to growing numbers of attacks against British forces by Jewish organizations in what was still the British Mandate of Palestine, by urging Britain to engage in retaliatory punishments. For every British soldier injured, he recommended, one hundred British Jews should be publicly flogged. It was an alarming echo of Nazi practice in occupied Europe.

In the wake of the revelations of the Holocaust, these groups were almost entirely marginalized, but their existence alone was enough to frighten Chimen and his friends. When the ten-year-old Raph Samuel and one of his friends, Peter Waterman, crept out onto Hampstead Heath in August 1945 to join in the celebrations of the victory over Japan, Chimen and Peter's father, Alec, rushed out in a panic looking for them. They feared that the Fascists would make trouble; that having lost the war they would wreak revenge by beating up Jewish children. When Chimen and Alec found the boys celebrating in the light of the bonfires at the start of what was shaping up to be an all-night party, they dragged them back to the safe confines of Hillway. Decades later, Mimi would express that same fear, in a letter that she wrote to me in September 1993, a month after I had moved to New York. "We have had a terrible political shock this week. In a ward by-election in Tower Hamlets the British Union of Fascists have won a seat by seven votes." Casting an eye back to the days surrounding the war, she continued, "Stepney was always a stronghold for the Mosleyites." Ironically, the same poverty and daily anxieties that had generated support for the Communist Party in London's East End had also made it fertile recruiting territory for the Fascists.

Perhaps more significantly, the activities of the British Union of Fascists and the National Front in the postwar years crystallized for Chimen his sense of terror that the Holocaust was, somehow, an incomplete project, that other vastly destructive political movements would arise to try to finish off the job of extermination that Hitler had begun. He worked, ever more feverishly, on trying to understand how to secure safety for Jews in a world of mechanized killing. He concluded, in the war's immediate aftermath, that the answer was not a Jewish state but a Socialist world. He put his faith in a universalist ideology and hoped that the new economic relationships he wanted to see created would be powerful enough to counter Fascism.

It was probably in the front room at Hillway, shortly after the end of the war, that Chimen helped to write a "syllabus" on the Jewish Question, for the Communist Party's Jewish Committee. Question seven asked, "What is the Party Attitude to Zionism?" The answer: "The influence and propaganda of Zionism is pernicious and harmful to the Jewish people and to general progress and must be combatted and countered." It was probably also in this room that the committee talked over their fourteen-page memorandum on how to oppose British rule in Palestine without endorsing Zionism. "Ever since the Balfour Declaration, Zionism has sought to be a lackey of Imperialism by forming a little loyal Jewish Ulster in a sea of potentially hostile Arabism," they declared. "For more than a quarter of a century it has kept the Jews apart from the Arabs in Palestine." These were arguments that would have been largely familiar to Jewish political thinkers and activists in the Eastern Europe that both Chimen's generation and that of his parents had been born into. Chimen and Yehezkel were on very different sides of this debate at that time, but by this point in his life Chimen did not argue about politics with his father; instead, he fought out these disputes with his secular friends.

"There were," remembered Peter Waterman, "loud and noisy discussions, and arguments. Because Chimen wasn't the only one who could get very annoyed at being opposed in an argument. My father [Alec] also could lose his temper. These were very highly politicised people." When, as schoolboys, Peter, Raph, and other friends poked fun at the Communist Party, Chimen, prickly on this point, quickly put a stop to it. Communism, in the 1940s and '50s, was not something to laugh about in Chimen's presence, any more than the Torah was something to be mocked in Yehezkel's.

All too often during these years, rigid political beliefs led to a willingness to defend the show trials, purges, and other arbitrary brutalities of the Stalin regime. Mimi and Chimen feuded with those who had grown disillusioned with the Cause; at times Chimen was even known to throw people who critiqued the USSR too vociferously out of their home. The more I research this period, the more I come to suspect that the front room of the 1940s and early 1950s was not a particularly pleasant place for nonbelievers to visit. And I think I am glad that I was not born early enough to test this thesis. Far better for me to remember the house as the tolerant and broad-minded place it would be throughout my childhood.

In 1949, when *The Jewish Chronicle* published an editorial accusing Stalin's Soviet Union of anti-Semitism, Chimen, outraged, typed out a response—or, since he could not type himself, he probably dictated it to Mimi. "You mention the attack on Zionism in *Pravda* and you write 'The distance from baiting Zionists to baiting Jews is short.' It seems you confuse criticism of Zionism with anti-semitism. The Soviet government since its establishment always had an antizionist attitude, but at the same time it was the first Government in the World to introduce legislation making antisemitic propoganda [*sic*] a crime, a crime not only against Jews, but a very serious offence against the Soviet State as a whole." He continued: "It seems to me, Sir, that you are deliberately deceiving your readers by attributing antisemitic motives to the Soviet Government." He fired off another letter to his friend the journalist Ivor Montagu, who had recently visited the USSR, urging him to write an article "refuting the allegations against the Soviet Union." And Chimen wrote angrily about how "reactionaries in the U.S.A. were using allegations of Soviet anti-Semitism in their own propaganda campaigns." That same month, Chimen and his comrades on the Party's Jewish Affairs Committee decided to revive a defunct publication called the *Jewish Clarion* (which Chimen had edited on and off since December 1945, and which had ceased publication a few months earlier due to financial difficulties) in part to deal with the growing chorus of "slanders" about the poor treatment of Jews in the Soviet Union.

And so, just as Stalin was unleashing a wave of anti-Jewish purges, marshaling the full force of the Soviet state against "cosmopolitan" Jewish intellectuals, just as the Jewish Autonomous Region was being purged and the dream of a Soviet Jewish homeland in Birobidzhan was destroyed, the Party's faithful in Britain, Chimen among them, were working to convince the world of the Soviet system's humanistic impulses.

It would take several more years before Chimen was willing to confront the awful truth: that anti-Semitism was alive and well in the Soviet Union—not to mention the fact that the system as a whole was light years away from being any sort of free and democratic beacon. And it was then, in that swirl of disillusionment, that he began to embrace Zionism. If Russia was not the place of refuge, somewhere else had to be. There had to be one country that could serve as what the early Zionist theoretician Ahad Ha'am, in the late nineteenth

century, borrowing from a biblical phrase, called Eretz Israel; or, as
Chimen explained the idea in a 1976 lecture, a place where "the Jewish spirit" could thrive, a spot on earth that could nurture "the
moral, creative forces of the Jewish people that were and are suppressed brutally in the diaspora."

If Communism could not deter cruel thoughts and terrible actions,
other ideologies had to be found that could. Much of Chimen's re-
thinking would have taken place while he pored over books from the
shelves of this front room and while he discussed his concerns with
comrades over cups of tea in the same room. In later years, he would
go on long, late-night walks around Oxford with his friend Beryl
Williams—then a young history tutor at the University of Sussex—
and others, talking about how guilty he felt for having stayed in the
Party for as long as he did. He told Williams that he lost sleep over it.
He denounced himself, in conversations with Eastern European intellectuals—many of whom were serving out their exiles at Sussex
and a handful of other British universities—for having bought the
Stalinist line that one could not make an omelet without breaking
eggs. "He saw the Revolution as something that went wrong rather
than something that shouldn't have happened at all," Williams concluded. "He became anti-Soviet, but he always remained a Socialist,
in a vague way."

———

When I was a teenager, involved in the pacifist antinuclear movement
and other left-wing activism in London, Chimen—still in full flight
from his Communist past, still mortified by the nonsense that he had
written as a young man—would lecture me on my youthful follies.
It used to infuriate me. His fury, I thought, reflected a lack of passion, a calcification of his political nerve ends. Today, as I sit at my

computer, a middle-aged man trying to put together the pieces of my grandparents' lives into a coherent narrative, I think I understand why he became so suspicious of what he saw as the naïve idealism of youth. Wanting to change the world for the better, caring passionately about the human condition, Chimen, Mimi, and so many of those they loved and respected had spent years defending a brutal and totalitarian system. It was, I believe, Chimen's most humbling realization.

In an archive at the University of Sheffield, I sit and explore microfilms holding ten years' worth of the *Jewish Clarion*. They contain articles by many of Chimen's closest friends from the postwar period: Izador Pushkin, Alec Waterman, Hyman Levy, Andrew Rothstein, Sam Alexander, Lazar Zaidman, Jack Gaster. Under an array of names, Chimen wrote dozens of articles for this paper over the years. Sometimes he would appear under flimsy noms de plume: C. Chimen was the first, then A. Chimen. Occasionally, he would write as C. A. On rare occasions, mainly when he was publishing an innocuous historical essay or book review, he used his real name. For his most overtly propagandistic pieces, however, the son of Yehezkel Abramsky, exiled rabbinic scholar and head of the London Beth Din, went under the pen name C. Allen.

The summer I left secondary school, I needed to earn money to fund a rail trip around Europe. For some weeks, I worked at odd jobs—in a deli, cleaning tables at London Zoo, even scrubbing school toilets. Then Chimen took pity on me and hired me to spend a few weeks with him trying to bring order to the chaos that was his upstairs study. We spent those weeks together, in the tiny room, burrowing through piles of papers, filing letters, chronologically ordering articles. Chimen, who never threw any written words away, found piles of his old Communist Party writings. Over my protestations, he made an exception to his rule: into a big, black rubbish bag went the papers, one after the other. Once the bag was filled, Chimen double-knotted it, as if he were trying to seal away toxic waste. And then he put the bag in the bin outside the house that the dustmen emptied into their truck every week. At the time, I was flabbergasted. *What vandalism! What a reckless disregard for the past!* Now, having read the articles, I understand his horror. The writings were ghastly. Claptrap. Massively propagandistic. There is simply no other way to put it. I think that, had I known Chimen when he was writing them, I would have found it hard to remain on friendly terms with him. I know that Chimen felt the same way. For him, C. Allen and A. Chimen and the others were young lunatics with whom he wanted nothing more to do.

In July 1952, a certain "C. A." wrote a review of a volume entitled *The Jews of Russia*, a work that explored the changing condition of Russian Jewry before and after the revolution. "Only the revolution of 1917 put an end to the persecution of Jews," wrote the man whose father, two decades earlier, had narrowly avoided execution, had been sent to Siberia because of his religious work, and whose family had then been expelled from the Soviet Union. "The need to run away from the country stopped. Jews became equal in every sense of the word." In November 1952, summarizing the proceedings of the Nineteenth Congress of the Communist Party of the Soviet Union, the thirty-six-year-old Chimen reverted to his deeper alias, C. Allen. After explaining to his readers that Western economies were being destroyed by American militarism, and that the senior Soviet politician Georgy Malenkov had detailed how the Soviet economic engine was outpowering that of the "forces of capitalism," C. Allen concluded with an observation of his own: "The Soviet Communist Congress is a beacon of light for the peoples of the world. Its discussions and decisions will be studied by progressive people everywhere. It will render great assistance to the fight for peace and for socialism, to the inestimable benefit of the whole of mankind."

It is C. Allen's obituary of Joseph Stalin, published as a full-page spread on the inside back page of the May 1953 edition, that I most don't want to read. I know it's going to be awful; I know, from everything I have managed to reconstruct of Chimen's worldview when he was in his twenties and thirties that he was a dyed-in-the-wool Stalinist. What I don't realize going in is just how phenomenally awful it really is, just how much he had bought into the cult of the personality. It leaves me gasping for breath, makes me want to run into a shower and scrub myself clean. This isn't the sweet old man I loved so much; this isn't the insightful humanist, so suspicious of even a whiff of totalitarianism and who so prided himself on his friendship with the great liberal philosopher Isaiah Berlin. Titled "The Debt Jews Owe to Joseph Stalin," and written five years after Stalin had embarked upon his massive campaign to eliminate Jewish intellectuals from public life in the Soviet Union, the obituary begins: "Progressive Jews everywhere grieve deeply over the death of Joseph Stalin, leader of progressive mankind, builder of Socialism and architect of Communism. To Stalin above all goes the credit for the great change in the position of Jews, from the violent oppression which they endured in Czarist times to the full equality as citizens which they enjoy in the Soviet Union.... Stalin's leadership was a tremendous contribution to the ending of exploitation of man by man, the root cause of anti-Semitism and racial discrimination." C. Allen explained that, in an article written in 1912, Stalin had "analysed the position of the Jews, of whose life he showed outstanding knowledge." Stalin created the Jewish Autonomous Region of Birobidzhan. He allowed Yiddish culture to flourish.

The obituary outlines all of Stalin's achievements through the late 1930s, and then details how he heroically commanded Soviet forces in their battle against Nazism from 1941 onward. Of the period from

August 1939 to June 1941, the years of the infamous Nazi–Soviet Nonaggression Pact, there is literally no mention. C. Allen's obituary of Stalin concludes with a flurry of hyperbole, of the kind one still sees today when a Great Leader passes away in North Korea. "The world has lost one of the greatest geniuses in all history. But Stalin's heritage lives on in the mighty Soviet Union marching toward Communism. Stalin is dead but his ideas and his work will live forever."

———

I want to grab C. Allen by the throat and punch him. I want to shout at him for being a damn fool. I want to scream that he's sullied my memory of my grandfather. But C. Allen is nowhere to be found.

THE DINING ROOM:
RITUALS AND REBELS

In Western Europe there are hardly any people who have lived through revolutions that are at all serious; the experience of the great revolutions is almost entirely forgotten there; and the transition from the desire to be revolutionary and from conversations (and resolutions) about revolution to real revolutionary work is difficult, slow and painful.
—Vladimir Ilyich Lenin, "Letter to the German Communists,"
August 14, 1921

C. ALLEN HAS *taken off his disguise, washed the low-grade printer's ink from his hands, and returned home to Mimi's warmth. Once more he has become Chimen Abramsky, bookseller, husband, father, and historian. And he's sitting at his simple wooden dining-room table, his children telling him about their day at school, while Mimi gives them dinner. At some point the doorbell will ring—he knows it will, it does so every night—and one or more of their friends will come through the entrance, barely breaking into their conversations and spirited political debates long enough to say hello, heading down the hallway and into the dining room to join the meal. There will be enough food for them all: Despite post-war rationing and lack of money, Mimi can always stretch her meager provisions to feed her guests. There will always be tea and biscuits, perhaps some herring or cheap pound cake. There will be beer; maybe, if the money can be found, there will be wine, imported from Israel or Morocco.*

———

In these years after the war and into the 1950s, the members of the Historians' Group of the Communist Party were among the most regular visitors to Hillway. Even after several hours at the New Scala restaurant in Soho or at Garibaldi's, a little Italian place off the Farringdon Road, the historians would still be hungry; they had, after all, been expending their energy pondering great historical questions, exploring how societies down the millennia had evolved, and trying to understand how this all fit into their Marxist schema. Chimen was not a particularly active member of the Historians' Group, and he rarely attended the restaurant gatherings: Throughout his Communist years he remained rigidly kosher and reluctant, especially in London, where he might be seen by religious relatives or acquaintances, to eat in nonkosher restaurants. And, during these years, he frequently did not have two pennies to rub together, so in the circumstances, even a cheap meal with his Party comrades would have seemed an unreasonable luxury. But despite his financial straits, he was one of the twenty-two members who had scrimped and saved to come up with the five-shilling membership fee. After the committee meetings, Eric Hobsbawm, who was the group's first treasurer and also presided over the inelegantly named Polemics Committee, and various others would decamp from Garibaldi's, get on the Underground, and set off for Hillway to eat and talk into the night.

The dining room in those years, before the house was extended into the back garden by several feet, was quite cramped, almost all the space taken up by a little table and dining chairs as well as two or three armchairs. Mimi brought the trays of food around from the kitchen, into the hallway, and then through to the dining room. She had to sidle between the chairs, leaning over her guests to reach the table. Elbows jostled elbows. Used plates had to be rapidly cleared, not for etiquette's sake but simply to make room for incoming food.

The walls near the table were reserved for paintings, usually one work or another given to them by their artist friends. Those at the other end of the room, away from the table, were shelved. Increasingly, as the collection grew, they housed books on Jewish history, many in Hebrew or Yiddish. Here were rare books on Jewish artists, included among them collections of high-quality reproductions of sketches by Marc Chagall, "the central figure among Jewish artists" in the period of the First World War, as Chimen wrote in the essay that accompanied a catalog for an Israel Museum exhibition in Jerusalem, *Tradition and Revolution: The Jewish Renaissance in Russian Avant-Garde Art, 1912–1928*. The artist, Chimen wrote, painted "a dream world of poetry and magic." His imagery spoke to the experiences of the Jews of the shtetl, as well as to the heartache of a people torn between past and future, between the pull of modernity and the familiarity of the old ways. It was sometimes whimsical, but often deeply melancholy. Many of his paintings, wrote Chimen, were intended to convey Chagall's feelings of horror "after the pogroms against the Jews in the Ukraine during the civil war."

There was also a collection of colored, numbered, and signed lithographs by the Russian painter Anatoli Kaplan, illustrating stories by Sholem Aleichem, including "Tevye der Milkhiker" and "Mottel: The Cantor's Son"—stories that formed the basis for the musical *Fiddler on the Roof*. There were collections of rare woodcuts, books of illustrated poems, and graphic art from the early Russian revolutionary period.

Around the crowded table and amid the clutter of books and art-work, the seated guests during these years would have included E. P. and Dorothy Thompson; the Oxford historian Christopher Hill, whose wife, Bridget (also a historian), for some time implausibly thought that Chimen was an Irishman named Seamus O'Bramski; Hobsbawm; and, of course, Raph Samuel. The youngest member of the Historians' Group, Raph had joined the Young Communist League in 1942 or 1943 at the astonishingly precocious age of seven or eight, and by the time he began attending Balliol College, Oxford, in the early 1950s he was already a gifted polemicist and historian. Raph would bring his Balliol friends, as well as his girlfriend, who was Harold Laski's granddaughter. There also would be some of Mimi's female friends: Mimi liked to play her hand at matchmaking, though the eligible Hobsbawm did not take the bait.

I rather hope that, outside of the confines of the committee itself, this coterie of intellectuals relaxed enough around Mimi's dining-room table to acknowledge the absurd self-seriousness of its members. I wonder how, for example, they responded to a colleague's martial announcement, transcribed verbatim by the secretary in a purple-bound lined notebook, that "there were sufficient forces in London to form an orientalists' group, and that he would launch it"? Or to the resolution that "university members should consider atten-dance at period group meetings a definite Party duty, though the group secretaries should not demand apologies for non-attendance except in special cases"? I suspect, however, that far from chuckling at these announcements, they shared Chimen's lack of humor about the Party during these years.

At the time, Hobsbawm lived in a flat in Bloomsbury with Henry Collins, and as they dunked their biscuits into their cups of tea with Chimen, the three of them would talk about Marx, and about Chi-men's fascination with the minutiae of the texts of and about the

Socialist prophet. It was out of these conversations that Chimen and Collins's collaborative effort began, which eventually led to them jointly writing the book *Karl Marx and the First International*. It was, Hobsbawm came to feel, the fruit of the combination of Chimen's extraordinary knowledge and Collins's ability to winnow down sprawling arguments, to synthesize information on the printed page. Hobsbawm concluded that Chimen had problems condensing his thoughts into written form because he could never let go of details: "He was one of those great Marx scholars we used to have, who really knew the text. They've mostly disappeared now. They mostly came out of Poland, places like that. Learned chroniclers of every detail, analysis of every line Marx had written. He found it hard to put it down on paper. He was too scholarly to do that." Collins, by contrast, had no such issues. He was a pragmatic man, smart, funny, yet utterly orderly in his thinking. A public school–educated English Jew among impoverished Eastern European migrants, he could rapidly shift from belting out a comic song in Yiddish one minute to having a serious conversation about Marx's involvement with union organizers in Victorian England the next.

It was in the dining room, during those early postwar years, that one of Hillway's strangest annual rituals unfolded: the Communist Passover. Around the table some of London's most stridently antireligious thinkers would gather and, with nostalgic fondness, solemnly relive the salvation story that had played so prominent a role in their Eastern European Orthodox childhoods.

Most years Mimi and Chimen held two Seders—the ritual Passover feasts, held on successive nights, at which the Haggadah, detailing the exodus from Egypt, is read—one for family, one for friends.

It was a huge production. Strictly kosher, they kept an entire separate set of plates for Passover. Should the wrong dish be used, they would bury it in the back garden for a week to purify it. On the first night, all of Mimi's cousins and uncles and aunts, her mother, and her sisters and their families would troop in: At this time almost all the members of her family of her own generation were active Communists. Chimen's parents, his brother Moshe, and his cousins would go to more Orthodox houses for their Passover meal. On the second night Chimen and Mimi's closest friends, many of them also Communist Party activists, would be their guests. Among them were Chimen's good friend Izador "Izzie" Pushkin, who had left Russia as a child in the 1920s, and Alec Waterman, who had been born in the small town of Blonie, outside of Warsaw nine years before Chimen's birth, and as a young boy had spent seven years in a cheder, immersed in religious scholarship: Both men served with Chimen on the Party's Jewish Affairs Committee. They made up a cadre of Jewish Communists, schooled in religious Orthodoxy, wedded to secularism, suspicious of religion, yet devoted to the familiar rituals of Judaism. And with them were their wives (many of them, like Ray Waterman, also Party members and activists) and children.

The men would all put on yarmulkes and everyone would listen to Chimen's rapid-fire Hebrew reading of the Haggadah; despite their avowed lack of religious feeling, they closely followed the rituals around which food to eat and when to drink their wine. Only after they had feasted on Mimi's Seder dinner was their irreverence let loose. Late in the evening, Collins would sing his favorite comic song, "The Yiddisha Toreador." "Moishe Levy vent to Spain, but not in a yacht or an aero-plane. Oh no; he had to go as a stow-away..." Along the way, Moishe makes a fortune and buys the ship he travels on. "Moishe arrived in a Spanish sea-port and he sold the ship vot he'd recently bought. He pulled a few vires and started some fires and had a good veek in the bankruptcy court. And so to escape from the toils of the law, Moishe became a toreador. Vot? A Yiddisha toreador. Yes, a Yiddisha toreador." And so on, until the climactic scene when Moishe suffers an ignominious death, after losing a fight and ending with a "bull's horn up his *tuchiss.*" It was the Marx Brothers meets the Marxists.

———

Levity included, Passover was one of the central rituals on my grandparents' calendar, as well as that of their friends—on a par with, say, the May Day workers' holiday, when they would go to the union-organized rallies; or October 25, when they commemorated the storming of the Winter Palace in 1917. These were people who felt the weight of history—the pogroms of their parents' generation, the Holocaust of their own youth—and who did not believe that history gave them the luxury to pick and choose their deepest identities. They were Jewish to the core: not revolutionaries who happened to be Jews but Jews who chose to be revolutionaries.

They could—and did—debate the implications of this combination of Jewishness and Socialism: Should they be Socialist Zionists or internationalists, and should their primary emotional allegiance be to the Soviet Union or to the new State of Israel? For some, including Chimen, their views on these issues were not fixed, and over time they came to reverse their positions.

In July 1946, just before his thirtieth birthday, Chimen wrote that "For over a quarter of a century Britain has kept Palestine under an iron rule by, at one time, encouraging Jews at the expense of Arabs and, at another time, siding with Arabs against Jews, taking advantage of every situation." Rather than a Jewish state, he wrote, "Now is the time to stretch out a hand to the Arab progressives and fight for an independent, democratic, Palestine." Fourteen months later he wrote, presciently, that a partition and the creation of a Jewish state would result in a "precarious dependence of a partitioned Palestine on foreign imperialist forces, be they British or American." Yet the following year, in June 1948, just after Israel had declared independence, my grandfather edited a "Special Palestine Number" of the *Jewish Clarion*, which included his front-page article under the banner headline "HANDS OFF ISRAEL." In it he gleefully celebrated the new country's birth. "The new Jewish state of Israel is a fact," he opined. "It has been recognised by all the leading Powers and welcomed by all democratic Governments. Only the British Labour Government withholds recognition. The British authorities are, in fact, doing all they can to destroy the new state." His article concluded with a typical rhetorical flourish: "All support to the new state. Long live Israel!" He was, I am sure, writing from the heart. But it did not hurt that, over the previous months, the Soviet Union had performed a spectacular volte-face on the question of Israel, trading opposition for support, largely in order to irritate the British authorities.

Whatever the reasons for Chimen's changed tone about the creation of a Jewish state, it was the beginning, emotionally, of a crucial shift in allegiance. Ultimately, that shift would take him from a vision of international Communism to a vision of Zionism in Israel and social democracy in Britain; from a dream of revolution to a belief that most change in most countries at most moments in time occurs gradually. Ultimately, it moved him from Bolshevism to liberalism.

The transformation took years to mature, years during which he was still a largely uncritical supporter of the Soviet Union. It was partly a transformation born of shifting political beliefs, and partly one fueled by a personal tragedy that struck the family in 1948 when Chimen's nephew Jonathan (whom Chimen had last seen as a toddler in what was then still Palestine a decade earlier) was shot dead on the streets of Jerusalem during the Palestinian revolt that followed the declaration of the State of Israel. Chimen had helped his older brother, Yaakov David, his wife, and their infant son to find an apartment in Jerusalem when they moved to the city from London in April 1937, just months after finally being freed into exile by the Soviet authorities. At the time, Chimen recalled with amusement, Yaakov David spoke a rarified form of classical Hebrew, elegant, highly polished, yet virtually incomprehensible to ordinary people. It was, he said, as if his brother were choosing to speak Chaucer's English during everyday interactions on the streets of modern London. Perhaps starved of adult conversation as a result, he had monopolized Chimen's attention, preventing him from playing with the young boy. Chimen did not recall very many details about his lost nephew.

The author Amos Oz wrote about Jonathan's murder in his memoir *A Tale of Love and Darkness*. According to Chimen, Yehezkel poured out his feelings to a fellow rabbi living in Switzerland, in a long letter written in Hebrew, after the killing. Shortly afterward, Chimen told my cousin, Ron Abramski, in a 2003 interview about his life, Yehezkel apparently suffered a heart attack. For the family as a whole, Jonathan's death must have been a shattering experience. How did the murder of a child, so intimate both in its execution and its consequences, fit into a one-size-fits-all philosophy that preached that, if only everyone recognized the brotherhood of man, a universal, everlasting peace would inevitably follow? How did Comintern slogans, no matter how grandiloquent their phrasing, help with the intense grief unleashed by such a personal catastrophe?

Bit by bit, at first subconsciously, later quite explicitly, the ground was being laid for a new political perspective, for a new, less utopian understanding of the human condition. Decades later, Chimen attempted to explain this shift. "When I was involved in politics and had contacts with leading Arabs in every Arab country in the Middle East I realised, fully, the total hostility of all the Arabs that I encountered, and their leading representation of the Left in Arabian countries, to the existence of the State of Israel," Chimen wrote to his friend Walter Zander in June 1976. "Without exception, all were for its total destruction, and I became utterly despairing of discussing the Jewish question with them: they showed no compassion or feeling for it." He ended his letter by warning against "idealism in a vacuum." Many of the guests around the Seder table went through a similar change of heart.

But while they debated most things political—from Communism to nationalism, from Zionism to colonialism—what Chimen and this circle of first-generation Jewish Communist immigrants from Eastern Europe never questioned was their adherence to at least the rudiments of Jewish ritual, to the modes of behavior that had governed the lives of tens of generations of their ancestors in the little villages and shtetls of Eastern Europe. Such a line of questioning they would leave for future generations. They would leave it to their children and grandchildren, to the younger generations who were reared in democratic, assimilationist cultures, their realities far removed from the deadly violence of the pogrom, the Holocaust, and the wars of the Middle East.

———

In many ways that circle of friends around the dining-room table at Hillway were the latest incarnations of a long line of Jewish thinkers, scholars, and revolutionaries whom the writer Isaac Deutscher described in his posthumously published 1968 essay "The Non-Jewish Jew." "The Jewish heretic who transcends Jewry belongs to a Jewish tradition," he wrote, in a book to be found in Chimen and Mimi's dining room, to the left of the little piano. "Spinoza, Heine, Marx, Rosa Luxumburg, Trotsky, and Freud. You may, if you wish to, place them with a Jewish tradition. They all went beyond the boundaries of Jewry. They all found Jewry too narrow, too archaic, and too constricting. They all looked for ideals and fulfilment beyond it, and they represent the sum and substance of much that is greatest in modern thought, the sum and substance of the most profound upheavals that have taken place in philosophy, sociology, economics, and politics in the last three centuries." Initially Chimen had slammed Deutscher. Writing in a Party publication, C. Allen had penned a long essay accusing the author of being an anti-Soviet Trotskyist. Later he came to appreciate Deutscher's writings on the radical Jews of the modern era. For Deutscher, who saw himself within this intellectual lineage, "they were born and brought up on the borderlines of various epochs. Their mind matured where the most diverse cultural influences crossed and fertilized each other. They lived on the margins or in the nooks and crannies of their respective nations." In the immediate postwar years, one such nook was the Communist Party and its various committees.

The original mandate of the Historians' Committee was to update A. L. Morton's *A People's History of England*, which had served as the Communist Party's de facto reference guide for English history since its publication in 1938, and Maurice Dobb's huge book *Studies in the Development of Capitalism*. Dobb, a colleague of Piero Sraffa's at Trinity College, Cambridge, was a leading Marxist economist at the time. To those ends, the members divided the work, setting up committees on different themes, working to build alliances with historians around the country and, ultimately, around the globe. Some (including Christopher Hill) specialized in sixteenth- and seventeenth-century English history and the religious schisms, civil war, and economic transformation of that era; others (most notably Hobsbawm) focused on nineteenth-century imperialism; while another group, including E. P. Thompson, John Saville, and Raph Samuel, concentrated on the history of labor and the working class in the era of the industrial revolution. "It was," Hobsbawm recalled sixty years later, "in effect a ten-year seminar, in which we talked with each other and talked over historical problems."

Members of the group, convinced that their work would help establish the tone for the coming revolution in Britain, set up the influential journal *Past and Present*. When the revolution did not unfold as planned, they set out to understand why. And later on still, in the more critical, anti-USSR years of the late 1950s, as the Party line became increasingly hard to swallow, Chimen's good friend Saville, along with Thompson, established a heretical journal, *The Reasoner*, to challenge the party orthodoxy. In *The Reasoner* they tackled the issues laid out in Soviet leader Nikita Khrushchev's 1956 "Secret Speech" (a speech that was not, in fact, at all secret), which bluntly acknowledged the horrendous crimes that had occurred in the name of Communism under the rule of Stalin; they also used the journal to air grievances after the British Communist Party's Executive Committee attempted to stifle the burgeoning dissent that emerged within its ranks in the wake of that speech. R. Palme Dutt, the Party's leading theoretician and Chimen's friend from the war years, had gone so far as to dismiss Khrushchev's revelations as "spots on the sun."

Saville and Thompson insisted on their right to dissent from this view. The Party, used to absolute obedience to its diktats, was not amused. In a series of increasingly acrimonious letters, members of the Executive Committee ordered Saville and Thompson to cease and desist publication; to appear before the Political Committee to answer for their sins; and to acknowledge that the Party was "the envy of every other working class organization for the level of its activity and the devotion of its membership." There is an Alice in Wonderland quality to the language. As people around the world were shuddering at the horrors detailed by Khrushchev—and as Communists throughout the West were being forced to acknowledge that the critiques of the Soviet Union that they had so long dismissed as capitalist propaganda were largely true—the Party's general secretary blithely asked the two historians, "Can you seriously compare our inner-party democracy with that of any other organization? Do you honestly expect to find a better party elsewhere?" Used to living under siege, the Party could not tolerate any dissent, Pauline Harrison, a molecular biologist and the wife of Royden Harrison, another dissident historian, came to believe. Dare to strike out on your own, to think for yourself, to exercise your critical faculties, and its leaders immediately moved to censor you or, worse, to ostracize you: Your erstwhile friends and comrades would simply refuse to talk to you, to acknowledge your existence. "I wouldn't call it a cult exactly," Pauline noted wryly, in conversation fifty-six years after she left the Party, but "it was a tightly knit organization. There were Party lines, and you were supposed to obey." Unwilling to accept the Party's convoluted logic, and embittered by the revelations of atrocities, outraged by the Soviet invasion of Hungary which followed quickly on the heels of Khrushchev's speech, and sickened by the Party's authoritarian treatment of intellectual dissent in Britain, Thompson and Saville left the Party. A few months before his final resignation, Thompson wrote that the Executive Committee of the Party would, if it ever achieved power in Britain, instantly destroy liberties carefully nurtured over three hundred years.

During those same months of 1956–57, Mimi, her sisters, Raph, several of her cousins, and many close friends all joined Saville and Thompson in fleeing the Party, although, nearly forty years later, Mimi wrote to me that she did not like the word "flee" in this context. "People 'flee' when they are pursued by terror," she explained.

"The people who 'fled' were the people who lived in a modicum of freedom. They 'left' the party because they no longer believed it represented what they believed in." Yet it seems to me that "flee" is not too strong a word here. Forced to view the true visage of the Soviet Union, they shuddered in horror not only at the nature of the beast but also at their own complicity in its actions. "Crimes were perpetrated in the Soviet Union and in the New Democracies which in character (using physical and mental torture of the vilest kinds, terror against relatives and friends of victims, deportations of whole nationalities, etc.), and in results (frame up and murder of hundreds of thousands, and imprisonment of millions of honest communists and people friendly to Socialism, including some of the most outstanding fighters for our cause)—were amongst the worst the world has ever seen," Mimi's sister Minna wrote to her Branch Committee, on May 22, 1957, explaining her decision to leave the Party. "I know that most Party members, at all levels, are basically not only very good people, but people who have dedicated themselves to work for the betterment of mankind. It has shaken me to the core to find that they can view with comparative equanimity mass murder, torture, and unspeakable crimes committed in their name against their own comrades."

A year later, the Italian publisher Giangiacomo Feltrinelli (who was at that time involved in a long correspondence with the Russian author Boris Pasternak, encouraging him to fight Soviet attempts to ban Russian-language editions of his novel *Doctor Zhivago*, and who in 1957 had begun selling an Italian translation of the masterpiece) wrote, crestfallen, to Chimen that they were living through "a very difficult moment for all sincere socialist [*sic*] and communist [*sic*], for all those who trust fully to apply the great lesson of Marx and Engels." Intolerance and dogmatism, Feltrinelli continued, were "seriously tempering the progress of human society."

Somehow, inexplicably, for two more years after the invasion of Hungary and after Khrushchev's revelations about Stalin's crimes, Chimen remained a Party member. He struggled to take off the blinkers that had been so much a part of his daily existence for so many years. He was, I am sure, petrified about what the world would look like once they were removed; as scared as a blind man, who has finally learned to navigate his sightless world—even, like King Lear's blinded friend Gloucester, to marvel at the interior sight of the eyeless—being told that, with surgery, he might see again. "People so much wanted to believe in this idealistic future," explained Pauline Harrison. "It was a search for meaning. A religion that believed in people rather than an external being. A sort of religion, but not totally blind."

Gradually, though, the pressure became too much. Mimi no longer wanted anything to do with the Party. Good friends like Saville had been hounded for their refusal to toe the party line. Others, like Pauline's husband, Royden, a historian at Sheffield University, had simply decided that remaining in the Party demanded too many intellectual contortions. "You owed it an enormous loyalty," Pauline remembered. "On the other hand, it was an enormous relief—to give up something you were defending even though you no longer believed in it." In 1958, Chimen left the Party. He had finally come to believe that the liberal world of ideas to which he had already started to temperamentally tie his fortunes was ill-equipped to stand up to the tyrannical impulses of revolutionary leaders.

The events of 1956 had corroded Chimen's sympathy for the Soviet Union; yet the invasion of Hungary did not trigger his immediate exit from the Party. Rather, the trigger was the discovery that everything he had believed about the Soviet Union as a place where anti-Semitism no longer existed was wrong. And, by extension, it was the psychologically devastating conclusion that if he was wrong about how the Soviets were treating the Jews, he was probably also wrong about many of his other assumptions about life in the USSR. It was the work of his good friend Hyman Levy, and his treatment by the Party, that finally brought Chimen to this realization.

Levy, a professor of mathematics at Imperial College, London, was thrown out of the Party for having had the temerity to write that anti-Semitism was a problem in the Soviet Union. "I feel I must take my stand on the question of covering up anti-Semitism," he wrote to Chimen, on small letterhead paper from Imperial College's Huxley Building, in 1958. "I owe it to all those Jews who over many years have been assured that in the Soviet Union these relics of Czarism have passed." To true believers in the utopian, post-nationalistic qualities of the USSR, such sentiments were, quite literally, treasonous. Levy's outrage had been growing for several years already. In fact, five years earlier, on April 16, 1953, he had written to Chimen criticizing his unquestioning acceptance that the Jewish doctors accused of trying to poison Stalin must, by virtue of the fact that they had been put on trial, be guilty. "You suggested," he admonished Chimen, "that I ought not to suggest the possibility of the Moscow Doctors not being guilty, but should know that if the Soviet decides to go ahead the case must be complete." Since their disagreement over the Doctors' Plot, Stalin had died, the case had been dropped, and the new Soviet leadership had made it clear that there had never been any real evidence against the doctors in the first place. "Do you think it is now possible to say that that attitude on your part was mechanistic?" Levy asked, gently chiding his friend. "I don't mind being made to look a fool if it is absolutely essential—but I think it could sometimes be avoided by a little discretionary criticism. What do you think?"

Now, with Levy expelled from the Party, Chimen's eyes had been opened and, like Levy, he could no longer stay quiet. The Party would not publish Levy's book *Jews and the National Question* (which, behind the scenes, Chimen had helped to write), so Chimen decided to use a small publishing house, which he operated out of his home, to produce the volume. He had established Hillway Publishing Company several years earlier to translate and publish the dissident Hungarian philosopher Georg Lukács's *Studies in European Realism*. For Lukács's book, he had hired a freelance journalist named Edith Bone to translate the work into English; Bone had been accused by the early postwar Hungarian Communist leadership of spying and was held in solitary confinement for seven years before her release in 1956. Now Chimen worked to make sure that Levy's book was translated from English into a number of other languages. Parts of it were subsequently reprinted in French by Jean-Paul Sartre's magazine *Les Temps Modernes*, alongside a lengthy and very personal attack on Levy and Chimen by Dutt. As with his publication of Lukács, who for a time was one of Europe's most influential intellectuals, so with Levy's volume: The timing was right. The book was republished, to considerable attention, in New York, Milan, and Israel. Perhaps to remind himself of its importance, Chimen kept a little notebook, no bigger than his annual diaries, in which he meticulously recorded sales of Levy's book.

Previously Chimen had believed in reform from within the Party, in the idea of progress through a strongly Marxist organization. Now he increasingly felt that the political institution itself was a menace, that revolution was destined to become something nasty, almost cannibalistic. A few years later, as his estrangement from Communism deepened, he wrote a note to Isaiah Berlin bemoaning "the tragedy of us intellectuals. We are the ineffective forces in society: the Lenins, Titos, Maos, Castros triumph, and we poor liberals are cast aside."

———

Riven by a fit of fratricidal fury, he kills off C. Allen and all his other aliases. He becomes, again, simply Chimen Abramsky.

———

The salon temporarily collapsed in on itself. Old friends who remained in the Party wanted nothing to do with people they regarded as renegades. New friends had not yet replaced those who left. In Chimen's letters from this period one senses an uncomfortable silence settling over Hillway. As the Communist salon that was Hillway's first incarnation, its first republic if you will, imploded, Raph, who insisted on addressing anyone and everyone in his social circle as "Comrade," at twenty-three years old set up his own gathering spot, the Partisan Café, on Carlisle Street in Soho, as a more bohemian, albeit commercial, alternative to Hillway. "Raph could talk the hind legs off a donkey," Hobsbawm said, and he also could convince people to invest time and money in the most speculative of projects. Hobsbawm was persuaded to put up some money and ended up with the title of café director. He was not the only one to provide financial backing for Raph's venture. "Shoes!" Martin Mitchell remembered more than half a century later. "Without the shoes it would have been much more difficult to find a millionaire benefactor. It happened like this. We get an urgent call early one morning from [his wife] Lily's cousin Raphael, or Ralph [*sic*] as he later called himself. 'Lily, can you help me? My shoes are falling apart. My toes are showing. I need a decent pair of shoes. I'm seeing Howard Samuel this morning. I'm hoping to get money from him for the lease. I want to look presentable. I don't want him to see my toes sticking out. Please help.' 'Of course,' said Lil. 'Wear Martin's shoes.' And he did. And he raised a tidy sum from the left-leaning property millionaire. Money was also obtained from a meeting in a Parliament committee room."

"It was a wonderful place; everybody went there at the time," Hobsbawm acknowledged, as he recalled his foray into venture capitalism. "The idea was basically they were going to get this house; it was going to be the HQ of revolutionary debate and action." Upstairs would be the *New Left Review*; downstairs would be coffee and conversation. In an era when the notion of a political meeting house–cum–coffee bar was so exotic that the BBC sent a camera crew to interview Raph about his aspirations, the Partisan became a gathering place for penniless intellectuals, who would come to debate, to play chess, to read the newspaper... and to drink one cup of rather mediocre coffee, sparingly sipped over the course of a day. Architecturally, it tended to what Hobsbawm recalled as "brutal modernism," a cavernous, minimally decorated room, chairs dotted haphazardly around the floor. Thinking they were being clever, the directors hired, Mitchell recalled, a self-proclaimed burglar to run their security; after all, who better than a thief to make sure the locks could not be picked or the windows jimmied? True enough, the windows were not forced open, but fairly soon after the man was hired food started going missing from the kitchen.

Not surprisingly, the venture soon went bankrupt, closing its doors in 1962. "It wasn't short of people going there. It was short of having more income than expenditure. When we complained and said this is not a financial proposition, they waved it away until it went bust," remembered Hobsbawm, as we talked at his home in North London a couple of months before his death. Many of the Partisan's denizens, who had migrated from the comforts of Hillway to the bohemia of Soho, now returned to spend their evenings in Mimi's dining room. Order, I like to think, was restored. There, they still talked about Marx, but now, as the salon slowly reinvented itself, without the uncritical attitude to the political systems that claimed to operate in his name which had previously reigned at Hillway.

————

Working full-time, and with two young children to take care of, and quite possibly also having to cope with Chimen's post-Communist blues, Mimi nevertheless maintained her kitchen and dining room as something akin to a full-service restaurant for roving intellectuals, family members, friends, and friends of friends from around the world. Now, however, the conversation broadened, the cast of characters became more eclectic. Now, hints of nostalgia began to intrude on some of the conversations, a touch of regret at worlds lost, bitterness at dreams betrayed.

Keeping the salon going was a "monumental effort," remembered my Californian cousin Alice, who started visiting Hillway in the late 1960s, a decade into its reincarnation. And yet Mimi "appeared to take pleasure in the things that she did for people. Dinner had to start with soup. Chimen wanted soup. And it ended with tea, lemon tea or English tea. Chimen would ask 'And now, I have a very important question. Who wants tea or coffee?' Dinner would start with just a few people and by the end of the evening there'd be twelve, and Mimi would have caught all of them up with the courses of the dinner. It was the endlessly expandable table."

"The house was always full of people," my aunt Jenny recollected, long afterward, of a period that must, at times, have seemed more like a political education camp than a recognizable childhood. "From all over the world, all different kinds of experiences. And all the time, every evening, there was political discourse and debate going on around the table. Being the little person, no one ever paid attention to me. I remember saying, 'It's Marx, Marx, Marx, all the time! Why do we always have to talk about Marx?'" Some nights, the dinner guests and Chimen and Mimi would descend into violent verbal arguments—over interpretations of Marx's writings, over responses to events in the Soviet Union. Not infrequently, someone would push their chair back and theatrically storm out of the house. In reaction to this, Jenny made a point of deliberately not remembering any of the political theory that she was subjected to around the dining table. Worse still, when she was given a general-knowledge quiz at her high school in the late 1950s, and was asked to name the author of *Mein Kampf*, she confidently asserted "Karl Marx." Chimen, when he heard about this, was thunderstruck. I can imagine his eyes getting large, his jaw clenching. What I cannot quite see is whether he then smiles and lets his daughter's faux pas go with a mild rebuke or launches instead into a long political lecture. I want to think the former; in all likelihood, however, it would have been the latter.

Years later, as he reminisced about his life, Chimen would casually mention how so-and-so, who used to come for dinner, had been shot dead in an Iraqi prison or disappeared in a terrible dungeon somewhere. One of his close friends, the Italian publisher Feltrinelli, who had helped Chimen scour the world for rare Socialist texts during the 1950s and '60s, and who frequently visited Hillway with his wife, had moved into extreme left-wing political activism; he was killed by a bomb in 1972, during the years of political turmoil in Italy. It was never definitively concluded whether he was killed by his own hand while trying to plant a bomb intended to sabotage high-voltage power lines outside of Milan or whether he had been assassinated. Shloyme Mikhoels, the director of the Moscow State Yiddish Theater, whom Chimen had met during the war and whose presence had been a rallying cry for Jewish Communists in London (he was, Chimen later wrote, the "outstanding Soviet Jew of the second world war"), did not escape. On January 19, 1948, he was assassinated, at the behest of an increasingly paranoid and anti-Semitic Stalin, on the streets of Minsk, run over and killed by a truck in a way that could be passed off as an accident. Shortly afterward, fifteen leading members of the Jewish Anti-Fascist Committee were arrested: These were famous cultural figures within Soviet Jewry and the group had been formed on Stalin's orders, a year after Hitler sent his troops east into the Soviet Union, to help rally international support, especially in the United States and Britain, for the USSR. In a secret trial held in July 1952, they were all sentenced to death. It was a far cry from Chimen's correspondence with Harold Laski, shortly after the end of the Second World War, in which they celebrated the fact that anti-Semitism had been laid to rest once and for all in the Soviet Union.

Belatedly, Chimen had come to realize what the Russian revolutionary memoirist Victor Serge had recognized years earlier. Living in Moscow as Stalin's murderous rule got under way, Serge chronicled the way in which the revolution cannibalized its own, how one after another of the Soviet Union's top politicians, intellectuals, generals, and economic managers was arrested, disappeared, murdered. How any criticism could lead to death. How any pretense could be used to liquidate a faction or a group of friends. How millions could be condemned to death by famine as a by-product of Stalin's

Letter from Harold Laski to Chimen, praising the end of anti-Semitism in Stalin's Soviet Union, October 4, 1947.

collectivization plans. Of the show trials that characterized this period he wrote: "It was raving madness....The Politbureau knew the truth perfectly well. The trials served one purpose only: to manipulate public opinion at home and abroad." Later on, Serge averred that "totalitarianism has no more dangerous enemy than the spirit of criticism, which it bends every effort to exterminate."

Yet despite the radical change of heart that Chimen underwent in his political views, he nonetheless remained utterly fascinated by Marx's life and legacy, and was immersed, through all these years of turmoil, with Henry Collins in writing their book on Marx. No longer a follower of political parties claiming to act in Marx's name, Chimen continued to believe that Marx's understanding of history, and his account of the ways in which societies change over time, was unrivaled. At the same time, in full retreat from the totalitarian vision of the Soviet Union, Chimen looked elsewhere for an intellectual and political home. He found the latter in liberalism and the former, increasingly, in the manuscripts and texts of Jewish history and religious writings.

UPSTAIRS FRONT ROOM:
ROOTS

I believe in Spinoza's God, who reveals Himself in the lawful harmony of the world, not in a God who concerns Himself with the fate and the doings of mankind.
—Albert Einstein, *The New York Times*, April 25, 1929

WE NEED NOW to go upstairs again, under *Guernica*, back up the steps with the moth-eaten carpet. And at the top of the staircase, instead of turning left toward my grandparents' bedroom, we shall turn right, go down the hallway a jog, and then, opposite the tiny, fetid lavatory, enter the large, cluttered bedroom off to the left. It is time to pay a visit to the crown jewels.

Growing up, I knew less about this room than other rooms in the house. Its books were peopled by writers whose languages I did not speak or read, whose worlds and worldviews were faint

Glimpse of the floor to ceiling piles of books in Chimen's study, which he called "the jungle room."

shadows to me but not to Chimen. On his curriculum vitae he wrote, under Languages, "(other than Classical, Medieval and Modern Hebrew & English): Fully competent in Russian, Yiddish and German. Fluent reading of most of the other Slavonic languages and of French." All of those, and more, could be found on the shelves of this room. He once showed a Bulgarian text to the bibliographer Brad Sabin Hill, who remembered fondly, "He made a point of telling me he could read it—which he could, of course. It was in Cyrillic." I slept in that room sometimes, on an old bed with a sagging mattress, but its resident authors seldom spoke to me. Chimen talked only sparingly to me about the books on these shelves, though I do remember him once, after a great build-up, finally taking down a first-edition Spinoza to show me. Unlike the Marx volumes, which he would let me touch, I had to look at this one from a safe distance—and then only briefly.

Unfamiliar as I was with the room's nuances, however, I knew from a young age that it was a vital part of the temple of learning that Chimen had constructed. There was something reverential about the way he talked of this room and its contents—and while the Marx books, even the rarest of them, were easy to pluck off of the bookshelves, the volumes in the upstairs front room were kept locked away on shelves in glass-fronted cabinets, the keys for the heavy doors zealously guarded at all times. Unlike the other rooms, which Chimen willingly showed off to interested visitors, this room was dramatically more private. Even fellow collectors of Judaica, even close friends such as Jack Lunzer and David Mazower, were only granted ac-

Chimen's first edition of Spinoza's
Opera Posthuma (1677).

cess occasionally, grudgingly. In this room, the shelves functioned more like a treasury vault and less like parts of an active library. On the rare occasions when Chimen opened the doors for me, a smell of musty, contained, geriatric paper would float out into the room and, liberated, make its way up my nostrils.

When Jack and Jenny were children, this room housed a long-term lodger, a Scottish lady by the name of Georgie Finlayson, whose rent was a vital part of Mimi and Chimen's precarious financial calculations. They had met her through the Communist Party, and for many years she lived as a de facto member of the family, sharing their meals and even their summer holidays. Later, as the family fortunes began to stabilize, Georgie left, returning to Glasgow, from whence she had come, and Jack took over the bedroom. Without books covering every wall, it was a rather large space for him to call his own. He proceeded to clutter it up with schoolbooks; with Native American feathered headdresses and other paraphernalia from the "I Spy Club"; with chess sets (he was, for many years, a fanatical and very talented player, part of a school team that made its way to the national finals one year); and eventually with a makeshift table tennis table. He set up a record player, complete with large box speakers that he made from a kit, and started to build his own collection—not of books but of classical music and opera records. Jack's collection of hundreds of vinyl discs were, in their own way, as timeless, as removed from contemporary popular cultural currents—this was, after all, the era of Elvis and Cliff Richard, of Bill Haley and Jerry Lee Lewis—as the volumes that occupied Chimen's shelves.

Jack and his friends spent hours in that room, emerging periodically only to disappear again to play atop the rubble of the large bomb site opposite the William Ellis Grammar School that Jack attended, or to play tennis or cricket on Hampstead Heath. And then they would return to Hillway to be fed by Mimi. "The house had gravitational attractions" was how Jack's childhood friend Andrew Moss put it more than half a century later. "My entire life it's been true. It was the house you went and hung out at." When Jack left in 1961 to study physics at Trinity College, Cambridge—an event noted with happiness by Piero Sraffa, on the off chance that it would lure Chimen and his suitcases of rare books to the college more often— Jenny gleefully took over the room; it was at least twice the size of the box room at the back of the house, which, as befitted the younger sibling, had previously been hers. Over her bed she hung a thin rectangular reproduction of a Turner landscape, its muted colors testament to the quiet prettiness of the English countryside. The picture hung there until Chimen's death.

It was only after Jenny moved out that the room began to take on its final incarnation as the heart of Chimen's Judaica library. For when his youngest child left home, Chimen promptly colonized the additional space for his books and, now firmly middle-aged, what little hair he had left graying, took stock of his life. His mother, Raizl, died in Israel in January 1965 after a five-year struggle with the rare blood disease aplastic anaemia. In a little logbook, Yehezkel had carefully chronicled the hundreds of blood transfusions she underwent during these years. She had, Chimen wrote to Mimi from Israel, faced her death stoically. After being rushed to hospital with a lung hemorrhage, Raizl had told her youngest son, Menachem, who had moved to Israel in the 1950s, "where to find her identity card for the certificate of death. Within forty minutes after the attack she died peacefully. Her funeral was on Saturday night." Chimen was forty-eight years old. He and his father, he reported to Mimi, had had a "good cry" together when he arrived in Jerusalem. Raizl had been,

Chimen told his great-nephew Ron Abramski many years later, "very aristocratic." Because she was descended from generations of famous rabbis, "she felt somehow she is an aristocrat. And she *was*. But she was a tough lady, very clever, a good fighter, a good organiser. My mother knew a lot about literature, which she read voraciously. Read Tolstoy, Pushkin, Gorky, Chekhov. She read a lot of Russian and Yiddish, couldn't write a Hebrew letter—though she could understand it."

With the members of the older generation dying off, Chimen was, I believe, starting to think more about mortality, about his place in the great fabric of Jewish life down the millennia, about his own obituaries. How would people remember him? He did not want to be remembered simply as a disillusioned Communist Party propagandist, or even as the greatest private collector of Socialist literature in the English-speaking world. As the focus of his interest shifted from Socialism to Judaica, so the center of his library moved from the bedroom, down the landing, and into the upstairs front room.

———

By the late 1960s, Chimen had completed his intellectual pivot. Where once he had been an obsessive collector of all things Communist, now he became almost equally obsessive about collecting Judaica. So much so that in 1969, when he gave the opening lecture for London's eighteenth Jewish Book Week, on the emergence of Jewish history as a separate academic discipline, he was introduced to his audience as "possibly the greatest Jewish bibliophile in the world." The shift in emphasis was not purely caused by his changing political philosophy; the market for Socialist books and memorabilia had taken off and he could no longer afford the few Socialist items he did not already own. "I presume that you have seen that Sotheby sold

Marx 'Das Kapital' 1867 autographed to Ludlow, for two thousand four hundred pounds to El Dieff, the well-known bookseller in New York," Chimen reported to Sraffa on June 26, 1969. "A really staggering figure. Books of Marx and Engels are becoming literally extremely rare." Two years later he gloomily reported to his friend that over the past years he had not been able to purchase any more rare Socialist literature.

But if affordable Socialist works were no longer coming onto the market with any frequency, the world of Judaica was ever more attractive—although by the 1970s, in no small part because of his own work with Sotheby's, those collectibles, too, were starting to move out of Chimen's price range. He had been instrumental in building up a market that was now, ironically, pricing him out of the small club of top-tier collectors.

Chimen had begun developing this side of his collection in the 1940s, perhaps ten years after he started buying political and philo-

Chimen's mentor in the book trade, Heinrich Eisemann. Date unknown.

sophical texts, partly because he loved the books themselves and partly for their resale value. Under the tutelage of Heinrich Eisemann, he had learned how to acquire Judaica at bargain prices from libraries that had been left to rot in the United Kingdom or looted by the Nazis on the Continent. Jack Lunzer, a businessman and close friend who, with Chimen as his right-hand man, later built the astonishingly comprehensive Valmadonna Trust Library, recalled that after the war incunabula (books and pamphlets printed before 1501) could be bought literally for shillings.

Of course, even in those penny-pinched days, other acquisitions were far more expensive. As an investment for Shapiro, Valentine & Co. (which by now they owned), in 1948 Chimen and Mimi, along with several other investors, bought a medieval manuscript. It was a copy of commentaries written by the eleventh-century French-born and German-educated scholar Shlomo Yitzchaki, known to posterity as Rashi and widely acknowledged as the greatest Talmudic scholar in history. Hundreds of years before the advent of printing, Rashi and his students had written their comments on individual passages of the Hebrew Bible (or Tanakh) in the margins of the manuscripts of the texts that they worked with, using the great store of rabbinic lore known as Midrash to interpret particular lines in the Tanakh. So, too, the scholar had penned a vast set of commentaries to accompany the Talmud. For generations afterward, other scholars added in their own tosaphoth, or comments, on Rashi's comments. And scribes painstakingly copied those texts by hand and circulated them among Jewish communities throughout Europe and the Near East. Today, Rashi's notes, along with the tosaphoth, are included in all published editions of the Talmud.

The manuscript that Chimen and Mimi purchased, their fragmentary correspondence from the period suggests, was worth a royal fortune: £10,000 in 1948, the equivalent of several hundred thousand pounds today. Exactly what that manuscript was, however—who copied the Rashi and when, whether its margins were annotated with secondary commentaries, where the manuscript was made and who owned it in past centuries, even whether it was one of Rashi's biblical or Talmudic commentaries—is another of those mysteries from my grandparents' lives that I cannot unravel. Their correspondence about it dates back to those months in late 1948 when Chimen was traveling around America. Mimi's letters, which he kept, leave out the technical details. Chimen's, which almost certainly would have included them, were not saved. What does seem clear is that for a few months, at least, they owned a one-eleventh stake in something Rashi-related that was very precious. They were forced to sell it when one of their fellow investors needed to realize his investment, and the sale made a tidy profit, which they promptly plowed back into buying more stock for the bookshop. The purchase and subsequent sale of the Rashi manuscript seems to have represented a crucial leap forward in Chimen's book-dealing career. He was now entering the big time.

As his interests shifted, so, too, did his professional relationships. Chimen stayed in close touch with Eisemann, but by the 1960s, as Chimen's Judaica library rapidly expanded, his mentor was elderly and increasingly frail. They met for lunch episodically and discussed manuscripts; but Eisemann was no longer the dominant partner in their dealings. Gradually, as his health faded, the old expert left the stage; Eisemann died in 1972, at the age of eighty-two. By then, Chimen had long since found others to share his passion for rare manuscripts. Chief among these was Lunzer. Several years Chimen's junior, he had been at school with Chimen's younger brother, Menachem, for a while, after the Abramskys arrived in London as exiles from the Soviet Union. After the war he had occasionally wandered into Shapiro, Valentine & Co. to buy books. Now, a generation later, the Abramsky connection was reestablished by a shared passion.

Lunzer, a successful diamond merchant and an immensely cultured man, had the money to buy the most rare Renaissance Italian Hebrew manuscripts and books; Chimen had the understanding of the history out of which these works of art had emerged to appreciate the importance of the collection that his friend was so focused on building up. Lunzer hired Chimen, after his retirement from University College London, as a traveling consultant to the Valmadonna

Trust Library. They made a perfect, albeit somewhat incongruous, book-collecting couple: Lunzer, a large man with the air of a successful businessman; Chimen, a diminutive figure utterly absorbed in his academic pursuits. Between the eighth century of the Christian calendar and the mid-sixteenth century, Chimen wrote, scribes writing in Hebrew had created a vast written culture, much of which had been destroyed during waves of expulsions and book-burning spasms. What was left, though, was enough to show the vibrancy of Jewish communal life during these centuries. He continued, "The Jews not only copied lovingly, and sometimes illuminated the Hebrew Bible, or books of it, especially the *Torah* (the Pentateuch), the holiest book, but they wrote and copied the large number of volumes of the

Talmud—the principal embodiment of the Oral Law, and the second most sacred and important text, which guided, shaped, and molded Jewish life from birth to death. In addition they wrote treatises of commentaries on the Bible and Talmud; original works in philosophy, astronomy, medicine, mathematics, the natural sciences, grammars, lexicons, and excelled in remarkable poetry, both liturgical, lyrical and love songs. They composed homilies, wrote chronicles and polemical works, and created a vast branch of legal codes and Rabbinic Responsa. In a word they created a civilization of their own." In an essay to accompany

Illustration from an early eighteenth-century *Sefer Evronot*, from Central Europe, in Chimen's collection. This book was used to calculate Jewish calendar dates.

Title page of the first
complete translation of the
Bible into Yiddish, printed in
Amsterdam in 1678.

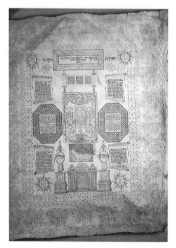

Illustrated manuscript wall
placard for Sefirat HaOmer,
counting the days between
Passover and Shavuot.

the catalog for the sale of the collector Michael Zagayski's books and manuscripts in New York in 1970, Chimen described how "Jewish scholars and philosophers wrote treatises on astronomy, medicine, mathematics, and the sciences. Philosophy was elevated to a royal throne. Poets composed deeply lyrical religious poetry as well as some of the greatest medieval love songs; Jewish mystics were engaged in fathoming the secrets of the universe, and seeking, sometimes desperately, a way to a universal and national salvation." It was this civilization that, in his upstairs front room, Chimen sought to resurrect.

For thousands of years, Jewish communal life had been organized around the spoken and written word. Virtually every aspect of behavior, both public and private, virtually every form of thought, every interaction—with kin, with country, with the earth, with the cosmos—was determined by the Holy Books, by an extraordinary body of commentaries, and by rabbinic musings and responses to those musings. Living in London, Chimen was at the epicenter of a different, much younger political culture, one which had built itself up around a set of common laws dating back to the thirteenth-century Magna Carta, and around a set of judicial writings dating back to Blackstone's work in the middle decades of the eighteenth century. Yet surrounding him in his own home were hundreds of thousands of pages of Talmudic texts, of minutely argued belief systems, that had defined Jewish life since at least the Babylonian exile. Here were contained millennia of arguments about how to understand the word of God, how to interpret history using these precepts, how to respond to any philosophical or ethical dilemma.

For Chimen, expertise in modern Jewish history meant having an intimate knowledge of at least five hundred years of history, from the time of the expulsion of the Jewish population from Spain under the Inquisition onward. In fact, of course, he sometimes lectured on aspects of Jewish life dating back much further. Once, he gave a talk on the development of Hebrew biographical writing in the ninth century of the Common Era; elsewhere he made reference to the expulsion of the Jews from England in the thirteenth century. What fascinated him was the texture of communal life, the ways in which individuals intersected with their milieu, the mechanisms by which the wheels of history turned. And, overwhelmingly, he was obsessed by the written evidence left by past centuries: books, Torah scrolls, manuscript fragments, letters, diaries, edicts, newspapers, poems, and songs.

Until he was well into his eighties, and already suffering from Parkinson's disease, Chimen traveled with Lunzer to visit the great Hebrew manuscript collections of Europe, sharing with Lunzer his excitement over the books and manuscripts that they saw. After one of their expeditions to a collection housed in Parma, Chimen wrote, in spindly, almost out-of-control handwriting, to his friend, "I could have spend [sic] there not two and a half days, but a few months. Again, my profoundest thanks for such an exceptional treat." Chimen wrote of examining the Pentateuch of Constantinople; Hebrew

Bibles from Soncino, Brescia, Naples, Pesaro, Lisbon, and other cities; books from as far apart as Kraców and Salonica, Tubingen and Mantua. And, he added, he had "listened to the divine voice of the ten commandments and 'schma Israel,'" the most important of all Jewish prayers. Writing of Abraham Garton, an early Jewish printer, he noted, "I hailed him as the Jewish Gutenberg. And I saluted to my 'ancient' master—Rashi—who enlightened millions of Jews with his exquisite clarity and exceptional brevity." Where Lunzer could afford to buy such manuscripts, Chimen had, on the whole, to be satisfied with high-quality facsimiles. Every so often, however, Lunzer would ceremoniously present an original manuscript to his friend as a token of his appreciation. Chimen would express great embarrassment, but nonetheless the manuscript would be secreted away on the sagging old shelves that lined the walls of the upstairs front room of Hillway.

Just as this room's bookshelves were filling up with books and manuscripts printed and painted and penned hundreds of years earlier, in the early 1960s came the Jacobs Affair. When the 1956 Soviet invasion of Hungary split the British Communist Party, Chimen had been deeply engaged in the resulting debates. But when the Jacobs Affair fractured the Orthodox Jewish community in Britain, Chimen, despite his growing involvement with the study of Jewish history, did *not* become publicly involved in the theological dispute, and watched from the sidelines as British Jewry was split down the middle.

Louis Jacobs was one of the country's leading younger rabbis and a scholar of note. At a time when both Judaism and Christianity were faced with the conflicting demands of tradition and modernity, Jacobs argued for modernity within the Orthodox tradition. He believed that Orthodox education should be fused with secular education and wanted young Jews in Britain to know about the religion of their forefathers while also culturally assimilating into the British mainstream. In an argument that had something in common with the contemporary debates in both the Catholic and Anglican churches, he urged his co-religionists to recognize the trends of modernity and to embrace change rather than instinctively resist it. His difficulties with the Orthodox traditionalists arose from his 1957 book *We Have Reason to Believe*, in which he argued that the Pentateuch was not literally the word of God, as had been believed by the Orthodox for millienia; rather, he had written that it was divinely inspired, but also a human interpretation of God's will—of how to live ethically and worship righteously. It was a similar conclusion to that reached by Maimonides eight hundred years earlier and by Spinoza in the seventeenth century. Jacobs's work, however, created a furor, as questioning the divine authorship of the Bible was anathema to an ultra-Orthodox rabbinate.

Jacobs had hoped to be appointed the principal of Jews' College, the country's leading Orthodox seminary for rabbinic students and a stepping-stone to the position of chief rabbi. Instead, he found himself fighting for his professional survival. In 1961, Chief Rabbi Israel Brodie issued a proclamation preventing Jacobs from taking up the headship of Jews' College, and for the next three years, Jacobs and Brodie feuded, more or less in public. In 1964, Jacobs tried to return to a job he had held previously, as the rabbi of the New West End Synagogue. Once again Brodie intervened, refusing Jacobs a license to take up a rabbinic position in a United Synagogue. Shortly thereafter, Chimen's father stepped into the fray in support of the chief rabbi.

Yehezkel Abramsky had long since retired from the Beth Din and was living in Israel, giving weekly Talmudic discourses to enormous crowds of followers; but from a distance he helped orchestrate the opposition to Jacobs. Where Jacobs, like Spinoza, espoused a more critical vision of religious observance and the role of ritual, Yehezkel clung to the Orthodox understanding of Torah as the literal word of God, to be obeyed in all its details. Schooled in the Musar yeshivas, he had never tailored his pronouncements to meet the shifting mores of the moment, and only rarely had he doubted himself after taking a position. One such case had occurred back in Byelorussia, when a sick man had asked him whether he could drink a glass of water on Yom Kippur. Rabbi Abramsky had told him he could not, and the man had subsequently died. Whether the lack of drinking water had anything to do with his death was beside the point; Yehezkel felt guilty about it. His biographer reported that, while he was in Moscow's Butirki Prison waiting for the death sentence the courts had handed down against him to be carried out, he conducted a reckoning of his life and concluded that this was one of the actions for which God was punishing him. Of course, in the end the death sentence had not been implemented, and Yehezkel had had ample opportunity since to make amends for the Yom Kippur ruling. He was a stern dayan but was widely regarded as a kind and humane man. When it came to Jacobs, however, he saw no reason to compromise his beliefs. The man was an upstart, a modernist railing against millennia of carefully worked out ideas and traditions. The historian Miri Freud-Kandel believes that he considered Jacobs "an agitator." It was, for Yehezkel, simply unthinkable that Jacobs could rise up the rabbinic ladder to the point where he would become a viable candidate to be Britain's chief rabbi. Louis Jacobs was denounced as a heretic by Yehezkel and others who shared his views. Not only was he excluded from the job at Jews' College but, because of the opposition of the chief rabbi and of leading religious figures such as my great-grandfather, he was essentially barred from ever again serving as a rabbi of a United Synagogue.

The story caused a sensation in the British media and has been described as the greatest schism in Anglo-Jewry's long history. "The Jacobs Affair is *the* theological scandal of Anglo-Jewry," Freud-Kandel explains. "Nothing compared." Outraged at his treatment, Jacobs, along with defectors from the New West End Synagogue, set up the New London Synagogue, where he founded a Conservative Jewish movement known as Masorti, outside the control of the chief rabbi and the United Synagogue, promoting a modern Orthodoxy and eschewing the ultra-Orthodox beliefs that men such as Yehezkel had brought with them from Eastern Europe in earlier decades. Jacobs became something of a guru to religious Jews of an assimilationist bent in London, something even, given the moment, of a countercultural hero to them.

What did Chimen, in full retreat from Communism and starting out on a near half-century project to study and interpret the modern Jewish world, think about this? Without a doubt, in private he sided with Jacobs—although he did so without picking a public fight with his aged father. Nor did he take a public stand on whether Jacobs was qualified to be chief rabbi—throughout his life, Chimen, a nonbeliever, was averse to stepping into controversies within England's Jewish religious community. But quietly he did reach out to Jacobs, and over the years, the two men eventually became friends. They would meet periodically and discuss trends in modern Anglo-Jewry.

In December 2005, *The Jewish Chronicle* conducted a poll of its readers: Who was the greatest British Jew since 1656, when Jews had been readmitted to England after centuries of exile? The winner hands down was Louis Jacobs. No Orthodox contender came close. Seven months later Jacobs died, his reputation now secured. I doubt if Chimen voted in that poll, but at the very least he would have been intrigued by the result. It gelled nicely with the ideas he had developed in a raucous public debate with Chief Rabbi Jakobovits in 1977, in which he had urged Britain's rabbis to not shy away from the secular and to reach out to young Jews with a fresher message. One could be a good Jew, Chimen argued, without necessarily subscribing to Orthodoxy.

Indeed, despite his growing obsession with all things Jewish, Chimen never re-embraced Orthodoxy. To the contrary, what most interested him about the great Jewish religious commentaries was how they related to the march to modernity: how Rashi's interpretations of biblical texts had segued into Maimonides's ethics, and how Maimonides ultimately led to Spinoza, the greatest of all Jewish philosophers.

Nearly half a millennia after Maimonides published *The Guide for the Perplexed*, Baruch Spinoza was shunned by the rabbinate for his heretical views: his belief in a God that was, in essence, "nature"; his conclusion that the universe was bound by inviolable rules of nature; and his argument that those rules, rather than miracles such as the parting of the Red Sea for Moses, truly represented the infinite power of God. Maimonides had depersonalized God yet retained the possibility of miracles; now Spinoza was, to all intents and purposes, turning God into another name for "the universe." Spinoza's God was everything; therefore, in some ways, the religious leaders who rounded on him realized that He was nothing. He existed so far removed from human concerns, so remote from human lives that the rituals of religion, the codes of conduct embodied in the Talmud, ceased to have any purpose. Infuriated by arguments for a God who seemed to have no need for coteries of rabbis and scholars to interpret His will, the rabbis excommunicated Spinoza from Amsterdam's Jewish community; his very name became anathema. Ultimately, however, Spinoza's ideas largely triumphed over those of his critics. Of course, many continued to believe in an activist, personal God; but, in the centuries following Spinoza's death, an array of Jewish thinkers turned away from ultra-Orthodoxy and sought answers to ethical and scientific questions using Spinoza's framework for understanding the universe.

In Chimen's library, one could see how Spinoza, a man ahead of his time, had influenced the emergence of modernity. He was a philosopher of religion who helped pave the way for the triumph of the scientific mind-set: He set the intellectual stage for Albert Einstein and the theory of relativity more than two hundred years later, as Einstein himself acknowledged. His God and Einstein's—the god who did not play dice, the god who presided over the space-time continuum—would have understood each other all too well.

In that overheated upstairs room, the ceiling of which would periodically suffer water damage after a particularly heavy rainstorm, Chimen would occasionally consult his first editions of Spinoza: a *Tractatus Theologico-Politicus*, printed in Amsterdam in 1670, and an *Opera Posthuma* from seven years later, published by Spinoza's friends shortly after his death. Also in that same room, Chimen would lovingly examine his first edition of Descartes's *Meditations*, which he had acquired from his friend Piero Sraffa in exchange for a letter by Lenin and a rare book by Engels. Unusually for a book in that room, it was not written by a Jewish author, but apparently it had earned its place there by virtue of Descartes's intellectual affinity with Spinoza, a generation his junior. You cannot understand the Enlightenment without understanding how Descartes and Spinoza broke down medieval certainties. Nor can you understand the Haskalah and the emergence of modern Jewish culture and politics without understanding the Enlightenment. By extension, therefore, Descartes was as much a part of the modern Jewish story, or of Chimen's particular version of it, as was Spinoza.

As Chimen's curiosity grew, so he sought to venture down practically every byway of Jewish thought and history. He owned mystical Kabbalistic texts and gorgeous Haggadot, some printed, some resurrecting the arts of medieval manuscript calligraphy, from the seventeenth, eighteenth, and nineteenth centuries, as well as a trove of rare documents relating to Sabbatai Zevi, a seventeenth-century mystic who had allowed his followers to believe that he was the Messiah, only to grievously disappoint them by converting to Islam at the point of an Ottoman sword. Zevi was one of only a handful of Jews forcibly converted by the Sultans during this period, and his conversion was viewed by much of the rabbinic elite with something approaching relief, since they had long maintained that he was a dangerous false Messiah. Perhaps because of Zevi's conversion trauma, many historians argue that he came to hold a profound appeal for Marranos in the Levant, those Spanish and Portuguese families forced by the Inquisition to convert to Christianity, who in secret had retained some aspects of their Jewish heritage. Zevi's humiliation was, they felt, theirs too. Spinoza's family, exiles who had moved to Amsterdam generations before the philosopher's birth, had been a part of this community.

The Kabbalah—the mystical premises of which intrigued, though never convinced, Chimen—expounded a doctrine of contraction: An all-encompassing, infinite God had, according to this theory, created the world by contracting Himself to generate an empty space. It seems to me that Chimen was trying to fill as much of that void as possible with words.

He had a Bomberg Hebrew Bible printed in Venice in 1521—the same year and place that the Tosefta (which Yehezkel spent a lifetime studying) was first printed and a mere five years after the city's Jews had been unceremoniously confined in Europe's first ghetto. That Bible was among Chimen's most prized possessions.

Daniel Bomberg was one of the great innovators of the printing press and created stunningly beautiful editions of the Bible, the Talmud, and other texts. In 1992, as Chimen wrote about a Babylonian

Talmud printed by Bomberg that he had been asked to evaluate, his joy at handling the volumes shone through. "Volume one has been affected by dampness, but otherwise the whole Talmud is in very good condition, wide margins, and with very few marginal notes. All the blank leaves have been preserved, which is most unusual for Hebrew books." The rarity of the Bomberg artifacts that he saw before him fascinated my grandfather: "Complete sets of the Talmud, whether of the first, second and third printing are known only in a limited number of sets. Perhaps a dozen or fifteen sets in the whole world."

Chimen's own Bomberg Bible was not the most famous version—those were published in 1524 and 1525, and came complete with essays by the editor, a Tunisian named Yaakov ben Hayim ben Yitzhak ibn Adonijah; extensive commentaries by both Rashi and Abraham ibn Ezra; and beautiful woodcuts. The margins were perfectly aligned and in some places the Hebrew commentary text spiraled around a verse in circles. But even if it was not quite of that caliber, Chimen's Bomberg was still extraordinary. Coming only three-quarters of a century after Gutenberg had first set his printing presses in motion, it was a technological marvel, a Stradivarius of the printing world. Bomberg was as far ahead of Gutenberg in style and technique, in the way he could manipulate space and play around with imagery, as the iPod was ahead of vinyl records half a millennia later. In the space of a few decades, printing had emerged from infancy into the full splendor of adulthood.

Chimen had another Venetian Hebrew Bible, this one from 1621, just a century later than his Bomberg. He had a Torah scroll from Prague, dating to 1610. And somewhere on those shelves were scraps from an even older Torah, this one from 1557.

In his bibliographic peregrinations, my grandfather had also acquired Hebrew texts printed in Constantinople in the early sixteenth century. One was a text from that city's greatest sixteenth-century rabbi, the Talmudic scholar, mathematician, and Euclid expert Elijah Mizrahi. This book, *Sefer ha-Mispar* (Book of the Number), was published in 1532, six years after Mizrahi's death, by his third son, Israel, and was one of the first secular scientific books to be published in Hebrew. Chimen had another Constantinople volume, too, from ten years earlier—within living memory of the capture of the Roman imperial city by Sultan Mehmed II's armies in 1453.

Paradoxically, perhaps, Hebrew printing in what would become the Ottoman capital developed centuries before Islamic printing in the city got a foothold, having been established as early as 1493 by two Portuguese brothers, David and Samuel Nahmias. In the decades that followed, the Nahmias press published more than one hundred books, in tiny editions that never exceeded three hundred in number, many of them written by Sephardic refugees from the Spanish Inquisition to the west. "Without the Inquisition," Paul Hamburg, the librarian of the Judaica Collection at the University of California at Berkeley, believes, "Spain would have developed as the center of Jewish printing in Europe. That didn't happen—because the Jews were expelled from Spain in 1492." On his mother's side, Chimen's rabbinic ancestors, he once told me, were among those who had fled from the increasingly intolerant Spain and headed east.

By the 1530s, the Nahmiases had been joined in Constantinople by Gershom Soncino, the scion of a famous Italian printing company. Gutenberg had printed the first books in Germany, but Jews within the Holy Roman Empire were not allowed to print Hebrew volumes. As a result, it had been in Italy that the first such books were printed, in 1475, thirty years after the German printing revolution. The Soncino family had been among the earliest of these printers. The Mizrahi book in Chimen's collection was one of Soncino's productions.

A generation later, these printers were joined by another Sephardic duo, the brothers Solomon and Joseph Yabes. With the Nahmias,

Soncino, and Yabes presses all working in Constantinople, the city became one of Hebrew printing's most vibrant locales, catering to the Jews living in Balat, a neighborhood to the south of the Golden Horn; in Haskëy, to the Golden Horn's north; and in Ortaköy, on the European side of the Bosphorus.

The leaves of many of these books were made of vellum, a thick, soft calfskin that sounded like small waves lapping up against the shore when the pages were turned; only the very best volumes were printed on vellum. The ink on these pages was as clear five hundred years later as the day they were printed. In a Bomberg Bible, even today, one can still see the black lines inked over certain words in the commentaries by Venetian censors, concerned lest anything remotely hinting at anti-Christian sentiment be allowed off of the presses intact. Originally, the pages would have been loose sheets tied together with a silk ribbon. Over the centuries, one owner or another had bound them in thick covers, the strongest of them made of pigskin (rabbinic rulings hold that, so long as the nonkosher animal is not eaten, its skin can be used to bind books). Some of the volumes had copper clasps, the metal blueing from oxidization, to keep them from flapping open. There were small symbols on many of the pages, instructions from the editors to the typesetters. There were commentaries running down both margins: Copies of Rashi's notes on the Talmud were typically given pride of place in the inside margin, or "gutter," while the less prestigious commentators' notes appeared in the outside margin. These were, in a sense, the original footnotes, a scholar's guide to how the text should be read. Chimen loved the detective-work quality of this sort of material, teasing out not just how the biblical text itself was understood, and how that understanding changed over time, but how the various commentators fed off of one another's ideas. Over the centuries, more and more commentaries were added. Today a Bible can include up to forty commentaries, the various authors' thoughts printed around the main body of the text in increasingly complex patterns.

I never asked Chimen how he felt when he touched Renaissance vellum, but given his ecstatic love of rare books it must have been an almost sensual thrill. "Look at the technology," Hamburg said, as he showed me a Bomberg that he had acquired for the Bancroft Library. "When you figure out all of it was done by hand—the straight lines and the columns, and the quality of the printing, and the fonts. I get very excited." Given the awful conditions in which he kept these jewels—Hillway was chronically overheated and the ceilings often leaked—I suspect that Chimen also experienced some relief knowing that these books were built to last. If they were going to reside in an environment as challenging as 5 Hillway, it was just as well that they were printed on a material as durable as vellum. Even so, the edges of the calfskin pages appeared mottled, as pocked by little brown spots as the arms of an old man.

One level down in the printed-word hierarchy were volumes printed on parchment. Slightly less expensive, but still beyond the price of an average sixteenth-century buyer, parchment was also made from animal skin (though usually sheep, goat, horse, or donkey, rather than calfskin) treated with lime and scraped and dried. The pages were still thick, but they felt crisper, more like card. They were more fragile, more prone to accidental ripping. Chimen had many parchment volumes too.

Most books, however, were made of rag-stock paper. Unlike wood-pulp paper, which came to be the norm from the mid-nineteenth century on, and which allowed for cheaper, mass-produced books to be printed, Renaissance paper had no acid content. As a result, instead of fading to brown after a few years and losing the integrity of its structure, as most modern paper does, the pages of a book printed four or five hundred years ago often survive intact and readable, even if kept in a place as climatologically unsuited to the storage of rare materials as Hillway.

The rare books on Chimen's shelves that were published in Ottoman Constantinople and elsewhere gave a sense of the tides of Jewish history—of who was being expelled from which country and when; of which ideas were deemed heretical and where; of regions of tolerance and lands of enforced orthodoxy. In his book purchases, Chimen was drawing maps of safety zones for Jews across time and space. In addition to his Constantinople treasures, his collection also included a number of volumes published in the Lombard city of Mantua, another safe haven for Jewish publishing in the sixteenth century. He had a Haggadah printed in Mantua and dating from 1560; there was also a Yiddish text printed there in 1560 or thereabouts. In his notes, Chimen gave no further details. Which means that it could have been a book titled *Yihus Bukh* (roughly translated as the "Ancestry Book"), a rare volume on rabbinical genealogy that would, very probably, have contained information on some of Chimen's rabbinic ancestors from Iberia. Except for the inconvenient fact that this book never existed and rumors of its existence were simply created out of thin air by a bibliographic scholar who mistakenly attributed a different title, in Hebrew, to this provenance; and, as rumors do, this error then circulated through the small world of bibliography, acquiring currency with the retelling. A careless mistake, a misreading of a few letters, and voilà, a quest for a Holy Grail. These were the sorts of mysteries that Chimen delighted in.

But while the volume was not the mythical *Yihus Bukh*, it may have been one of the early Yiddish imprints, from a couple of years later, of the Book of Kings. This unidentified volume, like the missing Voltaire letter, is a loose end: In the file-card indexes that he began compiling as a very old man, Chimen, in a rare slip for so meticulous a scholar, never provided a title for this book.

Completing his Mantua collection, Chimen also had several books on the Kabbalah. Mantua, along with Venice, had long been a hub for Jewish mystical thinking, and its printers had made a name for themselves printing the two most famous books of the Kabbalah: In 1558, they produced the first ever printed edition of the Zohar. This was a mystical Aramaic text on the unity of the Godhead, most probably written by the thirteenth-century Spanish rabbi Moses de León but attributed, by de León himself (on the time-honored assumption that in religion antique provenance confers legitimacy on an idea), to a rabbi from one thousand years earlier named Shimon bar Yochai. They followed that publication with bound books of the *Sefer Yetzirah*, a complex text divided into six chapters and thirty-three paragraphs, which claimed to have unlocked the secrets of the universe through a series of numeric and letters-based codes. Like the Freemasons several centuries later, they believed that extraordinary powers would accrue to those who could successfully decode these ciphers. Chapter six, paragraph six reads: "And from the non-existent He made Something; and all forms of speech and everything that has been produced; from the empty void He made the material world, and from the inert earth He brought forth everything that has life... and the production of all things from the twenty-two letters is the proof that they are all but parts of one living body." Everything, in this vision, is about the building blocks of written language, the letters that make up words, which make up sentences, which, ultimately, animate the cosmos. This is the poetry, the mystery, behind Chimen's obsession with the written word, with the construction of his House of Books.

Followers of the Kabbalah believed in a tree of life, linking ten central characteristics (or *sefirot*) of God's existence and of the universe into a complicated whole, bound together by a series of numeric and astrological mysteries: beauty, mercy or kindness, severity, knowledge, wisdom, understanding, kingship, splendor, victory, and foundation. Outside the tree was the all-encompassing divine will, which included not only the possibility of life but also the inevitability of death. Ten *sefirot*, and one crown, known as the *Keter,* and above the *sefirot* the *eyn sof,* the infinite divine. Eleven steps up the tree of life. Eleven times two equals twenty-two, the number of letters in the Hebrew alphabet, the magical number out of which all things emanated. Chimen was not a mystic, but he found something extraordinarily attractive about the notion of a world literally shaped out of letters and numbers. He kept, in that room, several beautiful, rare copies of the Zohar.

Behind the locked glass doors, there were volumes from Antwerp, from Kracόw, from Warsaw. As privileged visitors looked through the collection, they could see not just a history of the Jewish people going back five hundred years and more but also, and as important, a history of printing and of the variations in the Hebrew fonts used by printers on either side of the Alps, from its earliest days in Germany through to the establishment of great publishing houses in the mercantile cities of Amsterdam, Antwerp, and elsewhere. These books drew timelines weaving in and out of all these vanished worlds, chronicling the rise and fall of trading empires, the emergence of political centers, the passing of the torch from one hub of learning to the next.

———

Chimen's most valuable possession—valued for its rarity, its sheer beauty, and the name of the artist who had crafted it, and unknown to the rest of the book-dealing community—was nowhere near his oldest. It was a gorgeous, twenty-five leaf, illuminated manuscript Haggadah, complete with marble endpapers, lovingly designed in Hamburg—in 1829 according to Chimen's notes, in 1831 according to other scholars—by the scribe Eliezer Zussman Meseritch.

In an era of mass-production printing, Meseritch was a fish out of water, a connoisseur of the fine art of calligraphy, and a gloriously powerful artist. Several generations earlier, a few influential Court Jews in Germanic lands had commissioned manuscripts as status symbols, as signs of both their wealth and their culture. But by the time Meseritch came of age, the fashion had largely dissipated. He was determined to resurrect the dying art and used three different types of calligraphy: flowing, semi-cursive Rashi script; *mashket*, which was used in Yiddish and Judeo-German handwriting; and square Hebrew lettering. Within the manuscript were seven text illustrations, including miniatures of the four sons referred to in the Torah: the wise, wicked, and simple children who ask questions of their father during the Seder ritual, and the child who does not know to ask. At the end of Meseritch's manuscript was a striking image of the Temple in Jerusalem. Bound in thick red leather by the bookbinder Abraham Jacobson, Meseritch's Haggadah was, quite simply, extraordinary. How he had acquired it, Chimen never divulged. Nor did he explain its presence in his house on any of the myriad three-by-five index cards that were scattered in different drawers and shelves around Hillway, evidence of his stuttering half attempts to catalog his own possessions. As with so much else in the House of Books, the story of the Hagaddah's journey from Hamburg to Hillway was destined to die with my grandfather.

In a nod to practicality, for many years Chimen kept this Haggadah not at Hillway but in a bank vault. He could not see it unless he made a special trip to the vault, which must have offended his deepest scholarly instincts, imbued as he was with the idea that what he had in his house were his academic fields' greatest working libraries. But at least it was safe from flood and fire and all the other risks that came from living in an increasingly dilapidated old house. Later on, however, he brought it back to Hillway and carefully placed it in a green metal filing cabinet in his bedroom, the key to which he kept with him at all times. Meseritch's masterpiece now resides at the Center for Jewish History in Manhattan, where, one can only assume, it receives somewhat more delicate treatment than that afforded the manuscripts at Hillway.

———

While he was still a professor, luxuriating in his improbably late rush up the academic ladder, from adjunct lecturer to tutor to chair of a newly created department at University College London, Chimen proposed a book to several publishers on the great Hebrew manuscript collections of the world. Many of those publishers were interested. After all, the little man from Smalyavichy's knowledge was unrivaled. His involvement in the Prague scrolls saga, his triumphant connection with the sale of the Sassoon library, his acknowledged role in creating the global market for rare Hebraica had proved it. Chimen explained, in great detail, that he would need grant money to visit libraries in Paris, Copenhagen, the Vatican, Israel, the United States, and several other countries; and he carefully laid out his vision for the book. But then, there followed silence. After generating interest from the publishers, he simply failed to follow through. When it came to actually completing the work, this project, like so many of his other large-scale writing ideas—the biography of Marx, his own autobiography—just fizzled out. He could not find uninterrupted time for the research; he would not set aside the hours needed to fill in grant applications; he had too many conferences to attend and too many lectures to prepare. Eventually it became clear that the book would never be written, and gradually his correspondence with the publishers about the project ended. Nobody doubted that he knew more about his field than any of his peers, but at the same time, nobody—himself included—really believed that he would sit down for long enough to write the definitive book of scholarship.

For as he neared the age of retirement, Chimen kept up a schedule that would have been impossible for most men half his age. Having only received in his fifties the academic recognition he had long felt was his due, he was loath to curtail his career now simply because he had five grandchildren and had reached the age where he could claim a state pension. He was having the time of his life. He wrote more articles than ever, edited a book on Polish Jewry, and, most lucratively, spent an increasing amount of time evaluating manuscripts for Sotheby's and, later, for Bloomsbury Book Auctions, an auction house established in 1983 by Lord John Kerr, who had previously been head of the book department at Sotheby's. The materials that Chimen pored over and evaluated were almost like his progeny, said Nabil Saidi, an expert on Oriental manuscripts who worked with him for many years at Sotheby's, helping to rearrange Chimen's chaotic index cards into a format suitable for publication as catalogs. "Everything you catalogue becomes part of you. For him, it was his life. It was not just making money. It wasn't just purely a job. It was his life, day and night. I don't think he ever stopped thinking of manuscripts and books and pamphlets." In his handwritten reports to Kerr, there is an intimacy to Chimen's words, a sense of private worlds hidden behind public façades. "On Friday I went to Great Yarmouth and examined at the Vicarage the Scroll of Esther, which is Dutch mid 17th century," he wrote in late November 1988. "It's an important scroll, illustrated, though not in too good a state. My estimate is between three thousand pounds to four thousand pounds. In case the church will decide to sell it will require a careful description. I promised that you will write a report to the vicar."

The excitement that Chimen experienced when he encountered a printed jewel was contagious. Friends would share his joy at, say, discovering a volume from the town of Shklov—an area of Medinat Russiya (the Land of Russia) that had been a part of the Polish-Lithuanian Commonwealth, with a thriving Rabbinic culture and a Jewish population of sixty-five thousand, until the partition of Poland had delivered the land to Russia in 1772. There, geographically cut off from the bulk of the regional Jewish population, a Polish-Jewish island in a Russian sea, an autonomous Jewish culture began to thrive, which generated a number of important Hebrew-language scientific and artistic works. As a result of this historical accident, wrote the historian David Fishman, the Jews of Shklov became "Russia's first modern Jews." "This book is extremely rare!" Brad Sabin Hill remembers Chimen shouting out, his Eastern European accent accentuated with joy, his right forefinger wagging, when as a young scholar Hill visited the House of Books in the 1980s to study bibliography with Chimen. Hill, who went on to become the librarian in charge of the Judaica collection at George Washington University, pictured the five foot one Chimen practically jumping out of his seat in his attempt to convey the importance of the moment. "All books from Shklov are rare! Extremely rare!" Or, as he pronounced it, *Ehksh-treemlee hr-ayre*. It was, thought Hill, a worldview as much as a bibliographic statement. What it meant was something like "I have in front of me an artifact from a vanished moment in time, a glimpse into the lives lived by a fascinating group of people, who helped, in a peculiarly important way, to shape the Eastern European Jewish world. And if you're not as bowled over by that as I am, well I'm not sure we can go on with our conversation."

Chimen continued to globe-trot, going to conferences, evaluating libraries, searching for rare pieces that he could add to his collection. He visited Belgrade to deliver a series of lectures on the British Chartists, went to Switzerland, to Frankfurt, to Canada. He lectured in Oxford and London. Being in demand suited his temperament and gratified the ego that had been frustrated for so long by his lack of academic recognition. Several times a year, he traveled to Israel. Frequently, Sotheby's flew him to New York. He was acknowledged in the world of the auction houses as the ranking expert on rare Jewish manuscripts, with encyclopedic knowledge and phenomenal powers of instant recall, as the Cambridge historian Christopher de Hamel discovered when, as a young man newly hired by Sotheby's, he consulted Chimen about a photograph that he had been sent of a fifteenth-century Hebrew Psalter. "Chimen glanced in the direction of the photograph I was clutching," wrote de Hamel decades later, in a ninetieth birthday tribute to my grandfather. Chimen told him, "'It was sold at Parke-Bernet, July 17th, 1956, lot 14, $18,000. It was previously in the Siegfried collection, Frankfurt, Baer sale, January 1922, lot 3, 90 marks. It is missing two leaves after folio 17, leaf 61 is a modern replacement, and the prayer at the end is unique. And it is now worth sixty three thousand pounds to sixty seven thousand five hundred pounds.' My whole visit had taken, on a generous estimate, about four seconds."

Chimen reminded Saidi of a "bumblebee, going from one place to the other. He couldn't bear not being in the center of things. If he didn't know about a book [coming up for sale] he would be absolutely beside himself. He wasn't laid back at all. It would have been very difficult for Miriam to keep him under control. He was doing a lot of things at the same time. He was everywhere at the same time." I picture my turbo-charged grandfather buzzing from place to place and from book to book. As an audio accompaniment, I hear the last few minutes of Dmitri Kabalevsky's manic orchestral suite *The Comedians*, the string and brass sections racing against each other in a frenzy of explosive energy. Faster and faster, around and around, the notes conjuring all of the chaos and wonder of modernity.

If there were mists of time at 5 Hillway, they bubbled up out of this spare room in which the most-prized Hebrew manuscripts and books were kept. They were the mists out of which had emerged centuries of rich, if now obscure, Talmudic scholarship; out of which had germinated the great yeshivas that had shaped Yehezkel; out of which, finally, had emerged the Haskalah—the Jewish Enlightenment that sought to root Eastern European Jews in the secular world, the secular history, that was reshaping human society so radically from the eighteenth century onward. There were elements of all of these ideas in Chimen.

———

It was in the upstairs front room at Hillway that Shmuel Ettinger died one night in 1988 from a massive heart attack, while visiting from Israel. I remember the look of absolute devastation on Chimen's face the next day as he talked about what had happened. For the first time, Chimen looked like a very old man. Dazed. Overwhelmed. Shrunken into himself. Ettinger was like a brother to him, an intellectual soul mate for more than half a century, ever since they had met at the Hebrew University in Jerusalem, back before the war.

To a man more prone to self-pity, such a loss could have been shattering. But Chimen did not let it destroy him. He mourned Ettinger, wrote about him, but then he managed to move on. If it was his fate to outlive his contemporaries, then he would refill his well of friends with younger people, with scholars such as Dovid Katz and the journalist David Mazower, who increasingly turned up on Hillway's doorstep to learn from the master.

Quite consciously, Chimen now used his books, his vast, unique knowledge, to bring fresh blood into his life, to introduce to Hillway people with whom he could once again discourse and debate. "What a gust of fresh air it was for me to study with a master of the bibliography of my field, with a man who was the master of bibliography of many fields. He not only knew all the Yiddish academic books and journals of pre-Holocaust East European Yiddish studies (particularly philology), but he had most of them," recalled Katz, an Oxford-based New Yorker who subsequently moved to Vilnius, Lithuania, to study the history of the Yiddish language and culture in situ. Whenever he came through London, Katz spent hours at Hillway debating with Chimen. Katz argued that Yiddish was a vibrant, living language while Chimen averred that it was essentially dead. Katz was one of those few to whom Chimen willingly granted at least partial access to the inner sanctum, to some of the books in the upstairs front room. "One of the first [books] he showed me," Katz wrote, "was a 1592 book, *Mysterium*, by the Christian (and missionary) author Elias Schade (or Schadeus) which included a description of Yiddish that has remained important for Yiddish linguists to this day. I nearly fainted when he said he would gladly allow me to photocopy the pages I need and return it to him. He saw that too, and said, 'You see, I trust you.'"

Like so many others over the decades, Katz and the other young scholars who began attending the salon in the 1970s and '80s, were irresistibly drawn into all aspects of the Hillway experience—which meant not just handling rare books but also staying to dinner. And so, like flickering candles that do not go out, Mimi's kitchen and dining room, denuded of so many of their original guests by political dispute, by dispersal over the world, and by the passage of time, once more roared to life. They came to learn, and, after Chimen gave them little porcelain cups of coffee and slices of strudel or coffee cake, they stayed to talk. Soon they were regular visitors, as welcomed into the house as Shmuel Ettinger or Abby Robinson had been in years gone by. Mimi, now increasingly crippled by diabetes, would cook them dinner, as she had for generations of scholars. It was a gargantuan effort, but she simply could not bear the thought of not being a hostess. And when the grandchildren came around to visit, they would be absorbed into these conversations just as they had been in earlier years with older groups of friends.

"I met him because of a book," remembered Marion Aptroot, a Dutch scholar of Yiddish, who was working on her PhD dissertation at Oxford in the late 1980s. She was trying to find the first edition of a Yiddish Bible, printed in Amsterdam in 1679. But wherever she looked, she could only find the second edition, printed almost simultaneously with the first, but, she suspected, containing a number of textual differences. None of the libraries that might have had such a book did so. A copy had, apparently, once been owned by the Jewish Theological Society in New York, but it had been destroyed in a fire. Finally, Katz, her supervisor, told her to write to Chimen. She did, and promptly got a letter back. Yes, he had the book in his collection, and she would be quite welcome to come to London to look it over.

Aptroot made an appointment to visit Hillway. She arrived, and Chimen immediately took her upstairs to the front room. There he subjected her to what she thought of as a kind of entrance exam. "He'd open a book and say, 'What is this?' Just to test me. I passed the test. We had coffee. And then he let me work upstairs with the books." She returned several times as she compared the texts of the two editions. "He'd invite me downstairs for lunch. I'd go back up-stairs and work. He'd invite me down for tea. And then I'd leave." She found, in her work at Hillway, that her suspicions were correct: The first edition—the only known copy of which had somehow ended up in Chimen's collection—had been financed by a man who had held back a number of its pages as collateral. After he quarreled with the original publisher, he decided to publish his own edition of the Bible, using some of the pages in his possession to differentiate it from the original. Chimen was thrilled by the discovery. It helped bring to life these publishers who had lived three centuries earlier, to add emotion and human drama to their names. He thought, said Aptroot, that "it was exciting, from the point of view of book lore." They began a correspondence in Yiddish. When she visited, they would often lapse into the *mamaloshen*. "He was just so friendly, and the house was open. He was just a wonderful person to talk to and to discuss things with. He knew a lot, and also became a friend."

For much of his adult life, Chimen had been guided by Marx's admonition to action: "The philosophers have only interpreted the world, in various ways; the point is to change it." Now, as he aged, a subtle shift occurred. Increasingly he looked not to Marx but to Spinoza for moral guidance. "To be is to do, and to know is to do," Spinoza had written at his desk in Amsterdam in the late seventeenth century. It was also a call to action, but it was no longer an explicit call to revolution. Chimen remained vitally engaged in the world around him, but he no longer felt compelled to shake the pillars of the temple.

Thus, in later years, the upstairs front room, rather than the bedroom, became the intellectual epicenter of Hillway. Eventually, when Chimen was a very old man, he needed live-in help to be able to continue living in Hillway. To pay for it he sent a page from a twelfth-century manuscript to auction in New York, and the room became a bedroom once more, for a succession of Eastern European caregivers, economic exiles from the ex–Soviet Union and its satellite states. Occasionally Chimen would still venture in, especially when his old Sotheby's friends came around to visit and to show him manuscripts. Then, his enthusiasm fired up again, he would order his caregivers to strap him into the chair lift that carried him up to the first floor, would press the start button, and—to the horror of those watching from below—would accelerate up the stairs as fast as possible. At the top, he would be un-

Interior of Chimen's "jungle room," which was adjacent to the room containing his rarest Judaica volumes. The door to this study was usually locked.

strapped and then, with infinite solemnity, would totter into the room in search of hidden treasures.

But that was all in the future. Chimen, building up his Judaica collection, still had work to do; and the salon in which he and Mimi lived still had years left to run.

DINING ROOM RESURGENT:
REBIRTH

*We could then say that rationalism is an attitude of readiness
to listen to critical arguments and to learn from experience. It
is fundamentally an attitude of admitting that "I may be wrong
and you may be right, and by an effort, we may get nearer to
the truth."*
—Karl Popper, *The Open Society and Its Enemies* (1945)

AS CHIMEN AND Mimi's politics shifted, and as Chimen's book-
collecting priorities evolved, so the timbre of the gatherings at Hillway underwent a metamorphosis. Many of their firmest friends from
the Communist Party had also left the party (in their minds, they no
longer referred to it with an uppercased *p*) in the years following
1956. But most of those who had remained members now disappeared from the Hillway scene. Some no longer wanted anything to
do with the Abramskys. Party leaders such as Harry Pollitt—to
whom, nine years earlier, Chimen had sent a copy of Churchill's
memoirs "so that you can enjoy yourself reading what that 'bastard'
has to say"—and R. Palme Dutt viewed those who handed in their
membership cards as turncoats, renegades, class traitors; and they

discouraged their acolytes from maintaining personal relations with such individuals. They were, wrote Dutt contemptuously in *Labour Monthly*, deluded dreamers. "To imagine that a great revolution can develop without a million cross-currents, hardships, injustices, and excesses would be a delusion fit only for ivory-tower dwellers in fairyland who have still to learn that the thorny path of human advance moves forward, not only with unexampled heroism, but also with accompanying baseness, with tears and blood." For those who had lost the stomach for that bloodshed, who felt that their ideals had been utterly abused, Dutt had nothing but vitriol. With others who were too quick to toe the party line, too quick to stifle dissent among friends, it was Chimen and Mimi who cut the contact. For still others, among them Eric Hobsbawm, it seems to have been a mutual decision: When they saw each other, they fought; life was more harmonious apart. After a while, the invitations to Hillway were no longer extended and the casual visits for a cup of tea and a chat about history ceased.

There was some continuity, however. Hillway remained an epicenter for the family; old friends like the Pushkins and Watermans continued to visit; Chimen's great friends from the Hebrew University days made their way to North London as regularly as ever. But over time the tone of the gatherings changed dramatically. Marxist historians and Communist activists were replaced by liberal philosophers and historians—or were, at the very least, expected to discuss events other than goings-on in the Soviet Union and the supposedly imminent revolution in Great Britain; by relatives visiting from America, taking advantage of the rise of affordable air travel; by a growing number of wealthy businessmen–cum–book collectors; and, within a few years, by a new generation—me, my siblings, my cousins. Hillway filled with friends and their grandchildren, and their grandchildren's friends.

Politically bereft, my grandparents began to fashion a new community. For Chimen in particular, who had spent nearly twenty years in the party's inner circle, it was not always easy. There was something plaintive about his post-Communist persona: Loathing his past, he felt grubby when he recalled his enthusiasm for Stalinism and his defense of the show trials, yet he was nonetheless anxious to maintain contact with it. To Lazar Zaidman, his fellow theoretician on the Communist Party's National Jewish Committee, he wrote on March 28, 1959, "Dear Lazar, members of my former branch are boycotting me as an untouchable. When I left the Party nobody cared a damn, and nobody came to talk matters over. I still feel rankled [by] the way Hyman Levy was, and is, treated." Chimen went on, his small, precise lettering slanting gently to the right, to say that despite the party leadership turning against him when he published Levy and Georg Lukács, "personally I want to remain on very friendly terms with all party members irrespective of the differences I have with the party, and when one meets [wish] that we could freely discuss political differences rather than avoid them." He, too, had finally stopped capitalizing "Party."

Chimen missed the camaraderie of that organization. For years he and Mimi had taken the children to the annual Communist Party–sponsored Russian Bazaar held in the austere Victorian surroundings of St. Pancras Town Hall, where they could buy Ukrainian and Georgian embroidered blouses and other exotica. They had gone on May Day rallies, at which the whole extended family would proudly march through the streets of London. They had stayed in Socialist guesthouses in southern England, where Jack had learned to play chess, and they all spent the evenings watching grainy black-and-white films on such topics as the life and death of Lenin. But to stay within the party culture while critiquing its policy positions was impossible. The Communist Party could brook no dissent. Its very raison d'être was orthodoxy, requiring the rigid, unquestioning submission of the individual to the needs of the organization. When they were die-hard party activists, Chimen and Mimi had themselves broken with several close friends, including Mimi's first boyfriend, who had dared to criticize the Soviet Union. For years, Chimen had even avoided contact with his dear friend Shmuel Ettinger, after Ettinger had returned from a trip to the USSR deeply critical of what he had seen. To live and let live, as Chimen was now proposing, was apostasy. Even though he was, at that very moment, frantically trying to complete his book on Karl Marx, traveling back and forth on research trips to Socialist historical institutes and libraries in Amsterdam and elsewhere, and was already planning to write the definitive English-language biography of Marx—the project left forever unfinished when Henry Collins died of cancer in 1969—he came to realize that the relationships that had come from his decades as a party theoretician and activist were finished.

Over the years, Chimen's attempts to stay on good terms with former comrades like Hobsbawm and Zaidman floundered. Sam and Lavender Aaronovitch, who lived around the corner from Hillway, ostentatiously crossed the street when they saw the Abramskys coming; hostility crossed generational lines—it seemed to the twelve-year-old Jenny that the Aaronovitches had instructed Lavender's daughter, Sabrina, to stop playing with and even talking to the Abramsky girl. Other party stalwarts from the neighborhood also deliberately cut off contact.

Yet for all the emotional turmoil the breach with Communism entailed, Chimen and Mimi didn't step back permanently from their role as hosts. They could not. Without company around her dining-room table, Mimi would have withered away; without a crowd of fellow philosophes in the front room, Chimen would have crumpled.

As Hillway began a long march to becoming a liberal salon, its formerly Red hues bled down to a more muted pink. Where once the house counted among its most frequent guests the Marxist historians of the Communist Party Historians' Group, their places were filled by rising stars in the world of Jewish studies, American academics and civil liberties advocates, and European liberals and intellectuals. Scholars such as the lawyer and writer Walter Zander took the place of Hobsbawm; Rabbi Arthur Hertzberg, of the World Jewish Congress and the American Jewish Congress, came instead of E. P. Thompson. There were other new friends, too, such as Leo Stodolsky, the head of the Max Planck Institute in Munich, and his wife, Cathy; and the Israeli poet and playwright Dan Almagor, who had made a name for himself translating Shakespeare's plays into modern Hebrew.

As time passed, dealers in religious manuscripts and books on Jewish history became more regular guests than the dealers in Socialist literature. Where once Piero Sraffa had eaten Mimi's food and discussed rare volumes by Marx, Lenin, or Rosa Luxemburg, now Jack Lunzer popped in for conversations about incunabula. On occasion, Isaiah Berlin visited Hillway, although Chimen and he more often met either in Oxford or for lunch at the Athenaeum, Berlin's club in London, which Chimen regarded as practically hallowed ground. They would, perhaps, start with a drink in the bar, to the right of the entrance, its wallpaper patterned with gilded gold, a full-length portrait of Charles Darwin over the counter, settling into the deep-green leather armchairs as they began their discussion. After a while, they would move into the long dining room on the other side of the entrance, sitting at Berlin's favorite table, in the corner of the room by the windows overlooking Lower Regent Street, for a leisurely meal. After lunch, Berlin would escort Chimen upstairs to the coffee room, which was high-ceilinged with marble columns, quail-egg blue walls, and salmon-pink ornate draperies. On the shelves was a some-what random conglomeration of large antiquated tomes with titles such as *Illuminated Books of the Middle Ages* and *Spanish Scenery.* "In those days," Hobsbawm recalled shortly before he died, "the food wasn't particularly good. You sat down, nobody disturbed you. It's one of those grandiose buildings built in the days when the English ruling class was totally certain of its place in the world. 1835. Classical style. Great staircase. Marvelous drawing room on the first floor. With busts of the leading English intellects from the seventeenth, eighteenth, nineteenth centuries." Berlin would give long, very entertaining monologues "about everything: himself, gossip. Sometimes Isaiah would ask Chimen about Jewish matters. He may have asked him about Communist matters too. He liked to think he knew about what the Communists were doing. Primarily they would have talked about Israel." And in talking about Israel, in all likelihood they would have discussed their mutual friend Jacob Talmon.

Isaiah Berlin and Chimen, 1960s. Berlin's commitment to liberty was, Chimen said, "a beacon of enlightenment in a confused age."

Berlin had long been closely associated with Chimen's old friend from his Hebrew University days. Talmon had migrated permanently to Israel after the war (changing his name from Fleischer—the name by which Chimen had known him during their student years—to Talmon, taking the name of a biblical family that returned from the Babylonian exile to serve as gate-

keepers for the new Temple in Jerusalem) and had spent decades researching and writing a massive trilogy of books on Europe's violent
revolutionary history from 1789 onward. For Talmon, nationalism,
Fascism, and messianic Communist movements were all the heirs of
the Jacobins: As descendants of Robespierre and Marat, their casual
resort to extreme violence was the logical outcome of their admiration
for the Jacobin Terror and use of the guillotine against their enemies.
Carried away by their fervent rhetoric, intellectuals who defended
these movements were, Talmon argued, at least partly responsible for
spreading the virus of extremism that had done so much damage to so
many people throughout the twentieth century. "If modern ideologies were essentially a translation of old religious yearnings into secular and political frameworks," wrote the historian Arie Dubnov, in a
2008 essay on Talmon's life and work published in the journal *History
of European Ideas*, "then the intellectuals, who were functioning as
modern priests, were also responsible for this conceptual laicization."

In 1952 Talmon published *The Origins of Totalitarian Democracy*, the first volume of his trilogy. Perhaps he had Chimen—the
man who had helped him in England after he'd had to flee Nazi-oc-
cupied France, and who was now mired in Stalinist dogma—in mind
when he wrote that "Totalitarian Messianism hardened into an exclusive doctrine represented by a vanguard of the enlightened, who
justified themselves in the use of coercion against those who refused
to be free and virtuous." Chimen must have felt himself personally
attacked by Talmon's damning critique of those who participated "in
the pursuit and attainment of an absolute collective purpose" and
been dismayed by how his friend had lost his way and joined the reactionary ranks of the bourgeoisie. "Modern totalitarian democracy," Talmon sadly noted as he sat writing at his desk at the Hebrew
University, "is a dictatorship resting on popular enthusiasm." It was
an enthusiasm that he wanted no part of.

By 1960, when *Political Messianism: The Romantic Phase*, the second volume, came out, Chimen wholeheartedly endorsed its conclusions. Talmon, now firmly in the camp of Cold War liberals, explained to his readers that messianic politics "postulates an all-embracing exclusive doctrine, which is held to offer a binding view on all aspects of human life and social existence, including religion, ethics, the arts." Chimen might not have agreed with Talmon in placing all the blame for this development on Marx and the other great Socialist theorists of the nineteenth century, but, assuredly, he would no longer have argued with its central premise: that individuals, in terrifying numbers, had been sacrificed to false idols in the political conflicts that had spanned the course of the twentieth century. To him "freedom" now meant not the ultimate triumph of the working class but something much more individual, more classically liberal. It meant, he wrote in a tribute to Berlin in the mid-1970s, "freedom from chains, from imprisonment, from enslavement to other men—all other senses of freedom are an extension of this."

By then, Chimen was rapidly rising to the top of the academic world, propelled there in large part by the interventions of Berlin. Ten years earlier, it was at Berlin's recommendation that Chimen was invited to give a series of public lectures in Oxford in the early 1960s; and it was also at Berlin's instigation that he was subsequently elected to a senior fellowship at St. Antony's College, Oxford, in 1965. Chimen knew, all too well, how much he owed his friend.

———

As he approached the age at which most men slow down and gently slide into a well-earned retirement, Chimen grew increasingly proud of his academic achievements and stature, and quite self-consciously began modeling himself as an éminence grise. In the late 1960s, still

Chimen in his office at St. Anthony's College, Oxford, mid-1960s.

self-identified as a leftist of sorts—though he was no longer entirely clear of what sort—and now a part-time lecturer in modern Jewish history at University College London, he had tremendous cachet with the revolutionary graduate students. He would attend official meetings, tieless and in a rumpled jacket, and would sit with students in the basement cafeteria. By the late 1970s, however, he had graduated to wearing a suit and would hold court in the senior common room, surrounded by historians, philosophers, even physicists. His black-and-white faculty photograph shows him in a pressed black suit and tie, his gray hair bushy at the back like Einstein's, his eyes sparkling behind square glasses, one eyebrow raised slightly in what I take to be sheer delight.

In late 1974, Chimen reached an academic pinnacle when he was made the Goldsmid Professor of Hebrew and Jewish Studies at University College London. In the background, perhaps unknown to him, Berlin, the well-known Israeli historian Haim Hillel Ben-Sasson, and Hobsbawm had all lobbied furiously on his behalf. Hobsbawm went so far as to write a confidential memo to the university noting Chimen's "enormous erudition." Politically, he might have thought Chimen had sold out by abandoning the revolution, but he knew that Chimen was in a league of his own intellectually. As soon as the announcement of his appointment was made, Chimen, never one to embrace false modesty, made an addition to his passport. Under the space for his name, in which had initially been written "Mr. Chimen Abramsky," he added a proud amendment in bold, blue capitals: NOW PROFESSOR ABRAMSKY.

On April 25, 1975, at the age of fifty-eight, Chimen gave his inaugural lecture as Goldsmid Professor. Titled "War, Revolution and the Jewish Dilemma" and, somewhat incongruously, delivered in the chemistry auditorium on Gordon Street, it was a panoramic overview of the trials and tribulations faced by the Jews of Europe during the First World War. Among the huge audience of colleagues, friends, and family were Lord John Kerr (then head of the book department at Sotheby's, for whom Chimen was regularly evaluating Jewish libraries and manuscripts), Berlin, and chief rabbi Immanuel Jakobovits. Chimen spoke of political and literary movements in France and Germany; the role of Jews in science, music, literature, and commerce, both in Europe and in America; and the impact of "crude chauvinism" following the outbreak of war in the summer of 1914. "Even the Russian Jews, who experienced pogroms, blood libels, and ruthless discrimination, were drawn for a time by this wave of patriotic feeling," he explained. "The small, but very influential, group of Russified Jews became almost lyrical in their new patriotism." Of course, the newly minted professor continued, speaking quickly because he had to cover a huge amount of ground, that new state of mind was rudely intruded upon by the decision taken by Prince

Nikolai Nikolaevich, the commander in chief of the Russian army, to give more than 600,000 Jews twenty-four-hours' notice that they had to leave the border regions and relocate either to the Russian interior or to the cities inside the Pale of Settlement.

It was a tour de force. Chimen moved from Maxim Gorky to the poet Bialik; from the Balfour Declaration, which paved the way for the eventual creation of the Jewish State of Israel, to the Russian Revolution; from Lenin's nationalities' policy to Churchill's contempt for Russian Jewish Communists, for whom the British statesman "reserved his hatred, his passion, the powers of great rhetoric and, if one may say it, monumental exaggeration, bordering on grand folly." In 1920, Churchill had written an article in the *Illustrated Sunday Herald* in which he had denounced Communist Jews as "this band of extraordinary personalities from the underworld of the great cities of Europe and America," part of a "world-wide conspiracy for the overthrow of civilisation." Chimen approached the end of his lecture by quoting one of his favorite short-story writers, Isaac Babel. "I cry yes to the Revolution; I cry yes to her, but she hides from Gedali [the central character in the story] and her only messengers are bullets." Damned if they did, damned if they didn't, Jews ended up attacked from all sides: blamed for revolution; blamed for lost battles and failed wars; blamed, if they were Zionists, for not being internationally Socialist-minded enough; blamed, if they supported the overthrow of the tsar, for being too Socialist. He fell back on Spinoza for the final word. Historians, he now believed, like philosophers, had a duty "neither to laugh nor to cry, but to understand." It was one of his favorite quotations, one he would also include in a letter full of advice that he wrote me as I set out on my writing career in New York in the mid-1990s.

Four decades after Chimen's University College lecture, I can imagine how it must have felt to stand there, a tiny man on a large stage, close to sixty years of age, basking in the applause that built to a crescendo around him. I imagine him looking over at Mimi, tears starting to well up. I picture him looking at my father, Jack, and my mother, Lenore; at my aunt Jenny; at my cousins; and at a sea of luminaries from the worlds of academia and British Jewry. And in my head I hear him, I hear his wonderful accent, I hear him utter the words: "I am just a little man, but I know something about history."

———

Afterward, flushed with his success, Chimen engaged in a long correspondence with the university's publishing arm, eventually convincing them to contract with the publishing company of H. K. Lewis and Co. to print seven hundred copies of the lecture for public distribution; Chimen paid for the majority of the printing costs out of his own pocket. There was, he wrote to his university, a huge demand for the lecture. Contrary to his expectations, however, the booklets were not snapped up and decades later, dozens of copies—thirty-three pages in a simple gray stiff-papered binding, meticulously referenced with seventy-five footnotes (and containing a short acknowledgment that historians such as Martin Gilbert differed with Chimen on his interpretation of Churchill's anti-Semitism in the post–Russian Revolutionary years)—could still be found in boxes among his personal papers in the university's basement archives.

Now, however, nothing could contain Chimen's irrepressible intellectual wanderlust. After decades in the academic wilderness, he was at the top of his game. A decade earlier, Berlin had responded to the secret note that Mimi had sent him, begging for help in getting Chimen an academic job, by saying that it would take a miracle to get him the sort of job he merited, despite his erudition, his panoramic knowledge, and his skills as a teacher, because he lacked formal academic qualifications. Now, somehow, that miracle had happened. Exhibiting the energies of a far younger man, Chimen accepted any and all academic invitations with glee. He would lecture to large classes on everything from medieval Jewish literature—the shelves in his office were stacked with texts by Hebrew poets such as the eleventh-century Spaniard Levi ibn al-Tabban, the twelfth-century Spanish poet and rabbi Isaac ibn Ezra, and the sixteenth-century Syrian poet Israel ben Moses Najara—to post–French Revolutionary politics; he spoke on the role of the rabbinate over the millennia and the ideas of philosophers such as Spinoza, on the impact of the Jewish Enlightenment on Jewish communal life and on its destruction by the Nazis.

He lectured about the creation of modern Hebrew literature—one of his well-thumbed research books was a dictionary of all the words that the poet Bialik (some of whose original manuscripts eventually made their way into Chimen's collection) had introduced into the Hebrew lexicon; about Israeli theater; about modern-day Sephardic poets. His notes were usually handwritten, either fully worked out speeches written on lined paper or densely scribbled crib notes on index cards. His only concession to visual aids for his audiences was a list of names, dates, and places chalked onto the blackboard, in near-illegible handwriting, before the start of class.

Chimen's handwriting was almost as illegible, and his style as idiosyncratic, when he wrote up his index cards about the contents of the libraries that he evaluated for Sotheby's. They were written in what his colleagues at the auction house, simultaneously amazed at his knowledge and frustrated by his inability to write to their format, came to term "Chimenese." Those cards would, remembered Camilla Previté, who worked with him at Sotheby's for decades, later have to be "de-Chimenized," reworded to meet the requisite catalog style for the auction house. "Chimen would have the title of the book and then everything else was just thrown in," she said. "It didn't follow Sotheby's style at all. It was like every thought in his mind had just gone 'whack' onto the page." She laughed at the memory. He was, she said, a tiny man, but a dynamo, literally the founder of the modern auction-house market for Hebrew manuscripts and books, someone who knew everything about his topic and knew that he knew everything—which is why he had managed to negotiate an unprecedentedly high commission arrangement with Sotheby's. He was, recalled Nabil Saidi, "doing the role of many people—cataloger, negotiator, evaluator, seller, buyer, adviser. Chimen was all these things put together." Chimen would sit in the back rooms of the auction house, carefully evaluating materials, calculating their precise worth. Sometimes he brought the manuscripts back to Hillway, sitting at the dining-room table and poring over his reference books. "You could see him doing a mental calculation," Saidi continued. "He'd invariably quote in dollars. 'Twelve hundred and fifty-nine to three thousand and one.' You'd say, 'Chimen, that's not an auction increment!' He'd say, 'That's what it's worth.'" Stubborn as a mule and utterly convinced of his own abilities, he hated being talked into an approximation.

Back in the university setting, Chimen's lectures were always crammed full of information, far more knowledge being poured out than even the most advanced graduate students could absorb fully at one sitting. Standing half hidden behind a podium, he spoke fast, sometimes too fast, his encyclopedic knowledge, finally given a forum, rushing out from his inner depths. Like lava bubbling to the surface, it was a natural wonder to behold. In a talk on the emancipation of European Jewry and the rise of capitalism, he used his two hours to explore hundreds of years of history, from the rise of early capitalism, in the form of itinerant thirteenth-century Italian merchants, through to the immensely complex financial systems that developed in the nineteenth century. He talked of how the eighteenth-century French philosopher Montesquieu had posited the idea that it was Jews who had invented letters of exchange and bills of credit, vital forerunners to paper money that greatly facilitated international commerce; and then he debunked the idea, explaining that it was in fact Lombard merchants and bankers who had introduced these tools to the world of trade. He went on to detail how Jews had come to occupy crucial niches within capitalism as advanced economic systems evolved: as bankers, insurers, stockbrokers; as developers of the French and Russian railway systems and of the German shipping industry; and as vital players in the clothing, shoe, and furniture industries in England and America.

"What do we mean by capitalism?" he asks his audience on the scratchy audiotape of the lecture, cars honking and revving their engines in the background. There is no date on the tape, no location, no indication of whether it was given in a lecture hall or, as it sounds from the surrounding noise, outdoors. Perhaps it was given on the cobbled old university Quad, fronting onto a busy central London street, as part of a summer series, or maybe it was given in a pub, the doors open to the noisy metropolis outside. "We can talk from here till doomsday and still deal with abstracts. For Marx, it meant the decline of the economy based on agriculture. The shift from countryside to town, the mass production of commodities through new machinery. The changes in the mode of production brought also a change in the relationship of production. It broke down the old fetters imposed by feudalism." In that chaos, Chimen argued, many Jews, long acclimatized to urban living, long familiar with the world of banking, made good. Some, like the Rothschilds, became financial princes, able to make and break rulers with their money. In that ferment, as the old order broke down, universal rights were posited and marginalized groups such as the Jews gained a measure of civic equality; at the same time, a rabbinate that had been unchallenged since Roman times gradually ceased to command the absolute, unquestioning allegiance of young, educated Jews.

In that same lecture, Chimen explored the extraordinary population growth experienced by the Jewish community between the mid-seventeenth century, when about one-tenth of the world's one million Jews were slaughtered in a brutal series of pogroms in the Ukraine, and the Second World War, when upward of 30 percent of the world's Jewish population (then numbering between sixteen and eighteen million) were killed. He set out some of the cultural and public-health accounts that historians had used to explain how the Jewish population increased 1,500 percent, notwithstanding the episodic murderous violence leveled against them, during a period when the non-Jewish population grew by only 300 percent. He looked at urban demographics in Russia, Poland, Lithuania, Germany, Holland, England, and France; Jewish sexual mores; Jewish hygiene rituals that made the population less susceptible to epidemics in dense urban environs. He explored the rise of the Haskalah in Germany, and the influence, from the mid-eighteenth century, of Moses Mendelssohn. He discussed Jewish contributions to science and industry, finance, politics. And he gave his audience an overview of the various political movements toward emancipation, and the surge in the Jewish populations of cities that followed the lifting of residency restrictions: The Jewish population of Berlin, for example, increased from barely 1,000 during Mendelssohn's lifetime to more than 300,000 by the time the Nazis came to power 150 years later. He also discoursed on the rise of the highly political and ultimately deadly anti-Semitism that mushroomed in the twentieth century at least partly in reaction to the huge influx of Jews into Europe's great metropolises. It was a vast landscape to traverse. But traverse it he did, fearlessly, a man in total control of his subject.

He gave similarly authoritative talks to, among others, London's Spanish and Portuguese Congregation, on Sephardic Jews during the Inquisition. He lectured on the Holocaust (by 1977, he was co-chair of the British Yad Vashem Committee, whose mandate was to provide educational resources to schools and universities about the slaughter unleashed against the Jews by the Nazis); on Russian Jews in the decades after the Second World War; on recent migratory patterns into Israel; on contemporary Russian anti-Semitism. He appeared at conferences in Canada, the United States, Israel, France. He lectured in Yugoslavia. He visited archives in Holland, Denmark, Italy.

Staring compulsory retirement in the face, and not liking what he saw, in 1983 he spent some months as a visiting professor at the Tauber Institute at Brandeis University in Boston, giving a series of thirteen lectures on Jewish political move-ments and involvement in Social-ist and Zionist causes from the 1860s to the Second World War. He was housed in an expensive but empty apartment that, he re-ported to Mimi in one of his al-most daily letters, must have been owned by "an eccentric bachelor; it is empty of anything, no kettle, no telephone, full of empty cup-boards. I feel, at the moment, cut off from the world." Cut off he might have felt, but he was happy too. He was in demand, traveling

Chimen at rest. His concession to the Great Outdoors, as he sat with a pile of books, was to go without a tie and to wear sunglasses.

back and forth across the Atlantic. The strident anti-Americanism of his Communist years was by now a distant memory.

———

In 1982, Chimen retired formally from his professorship at University College London. The university threw him a dinner party. Salmon, peas, and salad; followed by a choice of strawberries and cream or apple strudel; topped off with coffee and petits fours. Then, after toasts had been raised to the Queen, to Professor and Mrs. Abramsky, and to the college, Chimen got up to speak. He repeated the formula that he had first penned to Berlin several years earlier, stressing the importance of "freedom from chains, from imprisonment, from enslavement to other men—all other senses of freedom are an extension of this." And, he now continued, "Men do not live only by fighting evils. They live by positive goals, individual and collective, a vast variety of them." Without choice, he told his audience, people's "lives will lack purpose, and, in the end, they will lose all that makes them human."

Chimen's retirement was merely fictive, the result of college rules on mandatory retirement at the age of sixty-five rather than any desire or intention to sever his ties to academia. Now officially a pensioner, he promptly negotiated a part-time teaching position at the university for several more years. He spent months more teaching at Stanford University, first in the early 1980s, then again in 1990. He traveled from Stanford to Israel, and back to Stanford, and then sent Mimi a plaintive letter saying that I [Sasha] was the only family member who had written to him since his return. "The rest of the family, including yourself," he wrote in reproach, "have ignored me as if I do not, or hardly, exist." Not surprisingly, Mimi sent an annoyed response explaining that she had always supported him as he went on his peregrinations around the world and, essentially, telling him to stop whining. She knew how important those journeys were to Chimen. Each trip served as a shot of adrenalin, making him ever more energetic, ever more enthusiastic for the academic world into which he had landed, late in life, with such a splash.

By now, Chimen regarded himself as a repository for all things Jewish, as a jack-of-all-trades when it came to understanding and interpreting Jewish life down the centuries in Europe and beyond. He bought and sold rare coins dating back to the Jewish revolt against Rome that began in AD 66, as well as coins issued by King Herod a generation earlier. He bought ancient prayer books. He even bought an original "petition against the Jews" published in London in 1661. Straddling the secular and religious worlds as he had his whole adult life—"I am very much more able to embrace and comprehend all sorts," he explained at a conference in which he jousted with England's chief rabbi over the role of secularism in Jewish culture—he traveled frequently to Israel; corresponded with prominent academics and political figures about how Israel should present itself to the world; and had meetings with London's leading religious figures. In private conversations and correspondence, from the mid-1970s onward, he frequently criticized Israeli government policy toward its Muslim population and Arab neighbors. As he aged, so he felt increasingly proprietorial toward Israel: He was proud of its accomplishments, embarrassed and shamed by its failures, and appalled by its increasingly heavy-handed response to Palestinian opposition to Israel's presence in the Occupied Territories. On June 22, 1982, he wrote, in pencil, an anguished letter to his friend Berlin, about the policies of Menachem Begin, the Israeli prime minister, toward the country's Arab population, and on the war in Lebanon. "I am off to

Israel to take part in the President's Conference on Zionist ideology," he concluded, "and I do hope to criticise some aspects of this policy which I find totally opposed to moral principles."

———

One after another, Chimen's utopias were breaking down: Forced to abandon Communism, he had put his faith in a Socialist form of Zionism. Watching Israel swing politically to the right, he feared losing that anchor too. His Eretz Israel, he was starting to see, would never be realized in a political community. It was, truly, a utopia, a nowhere-land. From the 1960s onward, he had sought solace for his political disillusionment in academia, the rituals of the university setting replacing political activism in his daily life, the culture of scholarship replacing the grand dreams of political transformation.

At a time when the world of English academia was still hidebound by tradition, he would hold graduate seminars in his book-lined office, ask the students to call him by his first name, and afterward, in a startling breakdown of academic hierarchy, invite the most promising back to Hillway to meet historians such as Shmuel Ettinger, Haim Ben-Sasson, James Joll, the classical historian Arnaldo Momigliano, and others—"all the great luminaries of the Hebrew University, and the emergent Tel Aviv university," recalled his onetime student and future colleague Ada Rapoport-Albert, who had come to London from Israel to study. At Hanukkah, Chimen would encourage his acolytes to come back to Hillway to drink red wine and sample Mimi's deliciously greasy potato latkes. For Rapoport-Albert, who was adopted into Hillway almost as a member of the family, "the way students like me were accepted and integrated in the crowd was extremely unusual. It was an awe-inspiring cocktail you got hooked onto." Hillway served as an incubator, fostering love of knowledge and backing up that knowledge with human warmth. Many of these young men and women from University College London were adopted into the ever-expanding Hillway tribe, and subsequently embarked upon academic careers in major Jewish history departments around the world. Decades later, Rapoport-Albert would become head of the department that Chimen had dominated for so many years.

Hillway was always overflowing with students and with friends and family from around the world. Elliott Medrich, the son of one of Mimi's first cousins, arrived from America in the summer of 1966: "I went alone, had an unusual experience—one of my traveling mates, who happened to be a female, her place to stay fell through; I arrived at Hillway and had her in tow, and Miriam wouldn't just find her a place to stay—she insisted she stay there—and we weren't a couple by any means. But we stayed together in the front room for two weeks. There weren't short stays. You were sucked into the life of the place. You thought of yourself as a member of the family. I thought of myself as totally belonging there." For Medrich, the table was the central meeting point at Hillway: "The endless hours spent round the table had something for everyone. The orchestration, the conduct of time, making sure everyone was comfortable, well-fed, and participated in the life of the evening."

———

The culinary arts of Mimi's kitchen and dining room cast a long shadow. Even at the height of his academic career, Chimen remained uncomfortable using the university's catering facilities. Or maybe, wisely, he just trusted Mimi's culinary instincts more. Whatever the reason, on days when he was presiding over a conference or had a guest speaker, he would arrive in Bloomsbury early, find a parking space, open the trunk (his vehicles were always well-worn, and frequently sported the dings collected during his creative driving ventures along London's increasingly clogged streets), and start unloading platter after platter of Mimi's home-cooked delicacies—doing his utmost to re-create the aura of the Hillway salon in the wood-paneled nineteenth-century conference rooms of University College London. On occasion, he took this practice to an extreme. There was the time, for example, when the Prince Mikasa, a younger brother of the Japanese Emperor Hirohito, and a man who had made a name for himself as a specialist in Aramaic, came to lecture. He was surrounded by bodyguards who had the physique of sumo wrestlers, colleagues recall. After the lecture was over, Chimen ceremoniously ushered the prince into the eating area and then proceeded to offer him Mimi's fishcakes and sandwiches. The archives are silent as to the royal personage's reaction.

Back at Hillway, Chimen would talk happily about High Table at St. Antony's or the senate faculty proceedings at University College London—in his head still astonished that the "little man," as he called himself, had made it to the big time. Talmon, Ettinger, and Robinson, his three closest friends from Hebrew University, had become renowned academics decades earlier—Talmon was described by the Dutch historian of ideas Frank Ankersmit as being among the twenty most important historians of the century; Ettinger, who had written his dissertation on the massacre of Ukrainian Jews in 1648, was widely hailed as Israel's leading modern Jewish historian; and Robinson, one of the world's most prominent mathematicians, ended his career as the Sterling Professor of Mathematics at Yale. Now, at last, Chimen was gaining similar recognition. To Mimi and the family, he would lovingly recall his conversations with Berlin at the mahogany dining tables in the Athenaeum; and on the occasions when he received a letter from Lord Annan, the chancellor of University

College London, he would almost caress the paper as he revealed its contents to his dining-room audience. That Annan, a peer of the realm, would communicate with the little man from Minsk, the ex-Communist without a formal degree, tickled Chimen pink.

What he would not, *could* not do, was talk about his own books. For although he had edited several volumes and contributed essays to many others on subjects ranging from Polish Jewry to Jews and chess, after the massive tome that he had written with Henry Collins on Marx and the First International he never wrote another book. The biography of Marx that he had planned withered once Collins died. The memoirs that others prodded him to embark on never made it past a few rough scribbles. Several other projects, either proposed by him to publishers or vice versa, in the latter decades of his life, never made it beyond the drawing board. He was, observed his former student Steven Zipperstein, "blessed and cursed by his inheriting the fabled capacity to actually have a mental photograph of a page when he read it. Chimen could actually do that." To Zipperstein, it appeared that that clutter of words in Chimen's head had an almost paralyzing impact. Like Funes the Memorious, the central character in one of Jorge Luis Borges's stories, "he remembered everything. Chimen never forgot. And that was responsible for his writer's block. He was a master without a masterpiece." Hobsbawm put it more prosaically: "He was enormously erudite and certainly not good at shaping it."

As Chimen and Miriam aged, the dining room grew hotter. With Mimi in poor health, she would crank up the central heating, sometimes to over eighty degrees Fahrenheit, and every few hours she retreated to a couch against the dividing wall with the kitchen to snatch a few minutes of quiet time and rest. While she lay there, sometimes recuperating from falls that she seemed to suffer with increasing frequency and which left her legs swollen and horribly bruised, other times just exhausted from all her duties as a hostess, the conversation around her would continue. So crowded was the room—with chairs, books, people, a large television, and the broken-down old piano—that the couch almost faded into the background.

Those few spaces of the walls in this room that were not covered with books were festooned with artwork and photos. Coming into the dining room from the hallway and looking out toward the garden, on the right-hand wall were two large pictures. The first was an oil painting by Sandra Pepys on an elongated, rectangular canvas, showing a panorama of Jerusalem's old city. It was a view similar to the one Chimen would have seen as a young student at Hebrew University, when looking down from the high slopes of Mount Scopus. The second, by Mordecai Ardon—a well-known artist and the father of Chimen and Mimi's good friend Mike—was ink on paper, framed and glazed. It was titled *Creation of the World* and portrayed the letters of the Hebrew alphabet extending outward from a core, spiraling away from the viewer. The effect was to present an image of energy rushing away at warp speed from the origin point. Next to these two pictures was a framed antique map of the eastern Mediterranean. In the top-left corner of the map was a lion perched atop a tiny island, a tree with a snake coiled around its trunk to the animal's left. It was, the note under the lion explained, "A Map, shewing Situation of Paradice and Country Inhabited by Patriarchs." Under these paintings was a heavy wooden bureau, with a roll-up top and dozens of little drawers. Cluttered to the point of overflowing, it served as Mimi's desk, the place she sat to write checks and, on occasion, letters; simultaneously, it functioned as a sort of stationery storage site—for rolls of old Green Shield Stamps; for half-century-old receipts and fading letterhead from Shapiro, Valentine & Co., which had closed in 1969 once Chimen's academic career gathered steam; all intermingled with yet more personal correspondence. It was one more hoarder's corner within a hoarder's house.

In the final years of Chimen's life, a huge original poster from the Paris Commune—issued during the heady days of revolution, before the army regained control of Paris and containing the black-and-white text of one of the Commune decrees—given to him on his ninetieth birthday by my brother, Kolya, hung in an imposing black frame with red borders on the wall opposite, above where in earlier years Mimi's couch had been placed. It was the one intrusion of radical political imagery remaining in a room that, otherwise, had banished such symbols of Chimen's past passions. He would sit in a reclining armchair, a large, heavy, old-fashioned television and video player perched on a table in front of him, and he would crank the volume up to watch the news. If all worked well, he would catch what the newscaster was reporting. But if his hearing aid was malfunctioning, or if his ears were particularly clogged, he would look around in discomfort, his eyes glancing toward the Communard poster, seeking solace in visual stimulation to make up for the fact that he could no longer hear what was being said around him. He would sit there, exhausted, his eyes flickering between the poster and the loud but unheard television. Frequently, he would doze off in that chair, lying completely still, his quiet breathing the only indication that he was still alive.

He dreamed, perhaps, of ghosts.

The old upright piano, which in earlier decades my sister, Tanya, and I had played at the behest of Mimi and her friends, gradually ceased to function as a musical instrument and became, instead, a shrine for photographs of friends and relatives now dead, along with images of the living—photos of children, of grandchildren,

Four generations of Abramskys. Left to right: Jack holding Sasha, Chimen, and Yehezkel. Jerusalem, 1973.

and, eventually, of great-grandchildren: my own children, Sofia and Leo, and Tanya's daughter, Izzy.

By the piano, in the last years of the salon, hung a watercolor by my cousin Maia and two pencil drawings that Tanya had sketched: One of Chimen, the other of Mimi. Both seemed to be smiling slightly as they looked out on the crowded room below. To the left of the piano, adjacent to a shelf that contained the collection of Jewish encyclopedias, there hung a matte ten-by-eight black-and-white photograph of four generations of Abramsky men: Yehezkel, Chimen, Jack, and me. It was taken in 1973 in Yehezkel's small apartment in Jerusalem. In the background is a window, the white slats of its shutters letting in the sunlight. I was one year old, sitting on my father's lap, a curly blond-haired toddler, smiling. My father, already balding, had let what hair he still had grow out; his beard was bushy, but in a 1960s rather than a religious sort of way. Chimen stood, hunched slightly, wearing a short-sleeved gray shirt, a yarmulke, his right hand gripping his left wrist, his watch-wearing wrist. Yehezkel sat to the left of the frame, in a starched white shirt, looking stern, his long white beard the focal point for the camera, the part of the image against which everything else was set. He was eighty-seven years old. It was the last time that my father saw him. It was the only time that I ever saw him.

On the other side of the piano was a wooden cabinet, the bottom

Four generations: Jack, Sasha, Sofia, and Chimen. France, 2004.

Four generations: Leo, Sasha, Chimen, and Jack. Hillway, 2009.

of which served as storage for some of Mimi's papers, the top part housing the few books that she claimed as her own in this mighty House of Books: some cookbooks, some detective thrillers, a few popular histories. After she died, Chimen kept her books there, never attempting to empty the shelves and fill them with his own volumes. There were more photos in front of the books, including one of me. I was thirteen years old, in my black school blazer, black trousers, white shirt, and red-and-black-striped tie; I was barely five feet tall, still prepubescent, my face cherubic, hairless. I was standing next to Denis Healey, one of the Labour Party's leading politicians, a cabinet minister in the governments of the 1960s and 1970s, and a man who had fought to keep the party on an even keel as it tacked ever further to the left in the 1980s. He was, in the middle years of that decade, the shadow foreign secretary—the opposition Labour Party's leading spokesperson on foreign affairs. A large man with extraordinary bushy eyebrows, in his gray suit he towered over me in the picture. We were on the terrace of the Houses of Parliament—an improbable visit arranged by Mimi's friend Rose Uren, whose dental services the MP used. (Calling in favors from other clients, she also commandeered hard-to-come-by tickets to the Royal Opera House and, to my father's absolute delight, Centre Court tickets to Wimbledon.) There were better photos of me, but I doubt there were any that made Chimen quite so happy. For, loathed by much of the left, Healey had become something of a political role model to the ex-Communist as they both grew older—a man of moderate Socialist convictions who was not afraid to stand up to the Soviet Union as well as to the ideologues inside his own political party.

Back in the dining room, and apparently at random, piles of books spiraled upward from the carpeted floor. Sometimes heaps would materialize on the dining-room table—a vanguard testing the waters, seeing how long it would take Mimi to swat them away. The tabletop itself was entirely her territory. "Frankly," recalled Medrich, "there was no such thing as you were done eating. Food was fuel. There was no question that she recognized this to be her first responsibility. The meals, as you well know, the next course was always in preparation. She always made sure that whoever you were, you participated. Always made sure that you were heard from, that there was a real effort made to assure the conversation wouldn't go on around you, that you became a part of it. The third thing she always did— whenever I would come, all the relatives at one point or another would be in the house." It was somewhere between an obligation and a delight: A distant cousin would arrive from overseas, and the entire extended family was commanded to attend them at Hillway.

Chimen held court at the dining table, and in between trundling in platters of food from the kitchen, Mimi would add the occasional pithy remark, puncturing academic bubbles as she saw fit. "The dinner table," noted Medrich, "was clearly a partnership between the two of them. They obviously honed this over many years—because it never changed. They'd figured out how to do this." It was a double act that kept their salon functioning even as the world of Marxist political ideas and the fascination with Marx's texts, which had first drawn so many to Hillway and into late-night conversations with

Chimen, came to seem increasingly irrelevant. At the height of the Cold War, the minutiae of Marxist and Socialist literature had mattered in a very profound way. The people of Hillway, in the salon's earlier incarnation, had not been debating esoterica: They were—or at least they believed they were—discussing the future, coming to an understanding of how the world was changing and of how society would be organized in the future. In such a world, Chimen's library had totemic, talismanic powers. It was, to Marxists, a Socialist Ark of the Covenant representing power, knowledge, the words of secular gods. No wonder scholars and politicians and revolutionaries from the world over flocked to Chimen's House of Books.

By the 1970s, however, not only was Chimen's infatuation with Communism a thing of the distant past; more generally, the world's fascination with the Bolshevik vision was in serious decline. Watching progressives the world over move away from the ideas that he had been so passionate about, Chimen must have had an inkling of how Yehezkel had felt as he published one majestic volume after another of his religious commentaries in a world that, outside of the enclaves of Orthodoxy, had less and less time for scholarship such as his. "Progress is destroying the Jewish religion," the itinerant Jewish novelist and journalist Joseph Roth wrote, sadly, as far back as 1926, in *The Wandering Jews*. "Fewer and fewer believers are holding out, and...the numbers of the faithful are dwindling." In his own circles, Yehezkel was a gaon, a Talmudic genius. Outside those circles, by the 1970s he was an old man from a vanished world. He had followers—tens of thousands of whom would attend his funeral in Jerusalem in 1976—but they lived in a self-enclosed universe, sealed off from the broader, secular society around them.

In Volozhin, Yehezkel had studied the Brisker method with the descendants of the famous rabbi Hayim ben Yitshak, who himself had studied with the Vilna gaon, one of the most influential Jewish

scholars of the eighteenth century. Under the guidance of Chaim Soloveitchik, students in the late nineteenth century learned to analyze
the context in which ideas were developed, as well as the literal
meaning of the words themselves. So influential, so coldly logical was
Soloveitchik's Brisker technique that it had revolutionized Talmudic
scholarship. It let in new ideas—it had room for scientific theory, for
medicine, for the ideas that were daily altering the lives of men and
women around the world. In contrast to this sophisticated methodol-
ogy, the students scorned what they termed "pilpul," the parroting of
obscure textual detail, the forcing of disparate quotations and
phrases into agreement with each other, without a deeper understanding of the issues being discussed. By the 1970s, the debates
about Marxist minutiae had taken on something of a pilpul quality—an obsessive reading, for hidden meaning, of tomes that no longer had the power to change the world. Chimen's Socialist library
was starting to lose its totemic power. It was becoming dusty.

When Chimen died in 2010, in a post-Marxist world, many of the
volumes that he had so prized had been reduced to curiosity items.
The inflated monetary value assigned to them at the height of Soviet
power was now as hard to comprehend as the six-figure prices ac-
corded tulips in the flower markets of Amsterdam for a brief period
in the seventeenth century. But despite these shifting sands, in the
decades prior to his death such was the reputation both of Chimen
and of his House of Books that the salon remained a vital part of
London's intellectual scene.

As more of his close friends and relatives started to die—Alec Waterman succumbed to a stroke in 1966; Collins, in 1969, to prostate
cancer; Robinson to pancreatic cancer in 1974; Chimen's brothers
Moshe and Yaakov David in 1975 and 1977; Talmon in 1980; Sraffa
in 1983—Chimen entered a new phase in life, as a grandfather. He
would take breaks from his work and entertain the children who

were, after a generation's gap, again running riot through the rooms of Hillway. Visitors popping in unannounced could find him balancing Yehezkel's gnarled old cane, its lineage traceable back into the eighteenth century, on the tips of his fingers and dancing around the dining room, to the amusement of his five grandchildren and the various other young cousins who were effortlessly absorbed into the house by Mimi and her mothering instincts. Or performing his other party trick: balancing stacks of plastic cups on his head and doing the Charlie Chaplin penguin walk. Given recognition and validation in the academic world, perhaps he felt able to relax just a little bit, to learn not to take himself quite so seriously.

In between meals, he would clear space on either the kitchen or dining-room table and take out the little wooden box of dominoes. Unlike regular dominoes, small black rectangles with indented white dots, these were large wooden dominoes, the dots painted in a different color for each number. For children, the colors made the game of Russian dominoes easy to learn. There are many variants of dominoes; in this one the aim was twofold: most immediately, to try to create a snake of dominoes, as well as side arms coming off of the first double-numbered domino to be crossed, the ends of which collectively added up to a multiple of five. If they did, that number was added to your score. As the double numbers were added into the equation, as the game unfolded, you could end up with numerous domino end points, and scores that, on occasion, went into the thirties. The second strategy was to get rid of all the dominoes in your possession. Once you were all out, you added up the numbers left in your opponent's hand to the nearest five, and added that score to your own. The manipulation of the numbers was endlessly fascinating to Chimen, the chess scholar. Usually we played to five hundred points, which could involve ten or twenty rounds. Sometimes we played to a thousand. The hours would vanish as we played. On occasion, like a

Family group at Jenny and Al's house,
late 1980s. *Back row, left to right*: Kolya,
Chimen's cousin Golda Zimmerman, Lenore;
Middle row: Al, Tanya, Chimen, Mimi,
Maia, Sasha, Rob; *Front row*: Jenny and Jack.

particularly long game of cricket, our matches would stretch across an entire weekend. Eventually Mimi would order us to stop so that she could use the table upon which we had ventured to trespass. When we were young, I later realized, Chimen would go easy, letting his grandchildren build up big scores, deliberately mis-strategizing. As we got older, he tried harder. By the time I was a teenager, my grandfather and I would pit our wills, endlessly playing this game conjured up out of the memory of the far-off decades of his own childhood.

Around the dining-room table, at huge family lunches and dinners, Chimen would ask a child's advice or comment on a matter of world politics, and would then say, in all earnestness, "I agree with every-zing you say." He'd smile slightly, as if infinitely amused by the interaction; amused, but not in a condescending way—rather he was happy that here was a young person capable of intelligent comment on matters of import. "The ways of

Chimen, Kolya, and Tanya with her
daughter Izzy, Hillway, 2009.

298

the world are mysterious, but everything works out in the end," might have been the sentiment behind that hint of a smile.

———

As they had done ever since they were first married, Mimi and Chimen continued to host enormous Seders—one on each of the first two nights of Passover. Some of their friends from the Communist days continued to come as guests. There were always a number of overseas visitors and, of course, the core of the family: my parents and us three children; Jenny and Al and their kids; and a profusion of relatives from Mimi's side of the family—Peter and Vavi and their children; Eve and her son, Tom. Sara would arrive with her platters of food. Lily and Martin would appear with their children and grandchildren, as would Phyllis and her husband, Max. Minna did not come often for Seders. And neither, by this time, did Raph.

The dining-room table, with the addition of three or four fold-up wooden tables ranged in a long row off of it, would seat nearly thirty people. There would be bottles of sickly sweet kosher Manischewitz positioned up and down the table—and, sometimes, far better wines conjured up by my wine-collecting uncle Al—piles of matzo, dishes stacked full of delicious haroses (a nut, apple, and raisin concoction), bowls filled with hard-boiled eggs, and dishes containing the ceremonial salt water, bitter herbs, and a lamb shank.

Chimen, as he had done for decades, would stand at the head of the table, dressed in his best suit, the unruly white hair that normally protruded wildly off the back of his bald pate tamed for the occasion, and read through the entire Haggadah. He did so at breakneck speed, alternating between Hebrew and English so often that it became almost impossible to determine which language he was speaking. Mimi continued to cook extraordinary amounts of food. There would be appetizers of smoked salmon on crackers and an enormous pot of matzo-ball soup, followed by a roast turkey, roast potatoes, and other vegetables: carrots, onions, mushrooms, perhaps some green beans. Into the mid-1990s, no effort was spared. "Our Seder was magnificent," Chimen wrote to me in late April 1995. "The culinary side was done by Jenny, your Mum and Dad, under Mimi's sharp eyes and major planning and designing. The dinner was supreme. The Haggadah part was well orchestrated. We finished after midnight."

While the reading progressed, my mother, Vavi, and other guests would start talking—whispering among themselves, telling jokes, laughing at, or with, the children. Predictably, Chimen would unleash a volley of orders to be quiet; as predictably, he would be ignored. It was a game that everyone happily played along with. I am sure that, had he actually had to conduct an entire Seder before a quiescent, silent, respectful audience, he would have been bored out of his mind. For while he took the ritual seriously, he enjoyed tweaking the traditions to meet the humors of his guests. In earlier years, that had meant Collins singing "the Yiddischa Toreador." Now it meant adding in songs such as "Three Crows Sitting on a Wall," sung, to general acclaim, in an impossibly Scottish accent by Al and his children. Yet Chimen's frustration was not all for show. Paradoxically, compared to the Communist days, now the participants (the younger ones anyway) knew far less about Jewish ritual life, were less familiar with both Yiddish and Hebrew, and were less patient of the eight days of dietary restrictions around Passover. And, in reaction, Chimen did get genuinely annoyed. At times his requests for silence sounded like screams of anguish. He would stop the reading mid-sentence and, looking up severely, order people by name to shut up. Then without a pause for breath, he would resume his recitation. After Mimi died in 1997, Chimen kept up the ritual for more than a decade, even as his voice began to fail him. Now, my parents, Jenny, and the cousins came over to do the cooking. Now, if Chimen's voice grew so hoarse that he could not continue, Vavi was ready to step in and read the Hebrew text. And as Chimen read, a respectful silence fell: The effort it took him to get the many pages of words out of his mouth was Herculean, like climbing a mountain, like running a marathon.

The size of the Seder crowd dwindled. Chimen did not seem to mind. Fast going deaf, he was far more comfortable surrounded by a smaller group—which might have been one of the reasons he took such happiness in hosting his "ladies' lunch club" each weekend. They would arrive like clockwork: his nieces Eve and Julia; his widowed sisters-in-law Minna and, after Steve died, Sara; his widowed cousin Phyllis; a couple of old friends, including Alec Waterman's widow, Ray; and Raph's widow, the author Alison Light (Raph had died of cancer in late 1996 at the age of sixty-one, only nine years after his and Alison's wedding, and a few months before Mimi's death). Occasionally my brother, Kolya, would be allowed into this ladies' club on sufferance. "Chimen was experimenting with cooking," Alison remembered, with a smile, more than fifteen years later. "He'd make a very nice aubergine dip; there was a soup he'd make; and he would do lemon sole with butter. He'd do all the courses. That was the thing that was impressive." Gently, my recently widowed grandfather (who had been taught to cook by Mimi in the last

Chimen taking a walk,
early 1990s.

years of her life, when she realized that he would outlive her and would need a way to keep the salon going) played the role of ladies' man to his gathering of widows. They would talk about politics, about old friends, about old quarrels. They would rehash the day's news, gossip mildly, and, most important, tend to each other's emotions. "He was looking after us," Alison explained. "And looking after himself at the same time. We were all bereaved. There was quite a lot of talk about people who had died. It was a way of bonding because of that. You could talk about anything. An amazing amount of frankness. There's a particular kind of warmth or sadness in an embrace. And I remember sharing that a lot at that time."

As a very old man, Chimen would sit on a simple wooden chair at his dining-room table, a pile of books and papers next to him. The effort it took, by then, to move from one room to another meant that once he was settled in a spot he would often stay there for hours on end, largely cocooned within the world of silence experienced by the elderly deaf. His eyes, watery and red, behind ever-thicker lenses, were his lifeline, his one remaining, largely functional link to the external world. He would take a book, lean upon it, hunch forward slightly. His glasses would slide maybe a quarter of an inch down his nose; his left hand, fingers slightly splayed, would hold the pages open. His right elbow would rest on the corner of the book, his right hand, fingers also splayed, would rest against his temple. In the biography of Yehezkel Abramsky, *A King in His Beauty*, there's a photo of Yehezkel. His beard is so fine that's it almost invisible, a vague shadow over his shirt and tie. In this photo, I see Chimen. It is the same pose, the same utter absorption in the Word. Both men were *talmidei hakhamim*, wise scholars.

FRONT ROOM REVISITED:
ENDINGS

In vain does the dreamer rummage about in his old dreams,
raking them over as though they were a heap of cinders, look-
ing in these cinders for some spark, however tiny, to fan it into
a flame so as to warm his chilled blood by it and revive in it all
that he held so dear before, all that touched his heart, that
made his blood course through his veins, that drew tears from
his eyes, and that so splendidly deceived him!
—Fyodor Dostoyevsky, "White Nights" (1848)

IN THE LATE 1950s, Mimi's mother, Bellafeigel Nirenstein, had often
sat stony-faced and angry-looking in the front room of Hillway. With
her health spiraling downward, she'd had to move out of her own
home and spent the last few years of her life living with Mimi and
Chimen. The solemnity of my great-grandmother's features in photographs from those years is almost a metaphor for the front room itself. This was, I think, an austere chamber, a room lacking whimsy.
Whereas the dining room, gorgeously lit by the sun coming in off the
garden and through the glass rear wall, was frivolous enough for
Chimen, in his old age, to dance around with plastic cups balanced
on his head, and whereas the kitchen was a place for endless gossip

and informal chatter, the front room was in general a serious place. It became weighed down by its own contents: overstuffed armchairs and books—volumes cascaded off the shelves and onto the coffee table, the floor, every available surface, and ultimately, in combination with a collection of heavy potted plants, blocked access to the fireplace. From the early 1990s onward, it served as a sickroom, first for Mimi and later for Chimen, its air poisoned by the smell of their medicines and ointments, by the odors of sickness and old age. Mirroring the physical decline of its owners, the basic infrastructure of the room (like the rest of the house) fell into greater disrepair. The built-in curved chest of drawers, which hugged the inside line of the windows overlooking the street, started to crack under the weight of generations of guests who used it as an extra seat. Its white paint started to fleck, as did the paint on the windowsills. The armchairs leaked stuffing. The lighting seemed to grow dimmer by the year as the lampshades grew dirtier. The couch-cum-bed that rested against the far wall seemed to sag a little more each year.

I remember the conductor Michael Tilson Thomas, during his sojourn at the London Symphony Orchestra, sitting on the window seat, his tall, thin body silhouetted against the window, singing songs and telling stories. In memory I see the maestro sharing the perch with a number of potted plants, their leaves drooping, under-watered but never quite dead.

***

As a young man, Raph Samuel spent endless hours in the front room, chatting with friends and fellow historians. Or arguing with Chimen—whom he viewed both as a second father and as his intellectual mentor, and with whom he ended up fighting as only close relatives can. By the time I came on the scene, he was no longer calling Mimi and Chimen "Comrade," but I have a peculiarly vivid recollection of him frequently bestowing that honorific on me. As a young woman, my aunt Jenny had loathed being reduced to "Comrade" by her elder, adored cousin. But it struck me as admission to a club; it meant that he was taking me seriously. He would say it in a slightly nasal way, his round glasses slipping down his nose, an ironic smile creeping up the corner of his mouth. I loved the frisson I felt as he sallied into the dining room or the living room—depending on the time of day—in his tan suede jacket, said "Hello, Comrade" to me, and watched for his now-anti-Communist uncle to flinch.

There was an almost unrelentingly high cultural tone to the front room. Even though the house was fashioned in the 1940s and '50s as something of a bohemian salon, what that meant sartorially was that the jackets were rumpled and the shirts occasionally weren't ironed, that ties were optional rather than mandatory. As the broader culture adopted the more casual, frequently flamboyant dress codes of the 1960s, the older habitués of Hillway never dressed more informally than in tweeds and corduroys.

Freethinking in theory, in practice Mimi and Chimen were re-markably traditional in demeanor. When they wanted to take Jack and Jenny on a childhood outing in the 1950s, it would be to a cultural event such as a screening of the film version of Laurence Olivier's *Henry V* or to Stratford-upon-Avon to see the bard's plays. Decades later, Jack and Jenny recalled once going to Stratford to see *Coriolanus* and driving back in a pea-soup fog so dense that Mimi had to get out of the car to feel where the road was.

When the family bought a television in the early 1960s, Jenny, seeking entertainment other than the classics, would watch *Bonanza* and other cowboy programs. Chimen lambasted her for wasting her time on nonacademic pursuits. "He couldn't understand," Jenny said, "how anything could be enjoyed that didn't have a basis in absolute reality." When, as a guitar-playing student in the late 1960s, Jenny decided to introduce the music of the Beatles to Chimen forcibly, by locking him in the front room and playing *Sgt. Pepper* at full volume, the result was not a success. Chimen, who was at the time busily trying to prepare a series of very learned, earnest lectures that he was to give at Sussex University to commemorate the fiftieth anniversary of the Bolshevik revolution, listened but was distinctly underwhelmed. Too old, too bruised by his earlier political experiences, the social revolutions of the 1960s and the changing enthusiasms of the young did not inspire him with any renewed revolutionary fervor. As students took to the barricades in 1968, Chimen watched from the sidelines or, at most, talked over events with some of the graduate students at University College London. This was not his revolt; it was not his utopia that was being stumbled toward. And its music and slogans and cultural priorities were not ones that he understood. When forced to confront modern popular culture, his nose wrinkled in disgust, and he looked as if he was being tormented by a particularly nasty odor. There was something *treif* (dirty, un-kosher) about the rhythms and sounds and colors of this new world. One year, after a particularly gluttonous Christmas feast—my grandparents had, over the years, reluctantly made their peace with the fact that the younger generations, not brought up religiously, enjoyed the festivities and gift-giving of Christmas—my brother decided to put on a video of the vomiting scene from the Monty Python film *The Meaning of Life*. There we were, stuffed to the gills, watching a waiter with an absurdly faux-French accent asking an overstuffed and projectile-vomiting diner if he wanted "a wafer-thin mint." The diner says he could not eat another thing; but the waiter presses and presses. Finally the diner concedes, eats the mint, and explodes. It is a vile scene, so disgusting, so over the top, that it forces anxious laughter from most viewers. Not Chimen. He looked at the scene, wrinkled his nose, and gave his verdict. "It has no aesthetic value whatsoever," he proclaimed, and turned back to continue his conversation about more serious matters.

About the only thing good that he saw in the myriad revolutions in personal behavior and artistic expression unleashed by the 1960s was that they broke down the boundaries of formality to the extent that it allowed him to call people like Isaiah Berlin by their first names. In their correspondence at this period each asked the other the gleeful question, "Do you mind if I call you by your first name?," and there followed a series of missives in which they experimented with just how to do so. Dear Isaiah, Sir Isaiah, Isaiah.

There *was*, however, one exception to the overwhelmingly high-culture rules of Hillway, and that was Mimi's addiction to the BBC radio soap opera *The Archers*. It had been running since 1951, and it was entirely possible that Mimi knew its plotlines better than those of any piece of great literature and understood its complex family relationships as well she did those of the extended Nirenstein–Abramsky clan. Like a religious ritual, every afternoon when the program came on, Mimi would retire to the front room, lie down on her sofa-bed, and listen to the radio. For a woman who never stopped cooking, hosting, counseling her numerous psychiatric patients from the Royal Free Hospital, and solving other people's problems, it was the one meditative moment in her busy day. No one was allowed to disturb her. If you telephoned at that time, Chimen would curtly tell you that Mimi could not talk, that it was "Archer's Hour." If one of the grandchildren made the mistake of barging into the front room during those minutes, they would be shooed away by Mimi; it was the only time when she showed impatience.

The wall against which Mimi's "Archer's Hour" sofa rested was the only wall in that room with no books on it. From the time of Chimen's father's death in 1976 onward, an intimidating black-and-white sketch of the rabbi hung there instead. It was drawn by the artist Hendel Lieberman in London in 1950, the year before Yehezkel retired from the Beth Din and, seen off by thousands of his followers at the railway station, moved to Jerusalem. The lines of Yehezkel's face were firmly inked, the long rabbinic beard pulling the head slightly downward, the eyes piercing in their intensity. Everything about that image was intended to bear witness: This was a portrait of a man who was used to observing the world around him and to having a crowd hang on his every word. This was a *gadol*, a great sage. While Chimen and Mimi were not religious, the placing of the portrait in their front room spoke to the fact that Yehezkel's influence over the inhabitants of Hillway was, until the day Chimen died, extraordinarily strong.

After the Second World War and the destruction of millions of Jews, the head of the Beth Din in London could lay claim to being one of the most—perhaps even *the* most—influential figures in European religious Jewry: Chimen certainly averred that his father had been recognized as the foremost contemporary scholar of the Talmud. It was a role in which the conservative Yehezkel excelled and one for which his followers would come to venerate him. As I write this, three-quarters of a century after he was made a dayan and nearly forty years after his death, Yehezkel's letters still turn up at auction houses; he regularly appears on lists of the most important rabbis of the last two and a half thousand years; and a Facebook page has even been set up for him by his admirers. Yehezkel's fame was quite a shadow for his sons to live under.

In religious Jewish circles, stories continue to circulate about my great-grandfather. One goes like this: Yehezkel was called to court to defend the practice of ritual slaughter. The judge looked at the deposition in front of him, and then asked, "Rabbi Abramsky, it says here that you are the foremost authority of Jewish law in the British Empire. Is that true?" Yehezkel answered, "That is true, Your Honor." The judge continued, "And that you are the most eloquent spokesman for Jewish law in the British Empire?" "That is also true, Your Honor." Probing more deeply, the judge threw out another question: "It also says here that you are the most senior rabbi in the British Empire. Is that correct?" Once more, Yehezkel replied, "That is correct, Your Honor." At that point, the judge apparently got a bit flustered. "Rabbi Abramsky, how do you resolve your answers with the Talmudic teachings of humility?" Yehezkel looked at the judge and, presumably with a twinkle in his eye, said, "It is indeed a problem, Your Honor, but I'm under oath."

When Yehezkel died in September 1976, Chimen immediately flew to Jerusalem and arrived in time to join the more than forty thousand mourners who accompanied his father's bier to its burial in the Har HaMenuchot cemetery, on the hilltops on the western edge of Jerusalem. It was one of the largest funerals ever to take place in Israel. In accordance with the instructions that Yehezkel left for those in charge of his funeral, two students walked behind his bier carrying all twenty-four volumes of the *Chazon Yehezkel*, his monumental commentary on the Tosefta, which had won the first Israel Prize for rabbinic literature. The Jewish Telegraphic Agency reporter assigned to cover the funeral noted that Yehezkel was the "dean of Israel's rabbis and [was] widely considered the foremost Talmud scholar of the age." In a tribute written for *The Jewish Chronicle*, England's former chief rabbi, Sir Israel Brodie, described him as "a Prince of the Torah." There is, today, a square named after Yehezkel in Jerusalem.

Wherever a person sat in the front room at 5 Hillway throughout the last three decades of the salon's existence, Rabbi Abramsky stood watch. The sketch weighed heavily on Chimen as he grew older, his father's presence almost as powerful in death as it had been during his long life. Chimen often looked at that portrait during those decades in which he tried so hard to distance himself from his earlier support for Stalin's world vision. He would stare at the sketch of his father's stern face and, I believe, silently apologize for the Communist Party autobiography he had penned in which he had insulted his father's character. Fascinated by Tolstoy's novel *Resurrection*, with its themes of sin and redemption, he was, I think, performing his own, very personal version of Teshuvah, the atonement for past wrongs that plays a central role in Jewish ritual life. It was why God did not punish Cain for killing Abel. It was a way to come back from moral death. It was how one could make oneself anew.

In 1971, Chimen attempted (successfully) to convince Isaiah Berlin to write an essay for the collection that he was editing in honor of the left-wing historian E. H. Carr, who had long been a close personal friend of Chimen's. Berlin expressed reservations and asked about the political leanings of other contributors. On June 1, Chimen wrote back that he did not know how to describe the contributors, "except for yours truly who could, possibly, be classified as an ex-communist, ex-Marxist, a mixture today of a radical-liberal-conservative-cum-counter-revolutionary; one who has lost his faith and has not yet found a new one, in a word a person who searches, gropes, doubts, constantly making 'post-mortems' on his own thinking... and somehow still believes in humanistic values." It was the most introspective note that Chimen ever hit. And it summed up the philosophical and political dilemma that he would be caught within for the rest of his life: All of the easy solutions, the formulaic responses to the messiness of life, had failed. Chimen knew this, knew that he could no longer subscribe to utopian beliefs; yet he could never quite set aside the dreams of his youth.

Eighteen years later, Chimen wrote another letter, equally frank, to Berlin. "We, your admirers see you as a great champion of liberty, of freedom as a profound value in itself, freedom from chains, from imprisonment, from enslavement spiritually and physically, to other people," he wrote, to commemorate Berlin's eightieth birthday in 1989, elaborating on both his earlier letters to Berlin on the topic of freedom and also his 1982 retirement speech. "Your skepticism and high moral ideals are a beacon of enlightenment in a confused age." It seems he was thanking his friend for having arrived early at conclusions that Chimen had only belatedly reached.

———

Into his old age, Chimen remained a man fleeing his past: his lonely childhood in the Soviet Union, his infatuation with Stalinism, his messy break with the Party and the friends who no longer talked to him. The flight—and the fears associated with it—had literal as well as metaphorical implications. Having left the Soviet Union in the early 1930s, Chimen avoided returning to Moscow for sixty years, increasingly fearful, he told friends and colleagues, that if he went behind the Iron Curtain he would be arrested or suffer some alternative, crueler fate, like those inflicted on other prominent Jews, some of whom had been comrades and visitors to Hillway. The only exception he made to this rule was in 1963, when he visited Prague to rescue the 1,500 Torah scrolls from their anonymous resting place in a disused synagogue. Notwithstanding the favorable reviews his book on Marx had received in the Eastern bloc, the Soviet press, he declared, in declining an invitation to visit Warsaw in the 1980s—presumably to discuss the book *The Jews in Poland*, which he had co-edited in 1986 with the Polish scholar Maciej Jachimczyk and the South African–born American academic Antony Polonsky—had personally and harshly criticized him in the past.

Finally, in 1991 he was persuaded to go back. By then Chimen had been absorbed for some years in studying the fate of Soviet Jewry, publishing a number of articles in the journal *Soviet Jewish Affairs*: there was an overview of Jewish history in Russia and Poland from the mid-eighteenth century to the late nineteenth; an article on Soviet Yiddish literature; and another on Hebrew incunabula kept in the library of the Leningrad branch of the Oriental Institute of the USSR Academy of Sciences. He had also devoted an increasing amount of his seemingly endless intellectual energies to studying the phenomenon of Soviet anti-Semitism. "Soviet Jews today are without an address," he said in a speech given to a gathering of English clergy in the Conference Hall of Westminster Cathedral on April 27, 1977, which included among the audience the Archbishop of York. "They have no means of expressing themselves either in Russian, or to revive the Hebrew national culture, or the Yiddish language." They were, he continued, "the only Soviet national minority that was deprived in this fashion." Worse than being vilified, he averred, Russian Jews and their culture were being ignored, "soon to become also a people that must not even be mentioned."

Now, in 1991, after decades of repression and stagnation, it seemed as if things were finally changing in the Soviet Union. And, despite his hard-earned cynicism toward all things Soviet, Chimen wanted to see what this meant in practice. Mikhail Gorbachev had come to power as the general secretary of the Communist Party in 1985 and had spent the next several years liberalizing the state's stagnant economy and opening up its political processes to scrutiny. These twinned experiments, known as perestroika and glasnost, were leading to extraordinary changes. The Berlin Wall, constructed in 1961 and the great symbol of the divide that had rendered Europe in two since the end of the Second World War, had fallen in 1989; a number of Soviet republics in the Baltic and Caucasus regions were moving toward declaring their independence from the USSR; and the Cold War, the game of nuclear chicken and proxy wars, played out globally between NATO and the Warsaw Pact for more than forty years, was drawing to a conclusion. The Soviet experiment would fast recede into the same mists of time that shrouded the key events in Chimen's historical landscape: 1848, Europe's year of failed revolutions, the formation of the First International, the Paris Commune, and the Russian Revolution itself.

In mid-August 1991, the new order was by no means settled. But putting aside his terror that KGB agents would start shadowing him as soon as he set foot on Soviet territory, Chimen boarded a plane at Heathrow. Trademark black briefcase in hand, he flew to Moscow to attend a conference on Soviet Jewry. His timing was, to put it mildly, far from perfect.

In the third week of August, the bitter remnants of the Communist Party's old guard launched a coup d'état. They placed Mikhail and Raisa Gorbachev under house arrest at their Crimean country dacha on the Black Sea coast and established a State Emergency Committee to attempt to restore the one-party state of Bolshevism in its heyday. Nearly two years after the fall of the Berlin Wall, with the Soviet state fissuring, the military, the police, and the KGB were attempting to seize control of the country, to put a stop to what they saw as a spiral of chaos. Suddenly there were tanks on the street. And in reaction there were enormous crowds of protestors, marshaled by the mayor of Moscow, Boris Yeltsin, furiously demonstrating their opposition. Chimen—who had been touring the Kremlin barely a few hours before—looking out of his hotel window must have suffered a sense of delirium, a shuddering, nauseating feeling of having entered a hideous time warp.

In a panic, fearful that he would somehow be recognized as an expatriate or, worse, as an ex-Communist, and held hostage as his brothers had been decades earlier, he phoned the BBC offices in Moscow, pleading with them to assist him in getting out. They all knew Jenny—she was, by now, rising far up the corporation's ranks—and they agreed to help him flee Russia. He paid a fortune but was able to get a flight out of Moscow, flying home via Israel. Adding a ludicrous twist to the adventure, as Chimen left Russia, he somehow found the time and inclination to stop at the Duty Free shop (which, bizarrely, had remained open for business throughout the days of the coup) to buy three jars of caviar for the family back home in London.

And so, for the second time in his life, Chimen retreated from Moscow, leaving unpropitious circumstances behind. As he fled, the coup collapsed in the face of Yeltsin calling out the masses into the streets and squares of the capital to block the tanks and paralyze the movements of the army. Far from restoring the Bolshevik old guard to power, the move to roll back the clock had been the catalyst for a massive revolt. Within four months, the Soviet Union ceased to exist; Gorbachev was shunted aside in favor of Yeltsin; and the Communist Party itself, heir to Lenin's 1917 revolution, was temporarily outlawed. The caviar that Chimen brought home for my parents fared no better. It sat, uneaten, in our fridge, waiting for what my father deemed to be a sufficiently important dinner party. One night, the refrigerator electronics malfunctioned and the insulation either caught fire or melted. When my parents came downstairs the next morning, the contents of the fridge were covered in a sticky, yellow gloop. The caviar, acquired at such a critical moment in history, had to be thrown away.

———

Chimen at the kitchen table,
photographed by his grandson
Rob Liddell for a high school
photography project.

Jenny and Mimi, a few years
before Mimi's death in 1997.

Chimen's visit to Moscow was one of the last long-distance trips that he took before Mimi died. She was, by then, increasingly ill, her kidneys failing, her heart unsound, her blood pressure gone haywire. Her legs, which had given her trouble since a horrendous fall down a flight of concrete steps during a trip to Israel more than a decade earlier, were now prey to blood clots and spasms. One hospital stay followed another; one pill after another was added to her daily regimen. When people asked her how she was, she would wave their question away, as if it was a fly buzzing around her head, ordering them not to talk about such matters. "At night (nearly every night), I write you page after page of letters," my grandmother wrote to me in early October 1994, a year after I had moved to New York. "I climb mountains; walk for miles over the Heath or through the City; cook mountains of food for throngs of visitors and rarely have a dull moment. During the day, I torment myself for not having written to you but I have a complete blockage. I do not know where to begin, what to put in and what to leave out. I have so much I would like to say and leave unsaid. The Atlantic leaves a big space between us."

To take her mind off the pain that was now her constant companion, Mimi continued as a hostess extraordinaire. It was as if she could ward off the imminence of death by cooking just one more meal, and then another after that. "But the main thing is she continues to smile, in spite of disabilities," Chimen noted optimistically in early December 1993. "We still entertain, visitors flock to the house, and she is busy preparing wonderful meals." Later, however, as her chronic pain worsened, her eyes started to look haunted when she answered questions about her health. Gradually, she wound down her cooking endeavors. Now, too weak to move about, she cooked vicariously, ordering her helpers to add a pinch more salt, to give a more assertive stir to a pan, to turn up the gas on the stovetop. Eventually, in her last months, she was so consumed by pain that she seemed to retreat entirely into herself, physically shrinking, cocooning into her skin, her eyes tiny, glassy beads in a mask of agony. She was, by the end, almost entirely unable to communicate with the friends and family who still trooped through her front door to visit.

As the decline in her health accelerated—she had suffered a "setback" was what Chimen would say euphemistically whenever I phoned from Oxford or, later, from America—the downstairs front room became Mimi's sickroom. It was the place where she lay, on the rickety old couch, before and after her awful visits to the hospital, three times a week, for dialysis; where she tried, and failed, to recuperate after a series of surgeries in the last years of her life; where visitors would hold her hand and talk. Eventually, it served as her makeshift bedroom, and the couch was replaced by a metal hospital bed when she could no longer make the gargantuan effort required to navigate her way to the stairs and up to the first-floor Marx library where she and Chimen had slept for so many decades. For the first time in many, many years the books were cleared from the tables in the front room, to be replaced by her bewildering array of medications.

"I have become, more or less a nurse, almost full time," Chimen wrote sadly to his friend Brad Sabin Hill, on May 15, 1996. To me, he explained, apologizing for a delay in sending me a letter, "The various functions I perform regularly, call on my time: doorman, semi-nurse, coffee and tea maker, handyman, washer up, 'entertainer,' and letters are postponed." As Mimi's health deteriorated, as her remarkable life collapsed into a drawn-out catastrophe, Chimen aged terribly. Three years earlier, on his birthday, he had written to me "So I am an old-man of seventy-seven, though in mind I feel younger, but age does creep on." Now the creep had become a gallop. When I visited Hillway he looked astonishingly small, his eyes red with chronic sorrow, his back more hunched than previously.

There was more sorrow to come. On December 9, 1996, Chimen and Mimi's nephew Raph Samuel succumbed to cancer. Too ill to leave home, Mimi stayed in the front room, while Chimen made the journey up the road to Highgate Cemetery alone. A huge crowd of mourners had gathered to see Raph off in the same cemetery where Marx was buried. Most of the broadsheet newspapers carried lengthy obituaries; it felt like a last hurrah for a dying breed of radicalism.

Four months later, in the last week of April 1997, Mimi entered the Royal Free Hospital for the last time. She had turned eighty only two months earlier. The place in which she had worked for so many years would be the place in which she died. Early in the morning of April 25, with Chimen by her side, she finally gave up the fight for life. I had arrived at Heathrow a few minutes earlier and taken one of the loneliest train journeys of my life to my parents' home in Chiswick. As I walked in the door, my father phoned from the hospital to say it was all over.

Chimen had always carried a tiny appointment book, sometimes clothbound, sometimes leather, with a miniscule pencil latched to the spine, in which he recorded his future commitments. From his late seventies, these little books had begun to double as diaries, as he tried to retain some control over the rhythms of his life by committing everything to the written word. When terrible things happened, the things that shred the fabric of existence, he noted them in the appointment book after the fact. On the page for April 25, 1997, there are two cursory notes, penned in blue ink, the handwriting almost microscopic. "7.40am, Miri passed away," reads the first. The second simply states "8.20am Sasha arrived from New York." Two days later he noted "12.30pm funeral of Miri at the Jewish Reform Cemetery Hoop Lane. Over 200 people attended. Service conducted by [Rabbi] Julia Neuberger. The speakers were Jack, Jenny, Sasha, Rob and Martin."

Four and a half years later, on September 11, 2001, there is the following note in his appointment book: "2pm ring urgently Arthur Hertzberg." Rabbi Hertzberg, one of Chimen's closest friends, lived in New York. At 2:00 p.m. in London, Chimen would have just found out about the attacks on the World Trade Center. The notes were sparse, barely emotional; the lack of expression, and the attempt to control the unbearable through committing its contours to paper, is almost heartbreaking. The memorialization of events on the page seemed to give comfort to a man whose whole life had been devoted to the written word.

Chimen was now well over eighty years old, but intellectually he was as sharp as ever. Mimi's long illness and death had forced him to confront his own mortality but had not inhibited his love of ideas, his yearning to be a part of the great discussions in the great universities. After a period of mourning, he returned to traveling for pleasure— the summer after Mimi's death my parents took him to Italy, from which he wrote long letters to me on the beauty of the churches and the violence of the history. Some time after that, he once more started attending overseas conferences; he finally traveled to Poland, to attend a conference on Jewish spirituality and to visit Kraców and other former centers of Jewish culture. "The shops are full of goods," he wrote in surprise, in a four-page essay that he never ultimately published. "The women are elegantly dressed. The restaurants and cafes are full of young people. There is liveliness in the streets. A feeling of freedom and happiness is felt in all the places we saw. A European atmosphere prevails." Yet at the same time, the journey deeply depressed him, the legacy of the Holocaust more apparent in what was absent than in what was present. In the city of Lublin, which had once housed Talmudic colleges and been home to great religious sages, he noted that "there is not a street named after a Jew. As if they have never been there." Poland, he wrote, "today is a desert for Jews. Before the Second World War Poland had over three million Jews."

Not content simply to attend conferences as one among many participants, Chimen also resumed his participation on the international lecture circuit. His old protégés at Stanford convinced him to fly out to California for one more series of lectures. He did so and was received with acclaim. He was, members of the audience felt, still on top of his game: His lectures, presented in a series of workshops to faculty and graduate students, were packed with facts, his memory as extraordinary as ever. There was, though, a poignancy to these meetings: His audience knew, as did Chimen, that it was almost certainly the last time he would have the stamina to travel so far for work.

Despite his public resilience, in private he was now a deeply lonely man. There was, he wrote to me, "little to report from an empty house. Empty, i.e. without Miri." But even without its hostess, the House of Books continued to exert its magnetic attraction for scholars and bibliophiles. Young scholars would make what was now effectively a pilgrimage to 5 Hillway, to the legendary house and its legendary occupant. "Pretty much any query I had to do with Jewish circles in London, Jewish books, Yiddish culture, he'd more often than not know the answers to," David Mazower remembered. "He sent me postcards occasionally, would ring up, say 'Why haven't I seen you? Come over.' He and the house were a time capsule that embodied everything I valued most about the Ashkenazi civilization."

———

In these last years of his life, Chimen returned more and more to the religious texts of his youth. He did not pray, did not go to synagogue on the Sabbath, but he looked to the great traditional texts for inspiration. Perhaps, even though he would never have admitted it even to himself, he began looking for a spiritual truth in these writings. On March 10, 1998, slightly less than a year after Mimi died, Chimen wrote to his good friend John Felstiner at Stanford: "As to prayer, there is a superb piece in the pseudo-Josephus—the Josippon. The anonymous author wrote: 'And Daniel prayed three times a day. He who prays to God he, man, speaks, but who reads the Torah God speaks to him.' An interesting comment on prayer."

Chimen did not believe that prayer brought one any closer to the sublime—nor that God, if He existed, responded to pleas by mortals. A few months before his death, I visited him. Well into his nineties now, he sat in his kitchen, stony-faced, every action a challenge, staring out onto the late-summer foliage in his back garden. "Every day that I wake up and do not feel too bad," he suddenly said, his raspy, faint voice fierce, his desire to impart some more words of wisdom to his oldest grandson painful in its intensity. He stopped, and I waited for him to say, "I thank God." But instead he balled up his face and, with a superhuman effort, almost shouted the words, "I feel that *I* have *won* another day." To the end, Chimen clung to his personal autonomy.

Nevertheless, while he did not believe in prayer, as mortality hemmed him in he did come to feel that the great religious traditions going back thousands of years that held his ancestors in their web of rituals, beliefs, and shared experiences were as close as he could get to touching immortality; he came to believe that homage to the past was a guarantee of a future. Perhaps, in his mind, he began hedging his bets. As a young man he had read works by Blaise Pascal, the seventeenth-century French mathematician and philosopher. Pascal had formulated a famous wager in favor of the existence of God: If you bet there is no God and you are wrong, a wrathful deity is likely to condemn your eternal soul to hellfire; but if you gamble that there is a God and there is not, your consciousness will cease to exist upon your death and you will never know that you were wrong. Much better, therefore, argued Pascal, to believe in God. A little over two millennia earlier, Plato had crafted a similar argument. Re-creating a conversation between Socrates and an old man named Cephalus in *The Republic*, Plato put the following words into Cephalus's mouth: "But you know, Socrates, when a man faces the thought that he must die, there come upon him fear and foreboding about things that have not troubled him before. Once he laughed at the tales about those in Hades, of punishment to be suffered there by him who has done injustice. But now his soul is tormented by the thought that these may be true." In precise Hebrew lettering, in the margins of the Everyman classic that had sat for so long on the front-room shelves, Chimen (always eager to draw connections from one seminal text to the next) had written: "This recalls the beginning of the *Phaedo*, where Socrates says almost the same thing."

In that dialogue, in which Plato reconstructs Socrates's last day on earth, the great teacher discusses with his students the possibility of an afterlife. "I ought to be grieved at death, if I were not persuaded that I am going to other gods who are wise and good (of this I am as certain as I can be of anything of the sort) and to men departed (though I am not so certain of this), who are better than those whom I leave behind," explains Socrates, as he waits for the hemlock that he has swallowed to take effect. "And therefore I do not grieve as I might have done, for I have good hope that there is yet something remaining for the dead, and, as has been said of old, some far better thing for the good than for the evil."

Death was cutting a swathe through Chimen's contemporaries. In November 1997, seven months after Mimi's death, Isaiah Berlin died. In 1999, Chimen's sister-in-law Minna died. Sara lived on after the death of her husband, Steve, in 1998, but as her health deteriorated she became a captive in her own home. When he could, Chimen would cut up a fresh mango for his beloved sister-in-law and, if he could convince someone to drive him over, would deliver it to her house. Later, as his own health declined, he could no longer make the journey to visit Sara. Barely a ten-minute drive away, she might as well have lived on the moon. He almost never saw her, instead checking in on her in short daily phone calls, unsatisfying minutes in which neither could hear what the other was saying. Chimen's younger brother Menachem became too sick to travel from Israel and died in 2006. One after the other, almost all of Chimen's cousins in England, in America, and in Israel died. Rose Uren was felled by cancer in 2005. Most of the other remaining close friends from his generation also died.

Time had finally caught up with Chimen. And as it did, as his eighties gave way to his nineties, the front room became his last redoubt: his bedroom, his retreat from the pain of his waking hours. It was where physical therapists tried to coax him to walk a few steps, where his night nurses helped him undress, where he lay in the dark, a small bell next to him in case he needed to ring for assistance, and thought about eternity. As his world grew smaller and smaller, these few cubic feet, surrounded by his books, became the epicenter of his tenuous existence. "As regards my family here," Chimen wrote to Felstiner in 2006, his handwriting larger and less precise as his neurological problems mounted, "I have Parkinson's, my movements are very slow, and one has to live with it. Walking is a problem. My children are as busy as ever. My grandchildren are divided between USA and England." Jack and Jenny were certainly busy, but as Chimen himself would have been the first to admit, they spent many hours a week—frequently many hours each day—at Hillway talking with Chimen, organizing his home help, taking him to the doctors' appointments that seemed to multiply by the week. As Chimen aged (exponentially, it seemed to me) so his children came to perform for him the roles that Chimen had earlier taken on in caring for Mimi. They became their father's lifeline; their ministrations allowed Chimen to remain in his home and, for a startlingly long time, to continue in his post as master of ceremonies at the now-diminished salon.

Of course, all of the family love on earth could not turn back the clock, could not drown out the endless drone of the second hand ticking away toward the end. Lonely, in pain, and daily staring death in the face, as he neared ninety Chimen had spilled his heart to Felstiner. "A huge biography, in Hebrew, was published of my father, in Jerusalem, full of documents and of photos of many rabbis. Two large volumes. And I remain a kind of bridge between the Rabbinic world and the world of Marx." He knew that these worlds out of which he had emerged and in which he had been shaped were vanishing; that much of the younger generations neither understood nor cared for the events, the great political and philosophical arguments and ways of thought that had so defined his nine decades. And he knew that when he died his mental universe would vanish with him.

Chimen's letter to Felstiner continued: "In September I shall be ninety, if I reach that date...My only pleasure is I read voraciously." He read, and when people gave him books, he added them to his piles. But he no longer actively sought out particular items to add to his vast collection. "Collectors' collections are like jigsaws," his Sotheby's friend Camilla Previté believed. "They're always looking for pieces to fill in. Five-million-piece jigsaws. Most collectors, their collections are near completion and they're looking for just a few more pieces." Sitting or lying in his front room, surrounded by books, Chimen knew that his life's puzzle, his House of Books, was almost complete.

On March 14, 2010, one hundred and twenty-seven years after Karl Marx's death, Chimen retired to that room one last time, was put into his bed, and did not get up. As he had requested months earlier when discussing death with my father, as he faded away Jack brought him a tiny Hebrew Bible, bound in cracked black leather, the endpapers water-damaged, to hold in his emaciated hands. He had, over the years, kept it in his jacket pocket as he traveled the world. It was not an expensive volume, nor one of his rare possessions, but it must have meant something powerful to him. Maybe it had been Yehezkel's.

Perhaps, as he held the Bible, the words of the Vidui, the prayer of confession to be chanted by the dying, floated before his inner eye. Perhaps, in extremis, he called up from his remarkable memory the words of the Psalms of Ascent or of the Adon Olam and Ana Bek-hoach prayers. "You who dwells in the shelter of the Most High, Who abides in the shadow of the Omnipotent," begins Psalm 91, "I say to you of the Lord Who is my refuge and my stronghold, my God in Whom I trust, that He will save you from the ensnaring trap, from the destructive pestilence. He will cover you with His pinions and you will find refuge under His wings; His truth is a shield and an armour." In the last moments, as infinity closes in, the dying person is supposed to make a supreme effort to declare as their final words: "Master of the universe, may it be Your will that my passing be in peace." It is the ultimate surrender of will when one can fight no more.

Or perhaps, a materialist atheist to the last, dying on the anniversary of Marx's death, he brought to mind the words of his former hero: "All that is solid melts into air." It is possible that both the religious and the materialist words flittered through his dimming consciousness. Or that, at the end, he saw and heard no words at all. There is, of course, no way to know.

———

I can still see Jack Lunzer, Chimen's confrere in the esoteric world of rare books, standing and quietly reciting Kaddish for Chimen in the little prayer hall in Hoop Lane where Chimen's body lay, in a coffin so small that it could have been a child's, before being moved to the grave site, to lie next to Mimi once more. Lunzer intoned the Hebrew words with infinite sadness, his large frame suddenly somehow grown small. Sick himself, he did not know if he could walk the distance along the pathway to the back of the cemetery where the newly dug grave lay waiting.

"All that is solid melts into air, all that is holy is profaned, and man is at last compelled to face with sober senses his real conditions of life, and his relations with his kind," went the fuller version of Marx's aphorism, penned in 1848, in a famous passage from the first chapter of *The Communist Manifesto*, as he sought to explain the creative and yet destructive forces unleashed by capitalism, the emergence of a world that never stood still. Chimen, by his own estimation, had at least forty editions of the *Manifesto* in his house, in most of the major European languages. He had volumes, he confided to those who knew enough to ask the right questions about his collection, which even the British Library lacked. Over the near-century of his life, Chimen sought to impose at least a modicum of stability and predictability on his ever-changing world through the collecting of books, building his House of Books as a repository of words. Collecting, preserving, reading, and transmitting the knowledge contained in books stopped, just for a moment, the onward march of time, the return to dust that is our destiny. Seven hundred years before Marx wrote his *Manifesto*, Maimonides had had a more optimistic philosophy: "Though the Sages state the Throne of Glory to be created they never say that it will cease to exist," Maimonides wrote in *The Guide for the Perplexed*. "Similarly the souls of the righteous are in our opinion created but will never cease to exist." Chimen had idolized both men; he had, I think, come to believe that both were somehow right.

The many hundreds of mourners, spanning four generations, walked to the grave site. And, the family members at the front of the silent crowd, we took it in turns to shovel dirt atop my grandfather's coffin. The earth was soft and made a gentle thudding sound as it landed on the wood several feet below. And then I returned home, back to my parents' house, back to a bottomless well of grief. To the blooming silence that says a life is over.

Within days, the experts would be at Hillway poring over the thousands of books—books that, in the end, Chimen had never managed to catalog, whose fate he had never determined before his death. Books that could no longer stay in the empty house, endangered by fire and flood and theft. Like a dream that flies away upon waking, the library, so lovingly collected over seventy-five years, was about to be dissipated to the four winds. Atlantis was submerged, so thoroughly that at moments I doubted it had ever existed. The salon's doors were shut for the last time. The House of Books was no more.

As I neared completion of this manuscript, more than three years after my grandfather's death, I had another dream. This time Chimen's books had been restored to their shelves, not quite in the right order but in something approximating his library's structure. They were stacked in strange formations, lying horizontally, many of the spines, with the titles on them, turned inward, away from the viewer. And Chimen had been resurrected.

One after the other, the books righted themselves. And as they did, Chimen got increasingly animated. His back straightened, his hearing improved. And with a slight, crooked smile, he began arguing again, talking about his books, debating his grand ideas. Outside his house was chaos. I saw, in my dream, huge encampments of the homeless, overcrowded trains, great, noisy restaurants. Inside Hillway, however, was a strange, musty order.

I woke up. It was 5 a.m. I was wide awake; as awake, as alert as a young child after twelve hours of sleep. As the dream began to fade, I did what Chimen would have done. I reached for a piece of paper and scribbled down the images. I filed the piece of paper in one of the boxes full of notes for my book. One doesn't throw away words. They might, someday, be useful.

Acknowledgments

THROUGHOUT MY DECADES as a writer, I have always known that one day I would write a book about my grandparents and their remarkable house. I didn't know what shape the book would take or how I would frame their lives, but I knew that theirs was a story I had to tell.

After my grandfather died in March 2010, telling that story became one of the driving forces of my life. It became rather more than an itch, something closer to an obsession. Chimen and Mimi's world, centered around the book- and conversation-filled rooms of 5 Hillway, was one that, by the day, was dying: The central characters in their lives were either very old or already dead; the political battles they had fought were increasingly seen as footnotes from the distant past; the books and ideas they valued were getting dustier by the day. If I were to tell their story, I had to do it sooner rather than later.

And so I set to work. I wanted to write *The House of Twenty Thousand Books* using the storytelling, descriptive techniques that I have developed over twenty years as a journalist, but I also wanted to tell it as a history, to use archives and libraries in a way that Chimen, a consummate historian, would have approved. I eventually decided upon a compromise: I would do deep research in archives and via interviews, but I wouldn't footnote my text. I would tell a story and trust my readers to trust me. I hope I have, in the telling, earned that trust.

The journey I embarked on took me nearly four years. Along the way, I read hundreds of books—many volumes from my grandfather's collection and also histories, biographies, and novels that brought alive the worlds Chimen and Mimi inhabited. I interviewed scores of people (in person, by phone, by e-mail) in England, the United States, Israel, Canada, Germany, Holland, Lithuania, and elsewhere, and spent weeks in archives in London, Oxford, Sheffield, and Manchester. It was a life-changing experience, opening my eyes to things I did not previously know or understand; introducing me to my great-grandparents and grandparents as children, as young adults, as middle-aged and elderly men and women, as well as to fascinating historical characters now long dead; and allowing me to see my grandparents' lives—and by extension my own—as part of a religious, cultural, political, and migratory history going far back into the mists of time.

None of this would have been possible without the extraordinary support of a vast number of people. First and foremost, I owe an immeasurable debt of gratitude to my parents, Jack and Lenore Abramsky—for participating, with me, in the joy of this project, and for having confidence in my ability to tie the loose strands together. My father, in particular, took to this project with the zest and enthusiasm of a young man, helping me with archival research, finding documents buried deep in family filing cabinets, filling the gaps in my knowledge of key people and key events, and, most important, trusting me to tell his parents' story with respect. On several occasions we visited key locales together, such as the street that had once been home to the Shapiro, Valentine & Co. bookshop; I shall always treasure those memories. Both my parents tolerated, with good humor, my endless requests for additional information. It cannot be easy having a son snooping around one's inner life; that neither my mother nor my father protested is a gift for which I will be eternally thankful. So, too, my aunt Jenny was generous to a fault—in opening up her house to me while I burrowed in her files, in talking to me about her childhood memories, and in providing me access to the thousands of letters written by, or to, my grandparents. My brother, Kolya, knew the Socialist side of Chimen's collection better than any other member of the family. His extraordinary knowledge and insights, his generosity in suggesting sources for me to read, and his insistence in gently but firmly critiquing some of my interpretations of events were of absolutely critical importance to me as I brought this book to fruition. We didn't always agree in our understanding of chapters in Mimi and Chimen's lives, but I never doubted for a moment his wisdom. My sister Tanya, my cousins Rob and Maia, Emma and Nick all opened their memory chests to me time and again over the years that I was writing this, providing a wealth of anecdotes that I had long forgotten or, in some cases, never known. So, too, did generations of other relatives: Eve and Julia Corrin; Alison Light; Lily and Martin Mitchell; Peter and Vavi Hillel; Elliott Medrich; Alice Medrich; Mildred Axelrod; Larry and Shirley Kedes; and many others. Late in the writing process, my cousin Ron Abramski provided me with a copy of an extraordinary filmed interview that he had conducted with Chimen in January 2003.

The number of friends and colleagues of my grandparents, and of my parents, who helped me by agreeing both to be interviewed for this project and also to photocopy or scan letters and other documents are legion: I cannot possibly list everybody by name, but you know who you are. I do, however, owe special thanks to Chimen's University College London colleague Ada Rapoport-Albert; to his friends at Stanford Peter and Suzanne Greenberg (whose wonderful hospitality and keen interest both in people and in ideas has always reminded me of that exuded by Mimi and Chimen) and Peter Stansky; to Helen Beer in Oxford and to Marion Aptroot and Efrat Gal-Ed in Germany, all of whom helped me understand, and in some cases translate, Chimen's wonderful collection of Yiddish literature; to Miri Freud-Kandel in Oxford and to Rabbi Elliot Cosgrove in New York, both of whom went out of their way to explain my great-grandfather's role in English Jewish religious life over the decades; to Pauline Harrison, whose insights into the psychology of the Communist Party of Great Britain in the years surrounding the Second World War fascinated me; to Lord John Kerr, who championed Chimen at Sotheby's and later at Bloomsbury Auctions; to Ormond Uren, one of the last of the lions; and to Chimen's great book-collecting friend and global travel companion in his later years, Jack Lunzer.

Tariq Ali, Gidon Cohen, Arie Dubnov, John Felstiner, Christopher Hird, Dovid Katz, Krishan Kumar, David Mazower, Kevin Morgan, Andrew Moss, Eilat Negev and Yehuda Koren, Jon and Michael Pushkin, Berel Rodal, Graham Thorpe, Peter Waterman, and Tony Yablon all provided reminiscences of life at Hillway and of personal and professional interactions with Mimi and Chimen over more than half a century. Beryl Williams arranged for the digitizing of Chimen's 1967 Sussex University lectures, given to commemorate the fiftieth anniversary of the Russian Revolution. Christopher Edwards was instrumental in helping familiarize me with the often opaque world of rare-book dealing. Camilla Previté and Nabil Saidi were similarly generous in helping me to understand the auction-house world of Sotheby's.

In addition to these friends and colleagues, I was immensely fortunate to have several extremely talented teams of archivists eager to work with me on this project: to the men and women who staff the libraries and archives at University College London; the Bishopsgate Institute, London; the People's History Museum, Manchester; the special collections room at the University of Sheffield; Stanford University, California; the Bodleian Library, Kressel Archive, and St. Antony's College, Oxford; and Trinity College, Cambridge, I send a huge thank you, which I hope will echo loudly and proudly through the silent chambers and reading rooms of your great institutions. An equally loud thank you to Philippa Bernard at Westminster Synagogue and, of course, to Henry Hardy of the Isaiah Berlin Literary Trust and Mark Pottle, who have edited Berlin's letters so skillfully over the years.

Beyond these circles, I repeatedly sought—and received—assistance from a magnificent brain trust: My friends Nathaniel Deutsch, and his wife, Miriam Greenberg, went far, far beyond the call of duty in researching answers to my questions and in correcting my sometimes flawed understandings of Jewish history and religious ritual. Without Nathaniel's enthusiastic assistance, and his translation of key documents from Hebrew into English, as well as his and Miriam's willingness to host me in their home in Santa Cruz while we discussed the project's evolution, I doubt very much that I could have brought this book to completion. So too, Steven Zipperstein at Stanford allowed me to pick his brain over a series of wonderful brunches in Palo Alto. I very much hope that he will continue to indulge me in these conversations after the publication of this book. At the University of California at Davis, David Biale never failed to generously respond to my requests for information and for book references. In Berkeley, Paul Hamburg, the librarian presiding over the university's Hebraica collection, both helped me to understand the importance of some of Chimen's oldest and rarest Hebrew books and manuscripts and also showed me equivalent books owned by the university. At George Washington University, Brad Sabin Hill, who many years ago apprenticed himself to my grandfather while learning the mysterious arts of Hebrew bibliography, conjured up a simply extraordinary amount of information and personal correspondence; Hill went so far as to draw up for me a complete bibliography of my grandfather's writings. I shall be forever grateful for this act.

Many of my oldest and dearest friends also made themselves available over the years to talk about sections of the book, to provide specific historical details, or simply to help me maintain my enthusiasm during what was sometimes an emotionally draining project. Particular thanks here go to Ben Caplin, Carolyn Juris, George Lerner, Eyal Press, Pete Sarris, Adam Shatz, Baki Tezcan (whose knowledge of Turkish history gave me an entry point into the world of Constantinople's Hebrew printers five hundred years ago), Kitty Ussher, Jon Wedderburn, and Jason Ziedenberg. My mentors at the Columbia University Graduate School of Journalism, Michael Shapiro and Sam Freedman, were also instrumental in convincing me that I had the wherewithal to tell this story.

In London, my editors Peter and Martine Halban embraced the concept of *The House of Twenty Thousand Books* from our very first conversation; and as the book moved toward publication, Kim Reynolds's historical expertise and first-rate editing skills were indispensable in knocking the rough edges off of my manuscript. In New York, my editor Susan Barba has shown a similar enthusiasm for the story of Hillway and its occupants. My agents, Victoria Skurnick in New York and Caspian Dennis in London, also deserve my warmest thanks.

Last but of course not least, to my wife, Julie Sze, to my daughter, Sofia, and to my son, Leo, my profoundest thank you for tolerating my workaholic tendencies during the gestation of *The House of Twenty Thousand Books*; for your belief in the importance of this story; and for your joyful interest in the sagas contained in these pages. Thank you, too, for always helping me to keep things in perspective. You make my home warm and my life full.

During the years that it took to write this book, many wonderful friends and relatives died. Among them were my uncle Al Liddell; my great-aunt Sara Corrin; Chimen's Oxford friend Harry Shukman; and his erstwhile Communist Party comrade Eric Hobsbawm. Every day, it seems, our past becomes more unrecoverable, the living links to that past more fragile. My book is, in many ways, a chorus of ghosts.

I hope that, in its own small way, *The House of Twenty Thousand Books* helps memorialize the men and women who collectively made up the world of 5 Hillway. They are, in the main, no longer alive, but their voices still resonate for me with the clear, loud tones of Bow Bells. They were, one and all, remarkable human beings.

Line of descent for Sasha Abramsky through both of his grandmothers

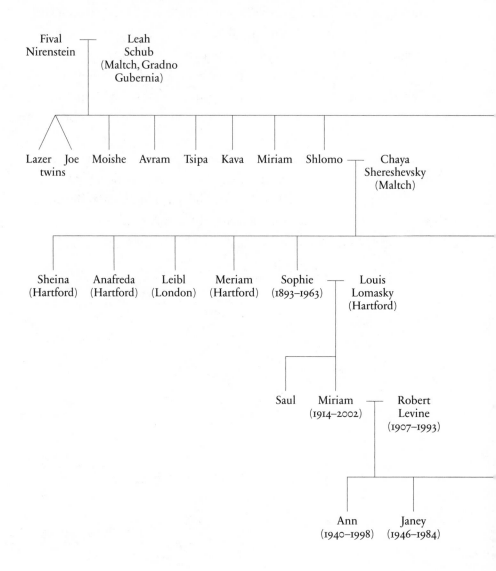

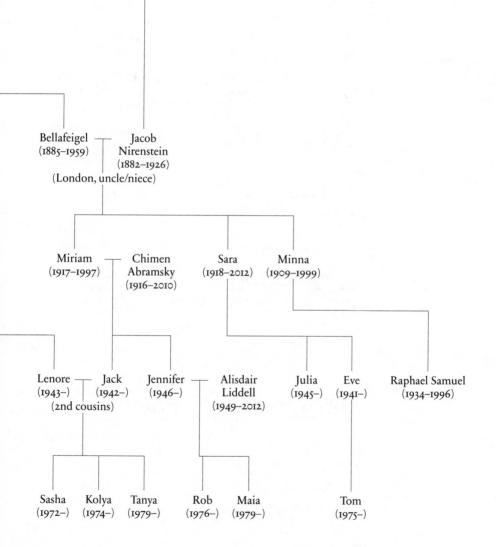

Bellafeigel
(1885–1959)

Jacob
Nirenstein
(1882–1926)

(London, uncle/niece)

Miriam
(1917–1997)

Chimen
Abramsky
(1916–2010)

Sara
(1918–2012)

Minna
(1909–1999)

Lenore
(1943–)

Jack
(1942–)

Jennifer
(1946–)

Alisdair
Liddell
(1949–2012)

Julia
(1945–)

Eve
(1941–)

Raphael Samuel
(1934–1996)

(2nd cousins)

Sasha
(1972–)

Kolya
(1974–)

Tanya
(1979–)

Rob
(1976–)

Maia
(1979–)

Tom
(1975–)

Line of descent for Sasha Abramsky through Chimen's father

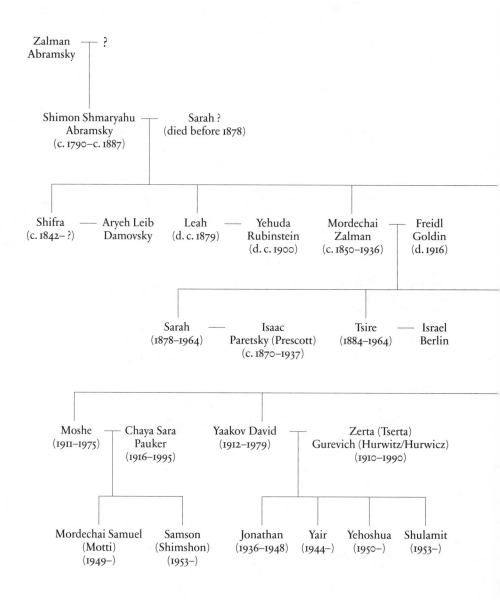

1. Shimon Shmaryahu Abramsky was a timber merchant and tavern keeper in the village of Dashkovtze, on the Neman River, a few miles from Most, southeast of Grodno, and east of Bialystok, where he was born.
2. Mordechai Zalman Abramsky was a timber merchant in Dashkovtze; he died in Zaludok. All his children were born in Dashkovtze. His wife, Freidl, was the sister of the writer Ezra Goldin.
3. Nephews and nieces of Mordechai Zalman Abramsky and Yehezkel Abramsky are not included in this family tree.

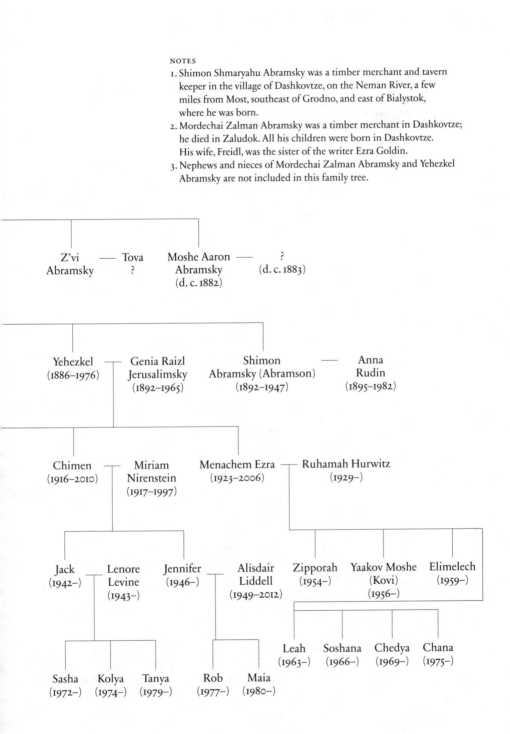

Line of descent for Sasha Abramsky through Chimen's mother

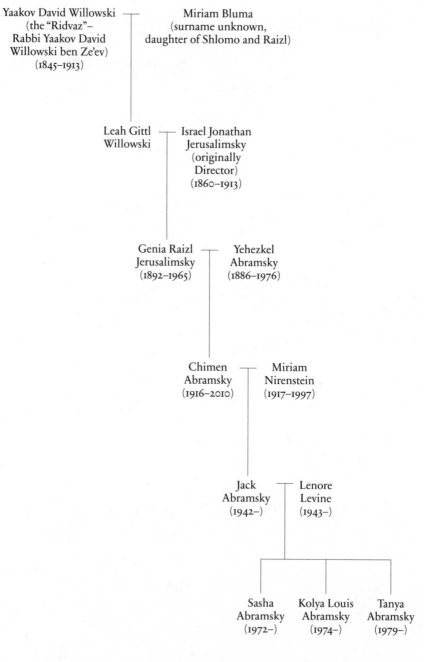

Index